Norway outside the European Union

In November 1994 the Norwegian electorate rejected membership of the European Union. Since then the country has struggled to adapt a range of policies to fit in with those of the EU. This book provides the first all-round coverage of the relationship between the EU and its oil-rich northern neighbour and sets out the options open to Norway in the future.

Professor Archer examines the background to the 1994 decision both in terms of an expression of interests within Norway and in terms of national feeling. He then investigates the subsequent interaction between Norway and the EU through the European Economic Area (EEA) – which allowed Norway access to the EU's markets; the Schengen agreement – dealing with justice and border matters and the Common Foreign and Security Policy. It includes discussion of policies that have had a particular effect on Norway, such as those of the Gas Directive, fisheries and the sale of alcohol and looks at how Norway has adapted itself to EU policy, noting the cases where the country has dug in its heels and when it has been acquiescent.

This book will appeal to students and researchers with an interest in European integration and Nordic studies in general.

Clive Archer is Research and Jean Monnet Professor in the Department of Politics and Philosophy, Manchester Metropolitan University. He is also Director of the Manchester European Research Institute.

Europe and the nation state

Edited by Michael Burgess

Centre for European Union Studies, University of Hull

and Lee Miles

The University of Liverpool

This series explores the complex relationship between nation states and European integration and the political, social, economic and policy implications of this interaction. The series examines issues such as:

- the impact of the EU on the politics and policy-making of the nation state and vice versa
- the effects of expansion of the EU on individual nation states in Europe
- the relationship between the EU and non-European nation states

1 **Poland and the European Union**
Edited by Karl Cordell

2 **Greece in the European Union**
Edited by Dionyssis G. Dimitrakopoulos and Argyris G. Passas

3 **The European Union and Democratization**
Edited by Paul J. Kubicek

4 **Iceland and European Integration**
On the edge
Edited by Baldur Thorhallsson

5 **Norway outside the European Union**
Norway and European integration from 1994 to 2004
Clive Archer

6 **Turkey and European Integration**
Prospects and issues in the post-Helsinki era
Edited by Mehmet Uğur and Nergis Canefe

Norway outside the European Union

Norway and European integration from 1994 to 2004

Clive Archer

Routledge
Taylor & Francis Group
LONDON AND NEW YORK

First published 2005
by Routledge
2 Park Square, Milton Park, Abingdon, Oxon OX14 4RN

Simultaneously published in the USA and Canada
by Routledge
270 Madison Ave, New York, NY 10016

Routledge is an imprint of the Taylor & Francis Group

Typeset in Times by Wearset Ltd, Boldon, Tyne & Wear
Printed and bound in Great Britain by MPG Books Ltd, Bodmin

British Library Cataloguing in Publication Data
A catalogue record for this book is available from the British Library

Library of Congress Cataloging in Publication Data
A catalog record for this book has been requested

ISBN 0-415-28279-9

Contents

Illustrations

Figure

Tables

Boxes

Foreword

Norway's relationship with the European Community, now European Union (EU), has always been of interest to outside observers. In many ways, the level of attention seems to be somewhat disproportionate to the size of the country in question, given that Norway represents a small state with a population of approximately 4 million.

Nevertheless, the focus upon Norway by political observers is, in my view at least, a valid and useful one. After all, Norway is something of a 'record holder' when it comes to how its political elite and general public have handled questions of European integration. The country hold records for applying for full membership status and, indeed, for completing negotiations on its accession terms the most times (twice). It also represents a prominent example of the difficulties that a pro-EU elite can have in securing full membership status, since the Norwegian electorate have rejected EU accession more than once (in 1972 and 1994). At face value then, Norway could be regarded as an official 'EU outsider', part of the periphery of northern Europe and, in many ways, content to stay that way.

Yet Archer's valuable study of Norway 'outside the European Union' illustrates that, for the most part, the Norwegian governing elite has adapted its country's political structures and policies to the demands of European integration as fully as possible, short of full membership status. Indeed, this in itself is not entirely new. However, Archer offers a coherent and comprehensive analytical framework also to understand the complexities of Norwegian–EU relations since 1994. Above all, he weaves together neatly substantive methods to explain Norwegian attitudes towards and adaptation to different types of EU policies, with a sophisticated interpretation of Norway in terms, of state, society and nation. The author provides us with a detailed assessment of Norway's impact in key EU policy sectors and outlines varying scenarios for future Norwegian–EU relations. From Archer we get a better understanding not only of how Norway 'thinks and works', but also of the challenges confronting European countries that prefer not to become full EU members.

This book forms part of the Routledge 'Europe and the Nation State' series. Written in an accessible style, the series invites leading scholars and ongoing researchers to explore the challenges that the European Union and European integration more generally imply for the political dynamics of nation states. Archer's book fits perfectly into the tradition of the series. It should be read by those wishing to understand not just Norwegian perspectives of European integration but also the complexity of attitudes that European integration often engenders.

Lee Miles
Europe in the World Centre
School of Politics and Communication Studies
The University of Liverpool

Preface

This is an account of Norway's relations with European integration since its electorate, in November 1994, turned down the opportunity for the country to be a full member of the European Union (EU). Despite this snub, Norway has managed a close relationship with the EU, almost appearing to be the 'sixteenth member'. However, it has not been part of the decision-taking process in Brussels and its privileged position may well be challenged by the 2004 enlargement, among other factors. This book seeks to examine the basis of Norway's relationship with European integration, seeing whether this has changed since 1994.

In writing the book I have received assistance from a number of institutions and individuals. The British Academy helped support research visits to Norway (Small Grant 33609) and the Norwegian Institute of International Affairs and the Norwegian Atlantic Committee acted as kind and supportive hosts. The list of individuals that assisted is much longer but particular thanks are due to Lee Miles, members of the Taylor & Francis editorial team and Anne Myrdal who, with me, carried out the surveys of Norwegian politicians and civil society (see Appendix 1). My gratitude is due to Dag Harald Claes, Erik Männik, Martin Sæter, David Scrivener and Helene Sjursen for comments on draft chapters. Others who helped are those who gave me their time for interviews (see Appendix 2) and those who assisted more generally, including at the Norwegian Institute of International Affairs, Valter Angell, Arne Olav Brundtland, Jeremy Ginnifer, Nina Græger, Janne Haaland Matlary, Andreas Kassekamp, Halvard Leira, Sverre Lodgaard, Martin Sæter, Iver Neumann, as well as the library staff; at the Norwegian parliament, Britt Fløistad; and at the Norwegian Atlantic Committee, Chris Prebensen and his staff.

However, in the end all views – and any mistakes – are my own responsibility. One final vote of thanks is to my wife, Elizabeth, who not only indexed the book but also supported me in many ways through the days of its production.

Clive Archer
Manchester Metropolitan University

1 Introduction

> The day of small nations has long passed away. The day of Empires has come.
>
> (Joseph Chamberlain (British politician), 12 May 1904, speech in Birmingham, reported in *The Times*, 13 May 1904)

In September 1972 and November 1994, the Norwegian electorate voted against joining the forms of European integration known, respectively, as the European Communities (EC) and the European Union (EU). After the first 'no', Norway signed a free trade agreement with the EC and before the 1994 vote Norway had already become a member of the European Economic Area (EEA) which extended the EU's Single European Market to Norway (and two other EFTA states) on a reciprocal basis. Since the second 'no' vote, Norway's relationship with the evolving EU has been based not just on the EEA but on the Schengen agreement and on an association with many aspects of the EU's Common Foreign and Security Policy (CFSP) of the European Union.

This book examines the ambivalent relationship between Norway and the process of European integration after the second Norwegian 'no'. It has been ambivalent because Norway – its people, its politicians and civil society – have been torn between maintaining the country's autonomy – the ability to do things *its* way – and increasing its influence in particular areas internationally. The latter strategy means greater involvement not just in international cooperation but, especially in the economic field, in European integration. This has never been an easy road for Norway to travel.

The nineteenth century saw a struggle for autonomy by Norway, first against Denmark and then against Sweden (see Chapter 2). Even after independence in 1905, this autonomy was threatened in the First World War and then, more dramatically, by the German invasion on 9 April 1940. Joining NATO in 1949 was a recognition that Norway needed outside help to secure the defence of the country in the long term. Membership of an alliance provided some elements of influence for a small state that were missing in Norway's previous security policy. However, in a range of other policies – social, environmental and economic – Norway steered its own course after the Second World War, with just a modest involvement in cooperative organizations.

The lead-up to the 1972 referendum was a major change in this approach. It was an attempt to bring Norway into what was becoming the mainstream of economic and trade cooperation in Western Europe, the European Communities. This move represented more than just a switch in trade and economic policy, it presaged a development in the political process that would require Norway to adapt to a new political system – that of the EC – to gain influence. It would certainly have meant a sacrifice of Norwegian autonomy as many understood it. The 1972 vote thus became a struggle between something Norwegian and something else. Norwegian sectoral interests may well have not benefited from membership as was the case in Denmark or the UK, but the referendum campaign only partly reflected that. It was also a fight between 'them' and 'us' over the soul of Norway. It was a continuing struggle between those representing government and those who claimed to voice the nation's feeling, with the battleground being in the realms of civil society. The background to this civil war, fought with slogans and epithets, can be seen in Norwegian history and institutions and in the identities, ideas and culture that they have generated (see Chapter 2). The referendum provided a modest little 'clash of civilizations' for Norway. It was not on the grand scale of Jihad versus McWorld or capitalism versus communism, but it was deeply felt within Norway. For many, it was 'Norway' versus 'Europe', and 'Norway' won.

Much changed between the September 1972 and the 28 November 1994 referendums (see Chapter 3). Norway became a more urban, richer country with a greater dependence on its oil and gas. Its politics became more fragmented. For over twenty years it had an industrial free trade agreement with the EC. The EC evolved, extending its policy remit and developing its institutions until it was transmuted into the European Union by the 1992 Treaty of Maastricht. Membership grew from six states in 1972 to twelve by 1994 and fifteen in 1995. The Cold War ended, completely changing the whole context of international relations in Europe.

By 1994 Norwegian society and the relative strength of its socio-economic groups had moved on from 1972 (see Chapter 3). These developments and the acceptance of the EEA meant that the 1994 referendum was much less a choice of identities than in 1972; it was more a policy choice of the exact form of relationship between Norway and the institutions of European integration. That Norway wanted a much closer involvement than that offered by the free trade agreement was decided when its government signed the EEA agreement in 1992. The European Economic Area seemed to offer some, albeit limited, influence for the EFTA states in the EU's Single European Market in exchange for a reduction in the autonomy of their economic policies. Though both the 'yes' and the 'no' sides tried to broaden the issue, the November 1994 vote was more a matter of a quantitative change in relations with the EU rather than the qualitative one of the 1972 referendum. Should the EEA be dropped for full membership? Did membership offer greater influence and was this worth the further loss of autonomy? What was the best way to adapt to the growing influence of the EU?

Since November 1994, the calculations have again changed for Norway. The 'pillar' structure of the Maastricht Treaty has allowed the EU involvement in a wider range of policies. The treaties of Amsterdam and Nice, followed by the efforts to create an EU treaty on the constitution, have developed the institutions and institutional balance of the EU. Enlargement, made reality in May 2004, has increased the size and weight of the Union. The original concept of the EEA has mutated. It became even more unbalanced as three of the EFTA states 'changed sides' by joining the EU and the 2004 enlargement further destroyed the notion of the EEA even having two 'sides'. Norway has also become more associated with the work of the EU, especially through Schengen and CFSP cooperation. In all this, Norway has attempted to exercise its influence, in particular in areas of greatest interest to it. The outcome of those strategies will be covered in Chapters 4 to 7. The book aims at addressing three sets of questions.

The *first* group will be covered in two opening chapters but will also be woven into the rest of the book. They involve the wider background to the more detailed questions investigated in Chapters 4 to 7 and examine the deeper relationship between Norway and European integration. Indeed, to what extent is it useful to talk about 'Norway' in this context or would it be better to look separately at the Norwegian state, Norwegian society and the Norwegian nation? What factors have determined any Norwegian approach towards the outside world, in particular to Europe? Has the self-understanding of what constitutes Norway changed since 1972 and 1994 and, if so, has this affected its approach to European integration?

The *second* are the specific questions about Norway's relationship with the EU during the time frame mentioned above. This relationship will be examined in Chapters 4 to 7 under three main headings that broadly correspond to the so-called three pillars of the 1992 Maastricht Treaty. The first is that of the Single European Market and its associated policies, the core of the Union, and much of that link has been in the form of the EEA. How successful has the EEA been in dealing with the mainly trade and economic elements? And what about other aspects, such as fisheries, not covered by the main body of the EEA? The second is Norway's relations with the EU's CFSP, in particular its evolving European Security and Defence Policy (ESDP). How has Norway fitted in to developments there? The final area covers Justice and Home Affairs (JHA) where a number of issues have, since the signing of the Maastricht Treaty, been transferred to the first pillar. What relationship have the two sides had on Justice and Home Affairs matters, including those covered by the Schengen Accords?

The *third* set of questions speculate about how Norway's relations with the rest of Europe may develop in the coming years. Will it be a secret suitor just waiting to plight its troth to the EU or is it as sure an outsider as, say, Canada? Is it merely marking time, adapting as best it can to the actions of the EU and waiting for changing undercurrents in Norwegian society and politics and for wider developments in Europe that could bring it into a more central position in the process of European integration? These questions will be picked up in Chapter 8.

These three sets of questions are interrelated, as will be explained in 'An overall framework' below. Before considering the theoretical background to the study, the actors involved should be identified.

Identifying the actors

In order to study the relationship between Norway and European integration, the two elements in the calculus have to be laid bare. The concept of 'European integration' is by no means an easy one to pin down. What is meant by 'Norway' may seem a lot clearer: it is, after all, there to be seen in the atlas as a long, thin north European country with a famously indented coastline. However, in relation to European integration it does need further definition beyond its geographical outline.

The factors affecting any consideration of the relationship between an individual country such as Norway and the process of European integration will be fashioned by wider global considerations and by the nature of the two interacting variables. There is clearly a size difference between the two: the population, wealth, power and area of the membership of the EU clearly overshadow those of Norway. However, the extent to which the attributes of its members are or can be transferred as fungible resources to the institutions of the EU when dealing with Norway, is doubtful. A closer examination of the two entities is worthwhile at this point.

Building Europe

European integration as such is scarcely an actor. It is a process, an aim and, for some, an aspiration. A dictionary definition of integration is that it is 'the act of combining or adding parts to make a unified whole' (Collins 1979: 759). The process of integration means that decision-making and taking, previously undertaken nationally, are now conducted at a different level, mainly that of the EU. 'Parts', either member states or new areas of policy, have been added over the years. The aim and aspiration is the unified whole, but its nature in Europe is a matter of disagreement. For some it is a Europe of the nation states and a trading group; for others a federal Europe similar to the United States of America, with a variety of options in between (see Chapter 2).

The EU's nature complicates any consideration of the relationship between a country and European integration. As the institutions and policy-making process have developed from the European Coal and Steel Community (ECSC) through the European Economic Community (EEC) and EC to the EU, they have involved more political actors. Government ministers, civil servants and technocrats have been joined by Members of the European Parliament, representatives of interest and pressure groups and regional voices. Local and regional administrations, sovereign state governments and EU institutions have become interlocked in what has been typified as *multi-level governance* whereby 'national governmental control became diluted by the activities of supranational and subnational actors' (Marks *et al.* 1996: 373).

A further complication is the difference in decision-making in the three pillars of the EU. Even within the *communautaire* pillar, decisions are made by a variety of methods, each allowing a different balance between the Community-based institutions and governmental ones (Galloway 2001; Nugent 1999: Part 2). In the second and third pillars, the state-based elements tend to dominate. As mentioned, some elements of the third pillar have migrated to pillar one. Furthermore, the Amsterdam Treaty introduced a number of 'flexibility' clauses that allow closer cooperation between some EU states, with others opting out (Warleigh 2002).

Clearly European integration, with the EU at its core, is a dynamic process. The developments in the main engine of integration – the EC and then the EU – have partly determined the menu of opportunities open for states such as Norway in their relations with the integration process, even before membership of the EEA. The list of policy areas dealt with by the institutions of European integration has lengthened over the years. At first this affected Norway only when it came to consider its trade relations with the early EC. As time went by, the environment, more social policy, research and development, health and safety, transport, education, and then justice and home affairs, economic and monetary union, and foreign and security policy were covered. In other words, some of the core areas of state activity – external and internal security – are now covered by EU treaties. This affects non-members when they come to negotiate such matters. The EU is also more likely to have greater influence in setting trends and determining values than its separate individual members acting alone. Indeed it has been suggested that the EU has become a 'normative power' (Manners 2002: 235–58). The structure of the EU will also mean that the relationship is not just an intergovernmental one. There is provision for involvement by Norway in the layers of multi-level governance, and the likelihood that the EU will interreact with the various sections of Norwegian society.

This leads to another point: the relationship is not merely one of government to government, of two billiard balls bouncing off each other. It cannot be seen as a relationship between two thoroughly bounded entities without consideration of what is happening within them. Because of the complicated institutional structure of the EU, the Norwegian side has to face not just the Council and the individual member states but also the Commission, the European Parliament, the institutions of the EEA, of cooperation in the field of Justice and Home Affairs and of ESDP, as well as a host of smaller EU-related institutions. Confronted with this labyrinth, there is a danger of any state suffering from institutional overload and confusion. A small state, with limitations on the size of its ministries and administration, could be at a greater disadvantage (Thorhallsson 2000: 232–40). The picture is even more complicated as neither side is a unified actor. The EU's Council has a variety of forms depending on subject matter while the Commission has various functional directorates, and its relationship with the Council and the European Parliament in the decision-making process of the EU is far from simple (Nugent 1999: Part 2). Norway itself can also be seen in terms that complicate the scene: emphasis can be placed on its government (which in itself may not be a unified actor), the wider civil society and/or on its people.

Constructing Norway

Norway, the land occupied by people, cannot relate to anything, except perhaps the flora and fauna that deck its dales and mountainsides or live in its fjords. In its relation to other parts of Europe it is normally its government that is seen as the interlocutor, though the wider population may also be heard, as may politicians not in the government, and interest and pressure groups.

The Norwegian government can itself be broken down into a variety of ministries, not all acting in coordination with their colleagues (Moses and Knutsen 2001). 'The Norwegian government' may be affected by bureaucratic nuances and by political divisions, sectoral concerns and public opinion. When considering Norway in terms of European integration, the Norwegian government (however defined) can be taken to speak for Norway, or specific Norwegian sectoral interests – both governmental and non-governmental – may voice the opinion of the country for their area. A wider consideration may be given to the Norwegian nation, with an emphasis on a group of people bound together by their understanding of their own history, culture and identity.

Thus when thinking about Norway, the state, and what it can do, a consideration of state capacity demands a view of not just the interests and organization of the government but also those of societal groups such as the socio-economic interests (Ribot 1993: 26).

The state can be seen to exist at a socio-political level, even as an idea held by a group of people (Buzan 1991: 63–4). Nevertheless, it is also a physical organism that gives flesh to the ideas of its occupants, or at least those that have access to the mechanisms of the state through its institutions. Thus a conceptualization of the state of Norway can be seen to involve not just the physical basis of the state, but also its institutional expression and what may be considered as the idea of the state (Buzan 1991: 65).

Neumann (2002a: 97–8) also deals with the *primacy of ideas and identity* in shaping modern Norway and its relationship with the rest of Europe. He portrays a battle between the paternalistic agents of the state, who considered the nation there to be moulded, and those who, one way or another, saw themselves as the voice of the people, the nation. In contrast, Heidar (2001: 6) talks of *the primacy of politics*, whereby, historically, 'politics and policies have been crucial in developing Norwegian society . . . Norwegian politics, social and economic change has often been initiated within the political sphere'. Väyrynen (1993) advocates the *primacy of sectoral interests*. While Ingebritsen (1998: 42–3) agrees that 'the political influence of leading sectors . . . is a systematic way to understand the politics (and economics) underlying the discourse about European integration', she brings together identity and interest, with the emphasis on the latter (ibid.): 'Nordic constructions of the EC are not just a discourse but also reflect the preferences of prominent, well-organized groups within each society.' Each of these approaches gives a different weight to the importance of the three elements outlined above, nation, state and society. Neumann's emphasis is more about the battle for the vision of the nation; Heidar sees Norwegian society as being fashioned in an important way by the political elite of the state, while Väyrynen and Ingebritsen show the capture of the political process by sectoral groups in society.

So what is meant by Norway when talking about 'Norway and Europe'? If it is to be treated just as a state that exists at the turn of the twentieth and twenty-first centuries, then the policies of the Norwegian government are the most important area of assessment, especially if they are seen as having a strong effect on society. Nevertheless, this might be a short-sighted view, as the electorate of Norway has in referendums twice rejected the European policies of its governments. Perhaps this expressed a more deeply embedded difference between people and elite about the concept of Norway, reflecting a historic distrust of the government in Oslo by certain groups. Also, given the all-embracing nature of European integration, it might be better to consider the wider views of Norwegian society, especially the economic, social and political groups active within it. Chapter 2 will examine the background to the three constituent parts of Norway: the state, the society and the nation. Meanwhile, a more limited attempt will be made to define 'Norway' as an interlocutor for the agents of European integration, especially the EU.

Defining Norway

From 1380 until 1905 the Norwegian realm either shared its ruler with other Nordic countries or, from 1536 to 1814, was seen as part of the Danish kingdom. Nevertheless, the country proved to be less in thrall to Denmark than may be assumed. Indeed, its distinctness 'was at least as strong in 1814 as it had been in 1536' (Dyrvik 1995: 123). It was certainly richer, albeit as an exporter of raw materials, and it had its own ruling class. Nevertheless, it was on the periphery not only of Europe but even of the Danish kingdom. There was no Norwegian state as an independent entity, though there was enough of a differentiation from metropolitan Denmark to represent a 'state in waiting'. Whether there was a Norwegian nation is disputable, but again there were elements (such as language) that could emerge and be seen as representing a nation. Society was predominantly rural and peasant-based, with merchants and administrators in the large towns and cities.

The events of 1814 by which Norway passed from the Danish to the Swedish crown may be seen as the results of international manoeuvrings, especially those between Sweden and Denmark at the end of the Napoleonic wars. Such a view would leave out the key element of the role of Norwegian interests. Although their attempts to obtain outright independence were thwarted, they nevertheless achieved considerable autonomy within the union with the Swedish crown and a liberal constitution by the end of 1814 (Riste 2001: 39–51). Norway had the trappings of statehood: a government, a parliament, its own currency and even a flag for its commercial shipping. The uneasy relationship with the Swedish monarchy was tested by the rising power of those who represented Norway's particular economic and trading interests. Neumann (2001) has also traced the nation-building of the nineteenth century, showing in particular its antagonism to the government in Oslo (then Christiania), even after the achievement of responsible parliamentary government in 1884. Nation, society and government came together in the lead up to 1905, when Norwegian independence was finally wrested from the Swedish monarchy after a referendum in which 99.95 per cent of the 85 per cent turnout of male voters cast their ballots for independence (Riste 2001: 70). The interests and the politicians had acted and the nation had spoken.

The nature of government and its relationship with wider society changed over time – the administration in Oslo was not responsible to the Storting until 1884 and full adult suffrage was introduced in 1913, with proportional representation in 1919. The growing 'corporatism' of Norwegian government that tied it more closely to the leading economic elements in civil society – especially the trade unions and the employers' organizations – was apparent from the 1930s until the late twentieth century. However, Heidar (2001: 6–7) suggests that the economic, political and social base was fashioned by the state from 1814 until well into the twentieth century. On the other hand, the cleavages in the Norwegian nation can be seen as having a political resonance in terms of civil society and in the parliament and government. This was apparent in the language and alcohol issues, in class differences and the attempt by the Labour Party to bring together the farm labourers and the industrial workers, and in the gap between the cities and the regions (Rokkan 1967).

These facets of the Norwegian nation, society and government have sometimes led to a varied and uneven approach to the question of autonomy and influence with regard to Europe, details of which are outlined in the next two chapters. Broadly, the history, culture and institutions of Norway have encouraged strong elements that have defined themselves in antipathy to Oslo, Copenhagen, then Stockholm, and certainly to the continent of Europe. When looking out, these Norwegian eyes have been fixed on the sea, especially the North Sea and North Atlantic. Governments have reflected this both inward-looking, in nationalist terms, and Atlanticist view but have increasingly had to deal with the events of the outside world. Sometimes when faced with a choice between the Nordic, the European or the Atlantic, a government has gone for the Atlantic option, as in 1949. On other occasions, governments have taken a European path but have found themselves blocked by sectional interests and national sentiment.

The representatives of civil society can be seen as interlocutors between nation and government, articulating the views and interests of certain parts of the nation. To some extent, these representatives have been able to capture branches of government (as could be seen in the case of agriculture) but they have also been compromised by their own proximity to power, as in the case of trade unions and governments, especially Labour ones. They have therefore been torn between elements of the nation and government when the two have parted company over relations with Europe. Voices based in the culture and history of the nation have called them to choose autonomy internationally, and thus keep their influence nationally, while those in government have wooed them with the promise of greater influence internationally, albeit at the price of reduced autonomy. The next section will examine the theoretical bases of the tension between autonomy and influence as factors that have contributed to moulding Norwegian attitudes to Europe.

Examining the theory

Kelstrup (1992: 17) remarked on how 'the way problems related to European integration "fall between" two major sub-disciplines within political science, international relations theory and comparative politics'. Indeed, as the concepts of Norway and of European integration are far from being simple, an examination of 'inter-state' relations between the two (which would already designate the EU as being state-like) is not enough. This section presents an overall framework that may be able to bridge the gap between the disciplines and thus cast a light on the relationship between Norway and the process of European integration. In particular, it pays attention to the concept of Europeanization and adaptation.

An overall framework

How can the relationship between Norway and the process and aims of European integration best be understood? Why has the relationship turned out as it has?

First, a few words are needed on the subject of the inquiry. It has already been mentioned that neither side of the equation – Norway, European integration – is simple. However, Chapters 4 to 7 will concentrate on the relations between the Norwegian government and the various aspects of the EU. In this context, the tactics of adaptation adopted by Norway in response to European integration come into play, and they will be given further consideration in the following sections.

Nevertheless, this more immediate relationship has to be placed in a wider context. The relationship between Norway and European integration since 1994 is contingent on what happened before that date, not least the events leading up to the two Norwegian referendums of 1972 and 1994. But those events, especially that in 1972, were reflections of earlier relationships between Norway and Europe and of a Norwegian understanding not just of interests but also of identity. To understand the relationship since 1994, one must dig deeper not just into the past but also into the causal links between past and present.

This process is helped by adapting a schema provided by Jepperson *et al.* (1996), which offers the following insights:

1. Cultural or institutional elements of states' environments shape the interests or, more directly, the policies of states (ibid.: 54).[1]
2. Cultural and institutional elements of states' global or domestic environment shape state identity (ibid.: 58).
3. Variations or changes in state identity affect the policies of states (ibid.: 60).
4. 'Configurations of state identities affect normative structures': this normally refers to the way in which states institutionalize their identities in such structures established between states such as regimes and security communities (ibid.: 62).
5. States' policies are part of a process and 'both reproduce and reconstruct' cultural and institutional structure (ibid.: 63).

The key variables feeding into policy in a complex web are thus cultural and institutional elements, identity and interests (see Figure 1.1). It should not be forgotten that Norway, in common with other 'smaller' states, is not taking policy decisions in the context of a mixture of purely domestic interests, identity, institutions and culture. The limitations are also set for the decision-makers by their international environment (Hey 2003: 186).

When considering how the agents of this state (or any other) act within the wider framework of world politics, the opportunities for action can be examined, as can the willingness of the agents to act one way rather than another, to take up one option and let another pass. Starr (1997: 13–14) defines the environments of decision-makers as providing a 'structure of opportunities, risks, and potential costs and benefits, constraining decision makers . . . Opportunity is the possibility of interaction because of objective conditions that may be perceived in varying ways by decision-makers.' On the other hand,

> [w]illingness is concerned with the motivations that lead people to avail themselves of opportunities. Willingness deals with the goals and motivations of decision makers and focuses on why decision makers choose one course over another. Willingness is therefore based on perceptions of the global scene and of the domestic political conditions.
>
> (Starr 1997: 14)

The interaction between opportunity and willingness can be understood as forming a 'menu for choice' whereby the environment provides a number of opportunities from which the decision-makers may make their choice (Russett and Starr 1996).

The decision-makers, whether they are representatives of the state or agents of various interest organizations or voices of national feeling, will want to maximize the control – the ability/power to regulate or determine – they have both within a state and internationally. The constraints of opportunity may mean that the possibilities for control are anyhow fairly limited, especially for those representing the interests of a small state or nation or of a group within such a state. Nevertheless, there will still be a range of opportunities, however limited. With regard to the actions of an entity within the wider system, control may be increased either by autonomy or by influence. Autonomy – freedom to determine one's own actions and behaviour – is made easier by the absence of others constraining that freedom. In other words, a set of opportunities that represent a limited range of interaction may be accepted as it means a lack of international constraints, allowing decision-makers to exercise a fairly unhindered choice, albeit from a limited 'menu'. Normally the extent of autonomy exercised by states is constrained by internal and external factors (Engberg and Lane 1980: 212–14). Another way of achieving control is through exercising influence on others, especially those that help mould one's own environment. This presupposes interaction with those others and giving up a certain amount of autonomy in order to exercise more control by influence (Bröms 1995: 109, 116). Thus the decision-makers widen the scope of the environment – the possibility of interaction – but thereby complicate the calculations concerning their actions.

A further complexity concerns the determining factors in the decision-making process within a state. Starr (1997: 14) writes that the willingness of the decision-makers deals with their 'goals and motivations' and is based 'on perceptions of the global scene and of the domestic political conditions', to which one might add 'and economic conditions'. But what factors shape these goals, motivations and perceptions that affect the choice between autonomy and influence? The answer given here is that an understanding of the dominant economic interests in a country is important but it is not sufficient to determine that country's European integration strategy.

Economic motivations and calculation of goals may turn the preferences one way or another, but how are these calculations determined and by whom? The roots of national feeling or culture may be shallow or deep. If they run deep, then they have had much to nourish them. This may be because the elements of national culture have been embedded over a period of time and are held in place by a number of institutions. They may be reflected in the national identity/ies and also supportive of particular interests. On the other hand, feelings of nationalism and their transmission into particular policies that attempt to support autonomy may be undermined. The nurturing soil may be washed away by outside elements but this may take time. As Elias (1978: 20) wrote, 'certain social transformations can only be achieved, if at all, by long and sustained development spanning several generations'. On other occasions the change may be swift, almost revolutionary. The important factors here are not just the material conditions but also the way that they are perceived as affecting the balance between the national and the international, between autonomy and integration.

Decisions about Norway and European integration have to be seen in this wider context. There are the immediate concerns of a group responding to a policy requirement, but this is just the foreground. It can be explained in terms of the interests of dominant socio-economic groups or sections within government. Interest-group politics and bureaucratic politics may help in understanding this process. The hinterland is the wider context for such policies, and consists of the culture and institutions of the country, that have helped to fashion the identity of its inhabitants especially in response to external identities and cultures (see Figure 1.1). This provides a particular interpretation of what are appropriate responses in terms of the match between autonomy and influence and which forms of adaptation are appropriate.

Chapters 2 and 3 will pay special attention to the way that both internal institutional and socio-cultural developments and external factors helped fashion the identity and interests of the Norwegian nation, society and

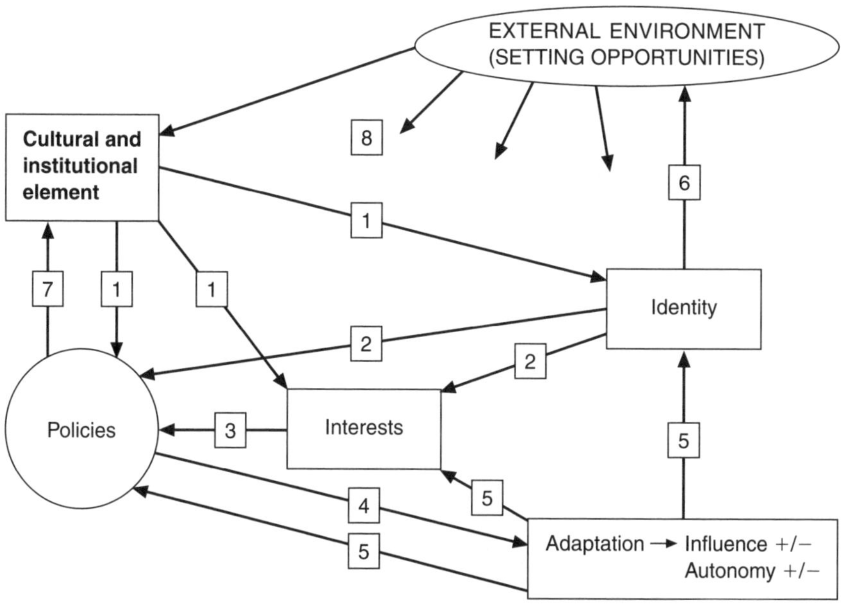

Figure 1.1 The complex mosaic of the pathways to policy.

Key:

1 Cultural and institutional elements in Norway's environment helping to shape Norwegian identity, the interests and policies
2 Changes in Norwegian identity affecting interests and policies
3 Interests directly affect policies
4 Norwegian policies on integration involve extent of willingness to adapt to European integration and increase/decrease in balance of autonomy/influence
5 Feedback from increase/decrease in influence to policies, interests and identity
6 Norwegian identity feeds into external environment
7 Policies reproduce and change cultural and institutional factors
8 External environment sets the 'menu for choice' for policy and also interacts with interests (strengthening/weakening some) and identity, culture and institutions.

state. Chapter 2 demonstrates how these factors, embedded over the years, took their toll on Norwegian relations with Europe. Chapter 3 will show how the changes wrought between 1972 and 1994 – both within Norway and externally – led to a different sort of question and answer at the 1994 referendum than at the 1972 vote, and will set the scene for Norway's response to European integration since November 1994.

Adapting and Europeanizing

The concepts of *adaptation* and of *Europeanizing* may help with the quest. Both these notions suggest ways that a country such as Norway may cope with a changing environment such as that provided by European integration. They are key ideas in other studies of small Nordic states and their environment and will find an important place here.

James Rosenau was one of the first writers to deal with the question of how a state's internal need may be balanced by external requirements, by suggesting four 'modes of adaptation'. Decision-makers responsive to both internal and external factors have a *preservative* orientation, according to Rosenau (1970: 5); they are *acquiescent* when they give preference to the external factors; *intransigent* when the internal is favoured; and when they only respond to their own values, they are *promotive*. Nikolaj Petersen (1979) again identified four 'overall patterns of policy behavior', those of dominance, balance, acquiescence and quiescence. Petersen's dominance seems to be equivalent to Rosenau's intransigence, his balanced policy to the preservative strategy, and acquiescence appears in both lists. Quiescence appears to be a neutral mode, typified by inaction, and Rosenau's promotive orientation, which he admits to being rare, is an extreme version of dominance (see Table 1.1 and also Mouritzen 1996: 4).

These represent strategies for agents to deal with their environments, and thus reflect choices made in the face of different opportunities set by that environment. It is not only states, or rather their governments, that choose from these strategies, but also associations, organizations, firms and national entities. Indeed, the leader of many commercial enterprises in a rapidly changing business environment will adopt the motto 'adapt or die'. Normally states do not have such an imperative, but nevertheless those that run the state and those encompassed by it may consider – on a fairly regular basis – how their choices fit in to the wider environment and, if there is a misfit, what may be done. A reasonable hypothesis is that in the international political and economic system, the smaller the participant in terms of resources, the smaller input it may have in formulating the environment and, on the contrary, large resource-rich states may have a greater ability to affect that environment. In the words of John Ikenberry (1991: 166) 'a small state with few resources will find structures at the international level more inflexible than a larger state with resources capable of changing regimes and arrangements...' Nevertheless, equally reasonable exceptions can be made to this hypothesis: if the system is divided into geographically or functionally more discrete areas, then a small entity within this division has a greater chance of affecting the environment in the particular policy area in which its resources are concentrated.

Table 1.1 Rosenau's and Petersen's modes of adaptation

Rosenau	Preservative	Acquiescent	Intransigent	Promotive	–
Balance	X = I	X > I	I > X	I	0
Petersen	Balanced	Acquiescent	Dominance	Dominance (+)	Quiescent

Key
X External requirements, I Internal needs, 0 neutral.

However, changes in the environment are normally independent variables for small states; it is something that happens to them. They can attempt to alter their international environment, or at least ameliorate it, by a promotive strategy, one rarely seen from a small state as it is a resource-expensive move with a high risk of failure. More often than not, the state or entity has to decide how to 'maintain a balance between internal needs and external demands' (Rosenau 1981). According to Petersen (1998: 45), the 'balanced policy mode is the archetypical integration mode' and the only one that is 'compatible with full participation in international integration'. Attempts are made to deal with the demands of the integration environment – in the form of new policy or a change in institutions – while at the same time speaking to the concerns of domestic groups that may be affected by the changes.

For much of the time and for many of the developments affecting them, the small state can do little. If demands are being made, it may have to acquiesce for a number of reasons. First, the changes could be seen by the state's decision-makers to be in their favour, albeit in the long run. Thus acquiescence is *willing*. Second, the changes may not be perceived as positive but there may be a recognition that nothing can be done to ameliorate them, so there is a *grudging* acquiescence. Third, though the changes are not seen as positive, an *expectant* acceptance is undertaken in that area with the hope of gains being made elsewhere (see also Wiberg 1996: 58).

Under what conditions do entities have to acquiesce? Rosenau (1981: 80–1) considers that when there is a much larger society 'intent upon imposing its will upon its neighbors', acquiescent adaptation persists. The other condition for its persistence is the 'absence in the adapting society of any highly potent societal, individual, or governmental variables'. This means that a society without the social groups, strong persons or decision-makers who have the willingness, and the ability, to oppose changes, has to submit to external demands. Strong civil society or national groupings – often ones with a strong identity – can provide just such resistance. They can articulate the sort of core values of the society or nation that can be preserved by a variety of responses to internal and external factors.

The concept of *Europeanization* can be related to the notion of adaptation. In the academic literature there have been a number of definitions of the term (see, for example, Featherstone 2002; Olsen 2002). It is here seen as a two-way process: one that stresses the evolution of European institutions, broadly concentrating on the process of integration at the European level, and that by which the process impacts on the 'political structures and processes of Member States' (Börzel 2002: 193). The first process has been alluded to above (see pp. 4–6). The latter aspect involves forms of adaptation and, to an extent, reflects the institutional relationship of the national political process with that of European integration. It has to do 'with the penetration of the European dimension in natural arenas of politics and policy' (Radaelli 2000: 3). The key idea is for member states to get as close a fit as possible between their national policy and that of the EU in order to lower adaptation costs. Börzel (2002: 194–5) outlines three ways in which EU states have responded to Europeanization in both the decision-making and implementation stages of the policy process – by pace-setting, by foot-dragging and by fence-sitting. These and a fourth option (least resistance) reflect some of the elements of adaptation as outlined by Rosenau and Petersen (see Table 1.2).

The pace-setters try to 'shape European policies according to their domestic preferences and priorities' (Börzel 2002: 197). At the EU decision-making stage, this seems similar to Petersen's dominance and Rosenau's intransigent and promotive strategies. However, at the implementation level it is more preservative, balancing external (EU) requirements with domestic needs. Foot-dragging is aimed at preventing other states from 'uploading' their domestic policies to the EU level or, most likely, trying to obtain 'some compensation in the form of side-payments or package deals' (Börzel 2002: 203).This resembles either the preservative (balanced) or intransigence (dominant) strategies. In the field of implementation, it is distinctly intransigent, trying to give favours to domestic elements and becoming preservative only if outside aid is available to improve domestic standards so that implementation is less problematic. Fence-sitting, 'taking an indifferent and neutral position' or building coalitions with pace-setters and foot-draggers (Börzel 2002: 206), is by its nature quiescent in the first case and preservative in the second for both policy-making and implementation. A fourth response can be added to Börzel's list, that of *least resistance*, when external demands dominate internal needs (or coalesce with them) at both the policy-making and implementation stages, and acquiescence is the response.

While Börzel's work refers to EU member states, it can equally be applied to an EEA state such as Norway. Furthermore, the strategies mentioned above are ones that can promote either Norway's autonomy or its influence within the EU system. Nevertheless, non-membership of the EU is bound to affect the balance, as Norway has fewer instruments available with which to implement its tactics. In EEA policy-making, foot-dragging and fence-sitting can be used to preserve autonomy and identity while

Table 1.2 Response to Europeanization and forms of adaptation

	Responses			
	Pace setting	*Foot-dragging*	*Fence-sitting*	*Least resistance*
Policy-making	Promotive Intransigent	Preservative Intransigent	Quiescent Preservative	Acquiescence
Implementing	Preservative	Intransigent (Preservative)	Quiescent (Preservative)	Acquiescence

pace-setting, least resistance (and possibly fence-sitting) can be used to promote influence. In policy implementation, foot-dragging (and fence-sitting) is a useful tool for maintaining autonomy, while least resistance (acquiescence) and a high level of implementation (pace-setting) could be part of the tactics of influence (see Table 1.3). Of course, different approaches can be employed in different functional areas.

What might determine the different tactics? The importance of the functional area to the economy could be one area. Börzel (2002: 196) points to the importance of the level of economic development. Also issue salience may affect tactics, with greater importance attached to those issues seen as having a heavier 'political weight' (Miles 2001). A state may be willing to adopt a tactic of greater risk – that of promotion or, at least of intransigence – when the issue is one of high domestic salience. A further consideration is the extent to which support of one's own view can be found on 'the other side'. Norway has had a presumed advantage in having its Nordic colleagues (except Iceland) as EU members (Sweden and Finland since January 1995). As will be seen, this has not always meant an increase in influence within the EU, though the presence of the old ally, the UK, has helped in distinct areas such as oil and gas and defence.

The *type* of European integration is a consideration. Knill and Lehmkull (1993: 3) make the simple distinction between positive integration, which is regulatory, negative integration, which is deregulatory (such as the single market, though that also involved a lot of regulations). They add the notion of framing integration that might 'change the domestic political climate by stimulating and strengthening the overall support for broader European reform objectives'. This in turn could affect policies and even identities (Vink 2001: 879).

The calculations that both government and civil society have to make concerning policy-making and policy implementation are different for all three forms of integration. While the strategies of pace-setting, foot-dragging and fence-sitting are all possible options for the formulation of policy in both the positive and negative form, implementation may be easier to hinder in the positive form, as it often involves detailed parliamentary legislation or, at least, national administrative rules. The implementation of the negative form requires the abolition of restrictions undertaken

Table 1.3 Tactics of maximizing autonomy and influence in the EU

	Autonomy	*Influence*
Policy-making	Foot-dragging (intransigent) Fence-sitting (quiescent)	Pace-setting (promotive) Least resistance (acquiescence)
Implementation	Foot-dragging (intransigent) Fence-sitting (quiescent)	Pace-setting (preservative) Least resistance (acquiescence)

multilaterally to an agreed timetable, leaving little room for manoeuvre. Framing integration is the most nebulous, both in its formulation and implementation, as it depends more on attitudes and common acceptance. It is therefore an area for action by civil society – whether in favour or against – as well as government.

Involvement in the process of European integration can thus have a feedback affecting the elements of state, society and nation that in themselves set some of the boundaries for integration.

A high level of integration can reduce the capacity of the state to intervene effectively in certain policy areas, especially those affected by negative integration once regulations have been dropped. It can change the nature of the state by requiring it to become more supervisory rather than *dirigiste*. Such integration can change the balance of interests within civil society by increasing (or sometimes decreasing) the economic incentives for certain groups to remain within the process of integration. It can also affect identity in a number of ways. It can provide an 'other' (the integrating forces) whose actions can threaten the values of the nation, stirring feelings of opposition and autonomy. However, it can undermine the willingness to pursue autonomy by placing a higher price on it and by making involvement in the integrative process to achieve influence more attractive.

Outline of the book

In summary, this book will examine three sets of questions (see pp. 3–4) about Norway's relationship to European integration, especially after 1994. These relate to the quest in Norway to exercise some control over its political-economic environment and the tension between greater autonomy or more influence in achieving this. The first set concerns how Norway has been constituted in relation to Europe and thus involves an overview of the building of Norway as a political entity and how those within the country came to see themselves in the European context. These issues have helped to determine some of the answers to the second set of questions which involve the strategy and tactics of the Norwegian government in its relationship with the EU since November 1994. Finally, there are questions that lead to a speculation about the future relationship of Norway and the EU.

Chapters 2 and 3 look at how the outlook of the Norwegian socio-economic interest groups and political groups about Europe has been fashioned by their identity and by the culture and institutions within the country, as well as by the external environment. Chapter 3 explores the interplay of the various sets of opportunities offered by the changing nature of European integration – especially the changes in the EU – and by the developments in Norwegian politics and economics, and the willingness to choose certain options by the decision-makers, the agents of civil society and 'the nation'. Chapters 4 to 7 investigate how this has manifested itself in policy terms after November 1994. Chapter 8 brings in the issue of the 2004 EU enlargement and examines the options for Norway in its relationship to the process of European integration. Finally, some broader observations are made about that relationship. Throughout the work the question will be asked as to the extent to which choices made improved on either the element of autonomy of or that of influence by Norway.

2 Norway up to the first application

Norsemen, whatsoe'er thy station,
Thank thy God, whose power
Willed and wrought the land's salvation
In her darkest hour.

('Ja, vi elsker' (Norwegian national anthem) by Björnstjerne Björnson, trans. G.M. Gathorne-Hardy; Royal Norwegian Government Information Office, 1943: iii)

The recent history of Norway's relations with the rest of Europe, and in particular with the process known as European integration, has been covered in previous texts (Allen 1979; Archer and Sogner 1998; Neumann 2001; Pharø 1991). The aim here is to give a brief account that places events and relationships since the turn of the twenty-first century in context. This chapter will examine the development of Norway as a modern state and will pay attention to its international context and to the internal factors that shaped the country. In particular, it will outline how the broad culture and institutions of the country affected the state, represented by the main policy-maker, the government; society, especially the socio-economic interests; and Norwegian identity, particularly in the form of the nation.

A number of motifs will emerge during the chapter. First, many of the socio-economic and political divisions that later emerged in the European debates have their roots in Norwegian history. Second, as a small state, Norway has had to adapt to its surroundings. Finally, at different stages there has been a changing balance between the two ways of trying to maximize political and economic control, autonomy and influence.

Norway up to 1905

This section will look at the formation of Norway as a social, economic and political entity in the period to 1905, to see whether there are any clues that may help in explaining the later attitudes of its government, interest groups and people towards European integration. Are there deeply embedded factors either in the placing of the country within a wider international context or in the socio-economic and political developments within Norway that left a lasting impression? Norway the state, the society and the nation will be examined to see what extent cultural factors affected their development and how these developments were reflected, if at all, in institutional form.

The international environment

Norway, first a joint kingdom with Denmark and then, from 1814 to 1905, with Sweden, was shielded from most European events. When it did spring on to the European stage in 1814 with its declaration of independence, it soon discovered the constraints of international diplomacy as it was passed unceremoniously from one royal hand to another. This process was moderated by events within Norway itself that led to the eventual establishment of a constitutional monarchy (Dyrvik 1995: 208–11).

The representation of commercial interest had consequences for the Swedish–Norwegian union. Norway was served by the Swedish diplomatic corps, who did not understand the needs abroad of a seafaring nation. Indeed, conflict over control of foreign and consular affairs provided the combustible material that eventually blew apart the dual monarchy of Norway and Sweden in 1905, though throughout the nineteenth century a rising Norwegian nationalism demanded increased control of Norway's affairs by the Norwegian parliament, the Storting (Danielsen 1995a: 304–9).

In short, the main international political elements that impinged on Norway from the thirteenth century were those of the immediate region, emanating from Copenhagen and Stockholm and, by the nineteenth century, from London. Distance, and slowness of communications, meant that Norway had to wait for the after-shocks of the continent-wide earthquake of the Napoleonic wars for the opportunity to break free of Denmark, and international control was sufficiently strong in 1814 to require a conditional transfer to Sweden. This also provided Norway, through Stockholm, with a presumed influence in the international system, though at the price of loss of autonomy in international affairs.

Norway the state

The claim that by 1274, the 'Norwegian king's realm' included 'one people, one territory and an independent political organization covering the country as a whole' (Helle 1995: 74) may have the ring of truth but is perhaps stretching the unity of each of the three elements a little far. It is certainly best to heed Helle's warning (1995: 87) that '[o]ne must not, however, confuse the state in the high Middle Ages with the state today, in terms of the latter's importance for and the control of society'.

Norway as a nation-state has scarcely been in business for a century. It drew apart from Sweden's embrace in 1905, though it had had a shadow existence in the form of the dual monarchy of Norway–Sweden for ninety years before then.

A number of theoretical works on state formation have traced the rise of the European states from the late Middle Ages to the nineteenth and early twentieth centuries and have placed some emphasis on the relationship of the nature of the rulers and ruled as well as on wider factors such as the geo-strategic or the religious element (Axtmann 1993: 21–45). How these attributes affected Norway may provide clues to its relations with other European states.

The rise of the Norwegian kingdom is often traced to the early thirteenth century, with its territorial power peaking in 1265. In 1380 it was united with Denmark, and further union with Sweden followed in 1397. Attempts to keep all three countries under one monarch were made throughout the fifteenth century but failed, with Sweden finally breaking away in 1521. By 1536 the Protestant Reformation was well under way and Norway became dominated by Danish nobles. The Norwegian kingdom was abolished by King Christian III, who decreed that Norway should be 'of the Danish realm and for ever under the crown of Denmark' (Neumann 2002a: 91).

Tilly identifies four factors whose various combinations provide the history of state formation: concentrated coercion, concentrated capital, preparation for war, and position within the international system (1990: 14). However, he scarcely mentions Norway in his study and, when he does, it is generally together with the other Nordic states (ibid.: 133–6). He notes that by the eighteenth century, in the four Nordic countries (Denmark, Finland, Norway and Sweden), 'the creation of a large military force on the basis of a small population, a relatively unmonetized economy, and an exiguous bourgeoisie had produced a very substantial state apparatus in which civil bureaucrats and clergy did a great deal of work for the crown'.

By the end of the seventeenth century a hierarchy in Norway successfully administered the place, not necessarily by means of coercion. Tilly's argument perhaps leaves out the effect of ideas, especially in the form of religion, Lutheranism in the case of Norway. Dyrvik (1995: 172) reckons that there were about 1,500 civil servants (*embetsmenn)* by the end of the seventeenth century, of whom 400 were ecclesiastical. The Lutheran Church was not only the source of the core of administrators, it was also a link with Denmark and provided education.

The concentration of capital in Norway was originally more in the hands of the Hansa traders, who were later replaced by Dutch and Norwegian merchants. The confiscation of Church property strengthened the position of the king in the country, though after a while much of this property was sold to Norwegians, representing a form of capital dispersion (Dyrvik 1995: 160). Preparation for war was also, appropriately enough, a two-edged sword. The Danish king had little or no nobility to rely on to raise his armies in Norway, and depended on conscription of the Norwegian peasantry for the Norwegian army and the bulk of the naval crews for both kingdoms (ibid.: 193). Furthermore the threat to Norway was different from that to Denmark: it was land-based, from Sweden (ibid.: 201–2). Indeed, it was through the wars of the seventeenth century and the early eighteenth that the borders of Norway were settled. Dyrvik (1995: 177) also sees the financing of the frequent wars of the seventeenth century, and the administration required to raise that money 'as temporarily accelerating a long-term trend, the hallmark of which was the greater involvement of the state in ever more aspects of social life'.

By the start of the nineteenth century Norway as a state was in a settled area and with governmental structures that were different from those of other provinces of Denmark. Dyrvik claimed that this fracture came because

> The elite saw itself as Norwegian, and this awareness, in the end, proved stronger than the close links with Denmark. Besides, there existed so little injustice and exploitation in Norwegian society that the most important social groups could agree on equal distribution of both obligations and benefits.
>
> (Dyrvik 1995: 199–200)

The settlement of 1815 left Norway with an exceptional constitutional position. True, the country had a Swedish king, but there had been a price to pay by Stockholm for this privilege which was the adoption for Norway of the liberal constitution that had been drawn up at Eidsvoll in 1814. The changes in this constitution resulting from the negotiations that led to the handing over of Norway to the King of Sweden weakened the power of the monarchy in Norway over matters of foreign and defence policy (Dyrvik 1995: 210–11). During this time the Storting was dominated by the administrative class, the *embetsmenn*, partly as a result of the electoral system and partly because of the lack of an aristocracy and the as yet disorganized state of the peasantry (Dyrvik 1995: 223).

Heidar (2001: 6–7) points to the vital role played by the state in shaping modern Norwegian society in the period from 1814 to 1884 when 'public officials vigorously advocated and put in place the vital institutions of a modern capitalist economy, such as banks and credit institutions. Bureaucrats and politicians, not entrepreneurs, created the foundations for private enterprise in Norway.' A battle from 1872 over the question of the responsibility of the government to the Storting proved long-drawn-out but ended in 1884 in victory for those who wanted such 'responsible government'. Reforms after 1884 led to a greater participation in the political system and a sharing of power between the Storting and the bureaucracy (Danielsen 1995a: 269).

Requests for a separate Norwegian consular system, an issue of direct importance for Norway's relations with the rest of the world, had escalated by June 1905 into demands for a Norwegian Foreign Office, and on this question the union finally split. The idea was that autonomy would bring greater influence in the precise areas of Norwegian interest, those of trade and commerce.

What does all this indicate about the Norwegian state compared with those in continental Europe? The indigenous agents of the state developed from the early sixteenth century to 1905. Tilly's four factors of state formation – especially those of concentrated coercion and preparation for war – pushed the process along but these were less important than in France or Prussia. The concentration of capital did not seem to be a strong factor when the Danish monarch started selling his land in Norway at the end of the seventeenth century. Norway's position in the international system condemned it to be a shuttlecock between Sweden and Denmark. Its place on the margin of Europe in 1809 to 1814 and then in 1905, together with the turn of events in the Napoleonic Wars and some judicious British involvement, led to the loosening of ties first with Denmark and then with Sweden. Nevertheless, the state of Norway that emerged in 1814 and in 1905 was not carved out of rock by international agreement – it was created from within by key societal groups in 1814 and by a sweeping national movement in 1905.

The Norwegian state, though appearing on the map as an independent entity only in 1905, was a long time in the making. Furthermore, the agents of the state – the administration – were heavily involved in society and, during the nineteenth century, were key elements in building the economic foundations of Norway.

Norwegian society

By the seventeenth century the social structure of Norway had some distinct differences from its neighbours, Sweden and Denmark. There was the familiar pattern of a nobility, headed by the king, and the civil service, including the clergy, controlling most of the resources in the countryside, and the merchants in the towns controlling trade, with a peasantry and labourers representing the less privileged sector of society. However, by the end of the seventeenth century the Norwegian aristocracy had declined in size, owning only 8 per cent of land, with Crown estates making up another 31 per cent (Dyrvik 1995: 158–62). Heidar (2001: 6) notes that Norway was 'unique in not having a viable aristocracy and in keeping a free peasantry all through the Middle Ages'. While Dyrvik (1995: 167) warns that 'one must not exaggerate the egalitarian aspects of Norwegian rural society', he admits that there was little of the 'feudal or manorial exploitation that was so common in the rest of Europe' and that the relationship between the general population and town elite was 'dominated by trade, not by the purchase of labour'. Both parties were 'mutually dependent' (ibid.: 171).

One of the distinctions between the peasantry and the administrative class and between town and country was language. In post-Reformation Norway, Danish was the language of the Church and of the government. From the eighteenth century it was the language of education and it would be regarded as a foreign language for the peasantry brought up with a dialect mother-tongue. It was only in the first decade of the nineteenth century that calls were heard for a national language (Neumann 2002a: 94).

By the end of the period of Danish control the administrative class was relatively small – some 1,800 – and, while distanced from others in Norwegian society, it was 'uncorrupt and impartial' by the standards of the Europe of the late eighteenth century and 'managed to balance the interests of the other groups in society' (Dyrvik 1995: 181). This administrative class was politicized as it found a *modus vivendi* with the new Swedish-based monarchy. This seems to back up the point made by Grew (1984) that by the nineteenth century the state was pulling society into its own political space and shaping it for its own objectives and Heidar's notion of the state fashioning society in the 1814–84 period. However, it gave the social groups an incentive to capture the institutions of the state for *their* own ends. How those groups reacted to the politicization of societal space rested partly on the nature of the interrelationship of these social groups. As shown above, by the nineteenth century Norway, relative to most European countries, had a harmonious society with a stronger basis for cooperation than for conflict between social groups. Without being starry-eyed about the nature of Norwegian society, it seemed less likely that conflict would serve one class. Certainly the presence of a strong peasantry meant that those living in the burgeoning towns would not have things all their own way.

The cultural separation of the administrators and the peasantry and labourers has been pursued as a theme by Neumann (2002a). Throughout the nineteenth century Norway had a strong peasantry and a powerful administrative class and only a small, but growing, urban working class and bourgeoisie. Also the two main class elements – *øvrigheten*, the authorities, and the peasantry – had different views of the relationship of the state and nation, with – to put it crudely – the former seeing greater state involvement in the business of the nation, and the latter wishing a national take-over of the state.

The nineteenth century was one of vibrant growth for Norway. The population increased from 885,000 in 1815 to 2.2 million in 1900. Whereas 9.4 per cent of Norwegians lived in densely populated areas in 1815, by 1900 the share was 35.7 per cent. These figures also mask emigration, mainly to North America. From 1880 to 1893 and from 1900 to 1911 between 10,000 to 20,000 more people a year left the country than immigrated (Statistisk sentralbyrå 2000).

The rapid economic growth that typified the Norwegian economy for the fifty or so years following the end of the Napoleonic Wars ground to an end by the close of the 1870s as 'the forces that had fuelled the growth in the Norwegian economy appeared to be exhausted' (Hovland 1995: 271). A deeper-water fishing fleet developed, a timber products industry was developed. Hydro-electric power gave Norway an advantage in the international market in electro-chemical and electro-metallurgical products and saw, in 1905, the creation of Norsk Hydro, supported by foreign capital. The shipping business continued to grow and the foreign currency it earned covered the commodity trade deficit (Hovland 1995: 277–87).

The economic changes were reflected in the social profile of the nation. A move from country to town was matched by the change from primary industries to secondary and, more gradually, into the service industries and public service. More women were employed, frequently as clerks, nurses and teachers in these services, as well as in the textile industry. Small businesses and the peasantry dominating the rural scene reduced the social distance between employer and employee. Blue-collar workers had organized themselves collectively by the end of the nineteenth century (Hovland 1995: 291). Voluntary associations gathered pace with the abolition of economic privileges in the 1850s and 1860s. Associations representing special interest groups became a facet of Norwegian life and training places for those interested in politics (Danielsen 1995a: 265).

The nation

Stenius (2003: 157) remarks that when 'modern political culture was in the making in the nineteenth and early twentieth century, it was the nation that was the obvious and indeed the only considered frame for social and political improvement'. This leads to the question about the pre-existence of the nation in the case of a country such as Norway. When did Norway become a nation? One core element of a nation is an understanding among a group of people in a geographical area that they have a common heritage, often seen in terms of language, culture and religion, and that these factors bind them together and usually exclude others. This Herderian view of a *kulturnation* was one common in the mid to late nineteenth century and by then Norwegians both saw themselves and were seen as a nation, separate from the Danes and the Swedes. One of the key indicators, according to Herder, was a distinct national language, it being the duty of nationalists to rediscover the nation's forgotten traditions, even when they had to be invented (Hobsbawm 1995: 96). Coexisting with this view of the nation in the nineteenth century was that of Hegel, who insisted that the ultimate mission of the nation was the creation of a state, the *staatsnation* (Gellner 1997: 65).

Joenniemi (2002: 196), writing about the case of Finland in the nineteenth century, sees the Herderian impulse taking a pragmatic view of the state: 'The state was not viewed as an anti-nation to be resisted if it did not bend to the needs of the nation. The nation was there for different things and its aim was to grow as a cultural unity.' Whether the concept of nationhood emerging in Norway had such a direction seems more doubtful, because of the different nature of the state in the cases of Norway and Finland, but also because the divisions between those who helped build the modern Norwegian nation made it less likely that 'the nation' would have such corporate 'needs' and 'aims' as suggested by Joenniemi. Neumann (2002a: 93) notes that from the 1770s certain markers – mountains, climate, the sagas – were being considered to be typical of all Norway and were thus being 'nationalized' and were used to strike a contrast with those from the south, whether Dane, German or other sort of European. Reflecting Grew's terms, the view of the civil servant culture, dominant from 1814 to the 1840s, tended to pull the nation into the political space of the state, whereas the populist nationalist saw the state as being open to capture: 'the nation should take over the state' according to Neumann (2002a: 97). The romantic nationalists were pulled between the two sides and divided in their loyalties.

Neumann (2002a: 90) outlines the consequences of this battle in political terms. The state–nation constellations were historical products and provided different benchmarks for interventions about Europe. One might add that the intervening role of particular elements of Norwegian society has been of importance as a 'conveyor belt' of attitudes towards Europe from nation to state and back.

In 1814 there was a Norwegian state and it almost managed to emerge as a sovereign country with its own king. Even so, it became part of a union but with its own distinct administrative and political system. However, it was not until the formation of the associations in the 1850s and 1860 that a wider sense of nationalism was created. Furthermore, the expression of this national feeling in political terms became entwined with the issues of the parliament obtaining the right to control the government and the representation of Norwegian economic interests abroad. National feeling became conjoined with notions of democratic control, representation abroad and opposition to union. These were spirits that were later summoned up by the opponents of Norwegian entry into the EC and the EU.

From independence to 1945

The international environment

Norway's debut on to the international stage after 1905 was modest and involved guaranteeing the neutrality and integrity of the country. The First World War taught Norway an object lesson in the realities of the international politics of the time. Though Norway maintained its neutrality, 'the fact of Norway's economic dependence on Great Britain had turned her into Britain's "neutral ally"' (Riste 2001: 109). In the inter-war period, the League of Nations seemed to provide Norway, and other small states, with a useful tool for promoting peace. However, by the mid-1930s the League's promise had faded.

The outbreak of the Second World War and the Winter War in which the Soviet Union invaded Finland brought the reality of conflict closer and forced the Labour government in Oslo to try to square the triangle of Norway's increased strategic importance, its hope of remaining neutral and its inability to defend itself on its own. The German invasion of Denmark and Norway on 9 April 1940 represented the nadir of Norwegian policy; Norway could not repulse the invader itself and Allied assistance proved unable to complete the task. Liberation in 1945 by British and Soviet armed forces underlined Norway's dependence on the strength of outside forces, but the inclusion of the country in the sphere of Western interest allowed a return to a political situation based on the pre-war pattern.

Norway, the state: the domestic political environment

The emergence of Norway as an independent constitutional monarchy saw the completion of the national revolution in the country. It was a bloodless change conducted by political means. From 1905 until the Second World War the political system was transformed from being based mainly on the town–country, centre–periphery split to one that reflected class interests more. It saw the decline of the Liberals and the rise of Labour.

An important issue after Norwegian independence was the question of control of the country's natural resources, especially the waterfalls, prolific producers of hydro-electric power. There was particular concern that foreign owners might buy up these assets, and the Liberals' 1909 Concession Law regulated the right to exploit natural resources, allowing for collaborative ventures for exploration but also for the reversion of installations exploiting resources to the state after a number of specified years (Danielsen 1995b: 311).

The increased strength of both the urban and rural working class found expression in the formation of the Norwegian Labour Party in 1887 and the main trade union organization (LO) in 1899. The party split on joining the Soviet-dominated Third International (Comintern) in 1921, but left in 1923, with a radical wing breaking away to form the Norwegian Communist Party.

The issues of temperance and language were politicized. The ban on certain alcohol sales introduced in the First World War was entrenched after a referendum on the issue in 1919, with the sales of spirits being allowed only after another referendum in 1926. The rivalry between the

Nynorsk and Bokmål languages also sharpened during this period. Generally, the Liberals supported Prohibition and Nynorsk and the Conservatives a more liberal alcohol policy and Bokmål. The two parties' economic policies alienated the farming population and in 1920 the Agrarian Party (later the Centre Party) was formed.

By the mid-1930s the political system was emerging as one of strong national consensus, with the Labour Party moderating its more socialist policies and the Agrarians supporting much of the Labour government's social policies in exchange for subventions for agriculture. This deal between Labour and the Agrarians reflected a town–country rapprochement, and the Basic Agreement of 1935 brought together the two sides of industry, the employers and the trade unions. Most important, the Labour Party had emerged as the dominant force in politics.

The Norwegian state was weakened in the period from 1920 to 1935. Internationally it depended on the UK and the League of Nations. Its economic policy was based on financial orthodoxy to pay off its debt (Danielsen and Hovland 1995: 320). However, haltingly in the 1920s and then increasingly in the 1930s, it started to intervene more actively in the economic life of the country with protection, subsidies and market regulation. The Labour–Agrarian political agreement strengthened the hand of the state in both country and town.

In international affairs the new Foreign Minister, Jørgen Løvland, stated in October 1905 that 'we want no foreign policy' in the sense that Norway should 'keep out of participation in combinations and alliances that can drag us into warlike adventures'. Nevertheless, it was very important 'to secure to the utmost possible our international material relations' (cited in Riste 2001: 75). The broad outlines of Norwegian foreign policy had been laid down: the country was interested in trade, not in diplomatic manoeuvring, less in general influence than in trying to promote its trade and commerce. Norway developed another aspect of its foreign policy, an emphasis on international law and the settlement of disputes by peaceful means. It became an active member of the League of Nations and joined the other Scandinavian states in advocating a greater say in the League for small states. Its 'new internationalism', again backed by the assumption that British naval power would protect the country against a threat, faded in the adverse conditions of the 1930s. The government seemed little concerned with events in Europe, accepting modest rearmament only by 1937. In Rosenau's terms (see pp. 14–15), Norway's security policy was one of intransigence, placing internal budgetary and political needs above those of external requirements. Indeed, this intransigence endured right up to and including the German occupation, when the Norwegian government rejected German attempts to 'legalize' the occupation.

In 1940 the government went into exile, where it responded to its new situation in two ways, reflected in Norway's post-war foreign policy. First, it embraced the UK and the US in an effort 'to nail the Anglo-Saxon great powers to their responsibilities in Europe' (Riste 2001: 165–7). The second trend, developed through 1943, was renewed stress on support for an international order based on a new universalist organization, the United Nations. In general there was recognition that autonomy in the 'quiet corner' of Europe was no longer an option, the question then being how and where to target Norwegian influence.

Norway the society

One account of Norway's inter-war economic experience suggests that 'events lent strong support to ideas for replacing the market's "invisible hand" with a state that regulated and planned' (Danielsen and Hovland 1995: 314). International events certainly encouraged intervention by government to save the people of a small country such as Norway from the turbulent economic seas of this period. Nevertheless, there were periods of rapid growth in 1926 to 1930 and from 1935 to 1939.

Agriculture was protected in the inter-war period by increased tariffs, and the state played an important role. A corn monopoly was made permanent in 1929 and increasingly the government and producers' organizations started to manage the agricultural market in Norway. Much of the management was undertaken by the organizations themselves rather than directly by the state.

Socially the period saw reactions to the change in material conditions for better and for worse. After 1911 Norway ceased to be a country of emigration as the US started to close its doors and conditions improved in Norway. The number of Norwegians living in densely populated areas rose from 35.7 per cent of the population in 1900 to 45.3 per cent in 1920 but as urban unemployment increased, rural industries were built up and farming stabilized, this figure increased only to 50.1 per cent by 1946 (Historisk statistikk 2000: table 3-3-1t).

The inter-war period was marred by high unemployment, with peaks in 1920, 1926 and 1931, each higher than its predecessor. Labour conflicts led to millions of days lost in strikes in 1921 and 1924 and a major national strike in 1931 (Danielsen and Hovland 1995: 315, 319).

Though generally Norway became a richer country in the inter-war period, there were groups, such as workers susceptible to unemployment, who suffered. Gradually the state built up the instruments to help alleviate this suffering, but the main emolument was the rise in economic activity in the second half of the 1930s. Norway was also becoming a state built on organization. This reflected not just the activities of local government and national government, particularly in state control of economic activity, but in the number of economic organizations, of farmers, labour and business, that helped regulate this control. This meant that by 1940 the government and national groups had an active joint interest in the control of part of Norway's economic life.

Norway the nation

If there was a cultural struggle in the inter-war period it was between the centre and the periphery. The language issue was reflected in the political life of the country, causing divisions between the Liberals and the Conservatives. The question of Prohibition was a reflection of different attitudes between the urban and rural areas and resulted in two referendums.

The country also saw the division between labour and capital which was reflected in the strikes of the 1920s and 1931 and the originally revolutionary attitude of the Labour Party. However, these social differences, as with those between town and country, were ameliorated by the late 1930s. Two reasons for this were the cooperative attitude of the political parties towards each other and the willingness of the two 'sides' of industry to come to an agreement in 1935. It seemed that these organizations and the politicians had realized by the mid-1930s that the resources of a small country such as Norway were too precious to be squandered in long-drawn-out internecine struggles. Also longer-term values of consensus and relative social harmony provided solid ground in which to root such agreements.

The achievement of independence in 1905 meant the fulfilment of the Hegelian view of the nation leading to the creation of the state. This threw open the question of whether the new state was ready for capture by the nation or vice versa. The language division was not solved and weak coalition governments into the early 1930s made few attempts to utilize national feeling in institutions for their own ends. By the latter half of the 1930s the Labour Party had gained support for its government from the Agrarian Party with its popular nationalism (Neumann 2001: 100). Divisions about language and alcohol were relatively marginalized, and special interest groups – workers, industry, farmers and fishermen – found themselves having the ready ear of the Labour government as it defined national interest in terms including the good of these societal groups, 'responsible negotiating partners' according to Ramsøy (1974: 8).

From 1945 to the first EC application

The international environment

In 1945 Norway was a founding member of the UN and hoped to see the wartime alliance of the Great Powers – the UK, the US and the Soviet Union – continue in peacetime. On the other hand, the special links with the US and the UK continued and became more important as the frost of the Cold War started to form in early 1948.

This dichotomy in post-war policy was eventually solved with Norwegian signature of the North Atlantic Treaty on 4 April 1949, but not until negotiations with Sweden and Denmark were held in a vain attempt to create a Nordic Defence Union. The move into the North Atlantic Treaty Organization (NATO) dominated Norway's security policy for the rest of the twentieth century. Increasingly the country became integrated into the military aspects of NATO. It brought the country into international diplomacy in a way that could not be imagined by non-aligned states: it had close regular defence links with both the British and Americans that seemed to guarantee the very existence of the Norwegian state.

However, Norwegian alliance policy had one external constraining element, the country's proximity to the Soviet Union. Norway was the only NATO member to have a border with the USSR in Europe and no Norwegian government wished to provoke Soviet leaders to take action that might raise the temperature in the Nordic region.

Norway's security position provides a number of relevant points in relation to the country's involvement in European integration. First, it gives a historical context. Second, it is a reminder that Norwegian foreign policy has always had an internationalist aspect that has sought to support international law and organizations, including NATO. Since 1949 NATO has presented an important institutional framework for Norwegian relations with the US in particular. Third, it addresses Norwegian identity. It demonstrates the physical separateness from Continental affairs that formed a considerable part of early Norwegian external policy and also a certain belief that Norway had something to contribute to wider world security. It shows that in the realm of defence Norwegian decision-makers from 1905 considered the country to be a maritime one, with interests shared by the UK and the US.

The international economic and trade context was, for Norway, one of wary cooperation. The Bretton Woods system provided a framework within which Norway's trade could be reconstructed after the war. The Organization for European Economic Cooperation (OEEC) allowed payments for trade in Western Europe to be settled on a multilateral basis.

The various discussions about a Nordic Customs Union and an OEEC-wide free trade area both collapsed under the weight of their own contradictions and were replaced by alternatives more acceptable to key participants. For Norway this was the creation of the European Free Trade Association (EFTA), a Swedish–Swiss brainchild adopted, or at least fostered, by the UK. The exclusion of fisheries from the free trade agreement annoyed the Norwegians but, even without that sprat, EFTA caught the Norwegian mackerel.

Norway the state: the political environment

The Norwegian state had been defeated in the Second World War. However, the occupation showed the strength of the state institutions. The monarchy, the government and the Bank of Norway, in exile in London, took on a strong representational element and displayed their economic power (with the Bank and the income from Norway's still free merchant fleet), political strength (most political parties were represented in the government-in-exile) and sovereignty (the government was recognized by the UK and the US, even if there were problems with acceptance by neutral Sweden).

The triumphant return of the agents of state in 1945, the abject failure of an alternative Quisling model during the occupation and the need to rebuild the economy presented government with a number of opportunities. The state itself was strengthened by the hegemonic position of the Labour Party, a party for a strong state. The domestic political scene after the Second World War and up to the first application for EC membership was one of some stability with the dominance of the Norwegian Labour Party. The party gained an absolute majority in the 1945 general election and maintained this position until the 1961 election, when it fell short of a majority by two seats.

The main opposition parties after the Second World War – the Centre Party, the Christian Democrats, the Liberals and the Conservatives – tended to represent different sectors of society. The Centre Party reflected the farmers' needs. The Christian Democrats espoused Christian and social values. These two parties fed on the three elements of historic counter-culture, the dominance of the speakers of Nynorsk, the evangelical church in opposition to the state-run Lutheran church and moral opposition to freer alcohol and abortion laws. The Liberals were supported by urban intellectuals and some rural voters (Rokkan 1967).

The Conservatives, with much of its support in business, commerce and those in managerial positions, was the main opposition party. Because of their beliefs, and their main source of support being on the opposite 'sides' of industry, the Labour and Conservative parties remained opponents during this period, but they had in common a concern for the state of industry and commerce and a more internationalist outlook in economic terms than most of the other parties. The Labour Party also tried to reach out to those in the regions, working on farms, in forestry and at sea; it was not completely an urban party but spanned a number of interests. It is perhaps not surprising that a good deal of legislation passed during this period did so with support from more than just the Labour Party.

Two main political issue areas after the Second World War were the organization of the economy and foreign and security policy. The Labour Party was prepared to take a fairly *dirigiste* approach to the economy after the war, and in this it received the general support of the centrist parties, whose main economic concern was continued support for agriculture and the regions. All these parties were satisfied that controls should only be liberalized cautiously, especially if it meant opening up Norway internationally. In 1952, the Labour trade Minister, Erik Brofoss, accepted trade liberalization and a multilateral payments system as long as this served Norway's economic interests (Eriksen and Pharø 1997: 110). However,

Norway was concerned lest schemes for economic integration, whether Nordic or covering Western Europe, should adversely affect these interests. There was still room for a choice between different approaches. The Norwegian representative to the OEEC, Arne Skaug, expressed to the Norwegian Foreign Minister the view that continental European politicians:

> are by and large opposed to income equalisation and frequently opposed to public investments. They see the freeing of trade as a goal in itself, but often counteract the results of this liberalisation partly through a deflationary policy and partly through attempts at protection of various sorts; they are not excessively concerned about holding to agreements about full employment. The Anglo-Scandinavian system is largely opposite to that of continental Europe.
>
> (Eriksen and Pharø 1997: 142, my translation)

This suggests Norwegian policy as then being in favour of income equalization and public investment and seeing trade liberalization as a means to an end, as stated by Brofoss. Thus plans for both a Nordic and West European-wide economic cooperation, customs unions or free trade areas met with Norwegian scepticism, even outright opposition, if they interfered with these goals or if they undermined Norway's autonomy in trade matters.

The main issue in foreign policy was Norway's security policy. After the war there was a consensus that the country should steer a route between any emerging power blocs, but when the Soviet Union seemed to become more aggressive in Europe – particularly with the communist take-over of Czechoslovakia in March 1948 – all the parties, except the Communists, supported the government's search for greater security in alliance with others. However, Norwegian politicians were aware that their people had reservations about new alliances. There were concerns about foreign troops in the country so soon after wartime occupation; and later there was fear about the nuclear aspects of the Atlantic alliance (Lindstøl 1978). Norwegian governments tended to mix the policy of deterrence, afforded through integration into NATO and the links with the US and the UK, with those of a certain screening against overbearing US or NATO requirements, thereby providing some assurance both to domestic opinion and to the Soviet Union (Holst 1966; Tamnes 1987). The 'Orientering' group of the Labour Party remained sceptical about NATO membership, especially as regards nuclear policy, and was excluded from the party in 1961. It helped form the Socialist People's Party (later the Socialist Left Party) in that year. Security remained a matter of consensus between most of the parties, though nuclear issues came to trouble the Labour Party during the 1980s.

The period from 1945 to 1962 can be seen as the era of the strong state in Norway. The political elite was dominated by the Labour Party which had a majority in the Storting until 1961. In economic terms the state directed the large public sector, regulated certain industries (especially fishing and agriculture) and facilitated the export industries (Grønlie 1995: 423).

Norway the society

During the period from 1945 to 1962 society developed along with the economy, and social cleavages within society became somewhat hidden.

Economic and trade policy also had to adapt to the new international realities after the Second World War. In the inter-war years Norway had relied on primary products as the mainstay of its economy – agriculture, fisheries and forestry, though the increase in general trade restrictions and the rise of home industries meant that '[t]he Norwegian economy became more insular' (Danielsen and Hovland 1995: 332). The main concern after 1945 was rebuilding the shattered economy and this was done, at home, by a broad political consensus about the control and planning necessary to reconstruct the country's infrastructure. By 1950 exports had returned to pre-war levels (Bjerve 1965), but controls were still kept on capital and labour costs and were managed through trade union–industry deals encouraged by the government (Ramsøy 1974: 8). Automobiles remained on ration until 1960 (Grønlie 1995: 361).

Given favourable international conditions, the economy and trade grew substantially until the 1970s. For twenty years from 1945, the Norwegian state carried out an economic policy that both assisted exports and reformed and reconstructed the economy internally. Cheap hydro-electric power and the extraction of minerals allowed the growth of a chemicals industry and processing such as that in oil refineries and aluminium smelting. The means for this transformation was the control of capital. Both the government and the banks channelled money into the export-led industries, and modernization of equipment, which took advantage of the movement of workers from the land into the new factories (Moses and Tranøy 1995: 109).

The Labour government, in power during the period until 1965, was in a good position to undertake this policy. It was a *dirigiste* party in the Nordic mould and had a strong political consensus behind its rebuilding policy after the Second World War. It could utilize the banks to control credit, direct industry through nationalized enterprises and regional policy, and guide labour through intermediaries such as the trade unions and housing associations (Hodne 1983: 142). Furthermore, the period was one of low unemployment, and low inflation helped to keep Norwegian products competitive internationally.

A major effect of the economic changes was a loss of some 17,000 to 18,000 jobs in agriculture and fisheries from 1950 to 1960, while industry and services picked up 23,000 extra places during the same period. The number of workers in national and local authorities rose by 135,000 from 1950 to 1970 (Grønlie 1995: 385, 396).

Welfare benefits were accepted as a right rather than as charity, and were dispensed on a universalist principle, in theory open to all who needed them. The infrastructure of the country was revitalized, with the outer regions, such as Northern Norway which had been so badly mauled in the Second World War, not being forgotten.

The economic policies carried out during this period helped to soften some of the cleavages in Norwegian society – between north and south, between countryside and town, between worker and peasant, even between labour and capital. Not all the policies were successful, especially when they encountered strong economic forces (such as the move from the land to the town), but the relatively successful attempt to build a welfare society owes much to the rooted cultural beliefs in Norwegian society in cooperation and consensus and, as noted in the account of the period up to 1905, the relative lack of exploitation of one group by another. What was becoming increasingly apparent was the role of the state as ringmaster in bringing together elements of society in harmony. The state was not just the central government. As Grønlie wrote:

> In many ways the welfare society appears as a dynamic interaction between local authorities strong on initiative and a state anxious to spread the benefits as evenly as possible. In many instances too, voluntary, religious and humanitarian organizations have played important roles in this game.
>
> (Grønlie 1995: 402–3)

Where did the concept of nation fit into this cosy relationship?

Norway the nation

The German invasion of 9 April 1940 was a sudden, violent and almost total disrupter of Norwegian life and identity. It made Norway an occupied country subject to the whims of the Third Reich. The social organizations – Church, labour, sports – that tried to oppose or ignore the new rulers were suppressed and Norwegians were forced to fall back on family and local contacts for survival. The surviving legal institutions of the state continued in exile, courtesy of the UK, keeping Norwegian hope and honour alive. It was a rude awakening for this small state in the 'quiet corner of Europe', demonstrating that events on its doorstep could spill over into its own house. The response in the re-forming of the nation after the Second World War strengthened the capture (or, at least, the taming) of the nation by the representatives of the state – predominantly the Labour government – often using the agents of society such as interest groups.

The nation had come under attack during the occupation, with the national understanding that had been emerging in the late 1930s being swept away by an attempt to create a 'pure' race-based Aryan nation. The Labour government of 1945 was able to rebuild the 1935–40 concept, which itself had the deeper roots mentioned in the first part of this chapter, but with more effective tools. The war had minimized much private space (thus making it more valuable) and had flattened many social organizations, such as the unions, the church and sports organizations. Their post-war rebuilding as national institutions could be undertaken at the same time as the reconstruction of the country's economy, and much more on Labour's terms. Once again, the trade unions, management, farmers and fisheries organizations worked hand-in-glove with the government. The issues that had split the nation in the past – language and alcohol – rumbled on but 'the people' were increasingly taken into the outstretched arms of the Labour Party, just as the agents of society became more involved in serving the ends of the state, especially those concerning the welfare society.

In the end, Norway benefited greatly from the Bretton Woods system which allowed the country to increase its exports in the twenty years after the Second World War but at the same time to restrict the flow of capital in and out of the country, to guide the labour market and offer support to the domestic sector of the economy, including agriculture. To paraphrase Lenin, during this period Norway was Labour Party power plus cheap hydro-electricity. Cheap hydro-electric power symbolized the natural advantage that allowed Norway to boost its exports. Labour Party power represented a plan to rebuild the country by the exercise of controls, hard work and enterprise. The environment had to be fashioned by political – and wider societal – choices.

All this was undertaken within the developing framework of economic cooperation and liberalization represented by Bretton Woods and the OEEC. Both the climate of economic growth and the inter-state institutions were permissive towards Norway's policy of guiding its economy. The Labour Party was able to exercise such control and achieve results partly, as noted by Skaug (see p. 34), because of its political choices, partly because of the consensus it had built with the trade unions and, to some extent, industry and agriculture, and partly because the international environment allowed it control of a number of important economic levers, such as control of capital movements. Norway could still give the impression of a walled garden in the post-war period. However, this Garden of Eden had its snakes.

The lead-up to the first application

If the 1960s saw a richer Norway, bedded down in the welfare state, they also contained the seeds of change that broke the post-war mould in the

1970s. In a roundabout way, two events in 1957 led international and domestic elements to interact in ways that eventually changed domestic perceptions and politics.

The first event in 1957 was a NATO summit in Paris, which, among other things, discussed the possibility of the emplacement of US Honest John nuclear missiles in Western Europe. One possible way of compensating for the supposed gap between the conventional forces of East and West in Europe was to place US nuclear-tipped missiles in Western Europe. That was seen as the most effective deterrent to any Soviet attack.

Though Norway was not specifically asked to host the nuclear version of the Honest John missiles, the 1957 conference of the Labour Party had adopted a rank-and-file proposal that Norway should not accept any nuclear weapons, a policy that the Labour Prime Minister, Einar Gerhardsen, reiterated in Paris later that year. Indeed, he pressed for the postponement of the emplacement of such medium-ranged nuclear missiles in Europe more generally (Riste 2001: 215–16).

By 1961, with nuclear weapons more in the public mind, East–West confrontations over Berlin and the increasing integration of West Germany into NATO, the left-wingers finally broke away and formed the Socialist People's Party (Lindstøl 1978). This party, as well as being anti-nuclear and for Norway's withdrawal from NATO, was also opposed to any Norwegian application for EEC membership after the UK had opened the gate to that path in June 1961. In the September 1961 general election the Labour Party, by two seats, lost its overall majority in the Storting and had to rely on the support of the two newly elected members representing the Socialist People's Party (Valen and Rokkan 1970: 287–300). Labour was never to regain the position it had from 1945 to 1961 when it ruled with an absolute majority in the Storting.

The second international event was the signing of the Treaty of Rome in March 1957 which established the European Economic Community (EEC). Norway, together with other members of the OEEC, was not party to this experiment. It seemed to encompass all the elements of 'continental Europe', as despised by Arne Skaug, and there was little immediate response in Oslo. Within three years Norway had joined EFTA but by mid-1961 the Norwegian Labour government was faced with the possibility of Britain ditching EFTA and joining the EEC.

The Norwegian government, supported by the representatives of industry, had followed their economic lodestone, the UK, to EFTA, and when the UK, together with Denmark from the Nordic region, applied for membership of the EEC the government in Oslo must have felt that its next step had been decided, and that it was on the road to Brussels. Nevertheless, the process, even of applying, was not so simple for Norway as for the UK, Denmark and Ireland. There was political resistance within Norway, though it is moot whether this was then stronger in Norway than in the other applicant states. Second, the constitution had to be changed.

The issue of application for EEC membership tore across the main post-war divisions in Norwegian politics which had been between the Labour Party (later joined by the Socialist People's Party) and the non-socialist parties of the centre-right, the Centre Party, the Christian Democrats, the Liberals and the Conservatives. On the whole, those favouring membership were drawn from the representatives of both sides of industry and were to be found in majority groups in the Labour and Conservative parties. Those opposing membership were from the outer regions and rural areas of Norway and were often close to agriculture and fisheries, those in public service, leftist groups opposing the EEC on ideological grounds and some right-wing nationalists. These groups were so strong, not least in the labour movement, that any quick response to the British application was deemed out of the question (Lie 1975: 223–9). Instead there was a nine-month debate.

The original report submitted to the Storting in October 1961 (*Stortingsmelding* 15, 1961) did not outline the government's preferred option in relations with the EEC as the matter needed to be discussed further within the Labour Party. After an overwhelming majority of the regional sections of the party supported the preference for full membership negotiations, the government delivered its report to the Storting in March 1962. Opposition within the party was still vocal and Labour was dependent on the Socialist People's Party representatives to keep it in power. Powerful figures such as Halvard Lange, the Foreign Minister, and Haakon Lie, the party secretary, had argued in favour of membership dependent on British adherence and safeguards for the primary sector (Lie 1975: 214–39). Negotiations were to be followed by a consultative referendum before the final vote on admission in the Storting. However, the Minister of Prices and Wages, Gunnar Bøe, resigned when the government's report was delivered to the Storting and, in committee, two Labour members opted for merely an economic agreement with the EEC. At the end of April 1962 the Storting agreed that Norway should apply for full membership by 113 votes to 37 with all the twenty-nine Conservatives and sixty-three of the seventy-four Labour members voting in favour. Two Liberals, seven Christian Democrats, fifteen Centre Party members, the two Socialist People's Party representatives and eleven Labour members voted against (Archer and Sogner 1998: 27).

For Norway to be a member of the EEC with its supranational institutions, the Norwegian constitution had to be changed to allow the country to delegate judicial authority to international organizations and for the direct applicability of Community law in Norway (Ramberg 1972: 49–50). After inter-party discussions a formulation was proposed to the Storting in March 1962 which agreed the changes by 115 to 35 votes. The discussion was heated and the opposition was similar in composition to that which had voted against the membership application a month later. The Norwegian application was submitted to the EEC in May 1962.

Both issues – nuclear weapons and EC membership – were imposed from outside Norway and both chipped away at the monolith of Labour Party rule and its claim to encompass a wide range of interests and opinions. Though the party attempted to keep sceptics within its embrace, a number lost faith. It was these groups that would challenge Labour's claim to define not just a government programme but also the 'national' interest, and they would do so by tapping into societal groups, that were coaxed away from a national consensus.

Conclusions

The above history of Norway up to 1961 brings out three points of relevance to the later study of Norway's relations with European integration. First, Norway had its own peculiar social and economic cleavages. Cultural differences associated with place and belief had their impact on politics in the nineteenth century and endured, albeit as a minor key, throughout the twentieth century. Class-based divisions may have been of importance in the first thirty years of the state, but increasingly it was only the shadow of the labour–capital division that was reflected in national politics. The reality was consensus and cooperation. The height of Labour hegemony was from 1945 to 1961 when the party dominated Norwegian politics and managed something not achieved in many other states (with the possible exception of Sweden); it orchestrated the agents of civil society and it coopted the symbols and the feelings of nationhood. It did this mainly by using the institutions of state and society to benefit materially a wide swathe of the country without obviously bringing detriment to business, capital or minority social groupings. The Labour movement used the assets of a small state (and a homogeneous one) to build its Norwegian home.

Second, Norway was born as a small state in the international community. It had little economic power and practically no military strength. Nevertheless, it had importance in one or two areas – whaling in the interwar period and merchant shipping throughout – and also tried, at an early stage, to build up moral influence based on its virtues as a small, democratic state.

Finally, the key dates of 1814–15, 1905 and 1945 represent triumphs in the struggle to establish and then maintain Norwegian autonomy. On each of these occasions, outside assistance was needed – diplomatic in the first two, military in the last – mainly from the UK and then the US. A final key date – 1949 – was more a recognition of the limits to autonomy and the need for institutionalized influence with Norway's main allies. In trade matters, within the general Western framework, Norway managed to retain a fair amount of autonomy. Nevertheless, the outside world was about to impinge on this land of the Norsemen.

3 Norway battles with European integration

The best laid schemes o' mice an' men
Gang aft a-gley.

Robert Burns

With the British application for membership of the European Communities in 1961 a battle started in Norway that was to last for a third of a century. It was not just over whether one country should join a particular institution, but a reflection of the mind, heart and soul of the country. It led to the downfall of governments and the undoing of the best laid schemes. It was also a tale of differing versions of how a small state might best flourish in a rapidly changing and potentially hostile environment.

Norway's first 'no'

The international environment

The period from the first application of Norway to the EC in 1962 until the Norwegian 'no' in September 1972 coincided with the move from the Cold War into *détente*. A Norwegian report stated that by the early 1970s the country's strategic situation had deteriorated because of the Soviet deployments, and stressed the need to maintain the allied military presence (*Stortingsmelding* 9 1973: 17). More generally the 1960s saw a move away from confrontation in Europe towards the creation of a *status quo* settlement, with tension eased between the two blocs, especially in Central Europe. Norway found itself in a period of diplomatic *détente* but with its own military situation not obviously benefiting.

In Western Europe, President de Gaulle blocked the UK's entry into the EEC in January 1963 on the grounds that the conditions of such an 'insular ' and 'maritime' country differed 'profoundly from those of the continentals'. The other applicant states, such as Norway, were merely referred to as being 'linked to her [the UK] through the free trade area, [which] for the same reasons as Britain, would like or wish to enter the common market' (cited in Stirk and Weigall 1999: 171–2). The decision allowed the Norwegian government to avoid a period of extended negotiations – the late application meant that Norway's had hardly started in Brussels before de Gaulle's veto – followed by what was foreseen as being a bout of political conflict. Instead Norway joined the other EFTA countries in reducing the barriers to industrial free trade.

A second British application in 1967 was again turned down by de Gaulle, leaving little time for discussion of its consequences in the other applicant states. The third round of applications started after de Gaulle resigned in 1969 and his successor, Georges Pompidou, considered that the time was right for the UK to be part of the EC.

The background to the negotiations for membership by the four applicant states, including Norway, during 1970 to 1972 was one of economic uncertainty. The system that had underpinned the economic recovery and growth of the Western world after the Second World War, the Bretton Woods institutions, was based on the strength of the dollar and it being tied to gold. By 1971 the dollar was devalued and its international exchange rate allowed to float. The hegemony of the dollar was challenged.

Norway the state: cracks appearing

The 1960s saw a weakening of the political hegemony exercised by the Labour Party in post-war Norway. The Labour Party had lost its overall majority in the 1961 election, and by the summer of 1963 the Gerhardsen government had been voted briefly out of office.

Many of the historic cleavages that had typified Norwegian politics[1] weakened and it seemed that the left–right divide was reasserting itself in the political system. However, the parties that made up the new centre-right coalition in 1965 still germinated the remnants of earlier divisions. The Conservatives were a more urban party, with the Liberals, Christian Democrats and Centre Party representing rural or small-town groups. The Conservatives and the Liberals were on one side on morality and religious issues, with the Christian Democrats and the Centre Party being more socially conservative. Most important, the Conservatives wished Norway to be part of the EC, and the Centre Party totally opposed this policy. Indeed, it was on this issue that the coalition was to collapse in 1971.

Nevertheless, the broad consensus about the welfare society that had existed since 1945 continued. The centre-right government's economic policies differed little from those of its Labour predecessor. Also the Labour Party, when in office, had continued its efforts at covering over the traditional cleavages. Both Labour and centre-right governments in Oslo continued to pursue regional policies that involved both subsidies and also tax equalization, leading central government to transfer tax income to the smaller authorities in larger proportions than to the bigger authorities (Grønlie 1995: 400–1).

Nevertheless, the agents of the state found their hegemony of the post-war period coming under increased stress from within (the change of government) and from outside with the intrusion of security and European issues into political life.

Norwegian society in a period of change

During the 1960s Norwegian society experienced social change similar to that seen in the rest of Western Europe as the post-war 'baby boom' generation grew up and consumerism became a part of life.

The service sector grew apace in the 1960s. The welfare state continued to expand and needed administrators as well as doctors and nurses, especially after the establishment of the inclusive social benefit system (Folketrygden) in 1967. Expenditure on social security and health increased fourfold during the 1960s and that on old age and disability payments fivefold. Many of the welfare activities that had been started by voluntary organizations and local authorities had been taken over completely by local authorities in the 1940s and 1950s and in the 1960s and early 1970s were taken on either by the counties or the state (Grønlie 1995: 403). The welfare state was becoming entrenched. A special effort was made during the 1960s to encourage growth in north Norway and in rural centres of population with the establishment of the Regional Development Bank in 1960.

Membership of EFTA allowed Norway gradual tariff-free access to the important Nordic and British markets for its industrial exports and for other favoured products such as frozen fish fillets. However, it also meant that the Norwegian domestic market would be opened up to Swedish and British exporters. So while, during the 1960s, Norwegian exports continued their steady rise as a share of GDP, reaching 22 per cent in 1970, imports as a share of GDP rose from 31.6 per cent in 1960 to 33.1 per cent in 1970. It was also a period of great economic growth for Norway (Statistics Norway 2000: 252).

The conditions that had prevailed during the first two decades after the war and had been so benign for rebuilding Norway in the image of the Labour Party started to change as the 1960s progressed. The social and political scene evolved and the international trade and economic situation also offered challenges. It became less feasible to shelter Norwegian economic life from the outside world, though the actual imprint of the international institutions, such as EFTA and GATT, was fairly mild during the decade. It was the unfulfilled prospect of membership of the EC that made a distinct impression on political life and threw into relief a number of points about Norwegian identity.

Economic changes were affecting Norwegian life. The country had long since ceased to be one with a sizeable primary product sector, though both agriculture and fisheries held sway among voters and politicians out of all proportion to their importance in the country's economic life. Many people in the towns and cities were but one generation away from the land or sea. Furthermore, the policy of expanding exports and imposing strong controls within the domestic economy met a number of challenges during the 1960s. Increased personal wealth and greater market choice afforded by the opening up of the Norwegian market led to a burst of consumer spending.

Grønlie (1995: 382) mentions that the economic growth in Norway 'had a more revolutionary feel to it' than that in the immediate post-war period. It was based more on exports and led to a rise in service industries and 'new urban societies and the development of built-up areas'. Nevertheless, the old links between the 'social partners' remained – the 'corporate pluralism', especially deals between the trade unions and employers' associations, by which Stein Rokkan (1967) typified Norway seemed little affected by these social changes.

Norway the nation: a warning

The general thesis of the previous chapter is that by the start of the 1960s the concept of nation was one that had been tamed and taken on by the labour movement in Norway, with the Labour government in the vanguard. Divisions had appeared during the nineteenth century, as there were competing visions of the nation. These seemed to be healed in the lead-up to independence, though some re-emerged in the inter-war period. As economic depression enveloped Norway, there was the danger of country and town, labour and capital, the centre and the regions fighting for scarcer and scarcer resources. Instead the moment passed as the international economy began to recover and the Labour Party assumed power with the help of the Agrarian Party. Labour became a national movement that brought together the urban and the rural, management and the worker, Oslo and north Norway. This was facilitated by the cultural heritage of unity of town and countryside.

The bitter experience of the war and the need for post-war reconstruction not only united the country further but also provided extra implements of social and economic control (Hodne 1983: 131). Neumann (2002a: 106) points to how the war had helped Labour by galvanizing its leadership, by marginalizing further the divisive elements of language and class and by allowing those parts of the state 'which had stuck it out in London' – the king and the government – to become symbols of the nation.

By the early 1960s the Labour Party was not just dominant in the political arena but also in many areas of the social and economic space. If 'the awareness of a national identity' involves 'the consciousness of belonging to the same nation, [and] makes distant people spread over large territories feel politically responsible for each other' (Habermas 1996: 286), then much of the glue of Norwegian nationhood in the two decades after the war was provided by the labour movement with its tentacles reaching into the country's societal groups. It was not too difficult as, even by the early 1970s, Norway had '*one* school system, *one* church, *one* secondary school system ... and *one* broadcasting and television system' (Torgersen 1974: 220, emphasis in original).

However, some of the adhesive started to come unstuck during the 1960s. The political changes removed Labour from the pinnacle of power, though it was still a force with which to be reckoned. International issues ate away at party unity, leading to a left-wing breakaway. Social and economic developments offered a more long-term threat, the rise of the consumer as king. Soon what Thorstein Veblen called 'the pecuniary canons of taste' – fashionable clothes, cars, televisions, foreign holidays – would start to challenge the symbols of nationhood. However, at that stage it was more the case that Labour's inclusive vision of that nation was beginning to be challenged. The original opponents of the first application for EC membership in 1961 were not slow to take up the flag. They noted that a united people had stood behind the great decisions of 1814, 1905 and 1940, but that 'the current *Storting* did not have the people's mandate to give up Norway's sovereignty and national independence for such a purpose' as EC membership (cited in Bjørklund 1982: 381–5). This group – 'the 143' – reflected 'the 43', being the forty-three organizations and associations that had sent a letter of protest to the German occupying powers in 1941, and those who had protested against nuclear weapons in 1960, 'the 13' (Bjørklund 1982: 21, 30). The decision to call on national feeling in the political arena was no longer the prerogative of the Labour Party.

Voting 'no' (1) A national revolt?

The applications and the campaign

From September 1965 Norway had a centre-right government consisting of the Conservatives, the Centre Party, the Christian Democrats and the Liberals. Of these, the Conservatives were in favour of EC membership, the Centre Party was against and the Liberals and Christian Democrats were split. Nevertheless, after the 1967 British move, the government decided to recommend that Norway should apply for negotiations with the EC for full membership, based on the 1962 conditions of British membership, safeguards for primary industries and a consultative referendum (*Stortingsmelding* 86, 1967: 99–100). This government report spoke of the application representing 'the best means of clarifying the basis for Norway's relations with the EC' (ibid.: 99) rather than a commitment to membership, thereby allowing sceptics to accept it, albeit holding their collective noses. However, the actual application – formulated by the

Foreign Ministry under the pro-membership Conservative minister, John Lyng – spoke of membership as the objective, with the negotiations serving to overcome any obstacles to that end (*Stortingsmelding* 92, 1970: 29).

The Storting voted in favour of the new application by 136 votes to 13, with the minority consisting of four Centre Party, three Christian Democrat, four Labour Party members and the two members from the Socialist People's Party (*Stortingstidende* 1967: 4557–8). Members of the government probably felt that the whole exercise was more like a stately political quadrille rather than the start of serious negotiations, as President de Gaulle was still in power and he had not changed his view of the 'Anglo-Saxons' (Lyng 1976: 213, 233). They were not wrong. In December 1967 de Gaulle again vetoed the British application without negotiations even starting.

So the Storting again voted for a renewal of the Norwegian EC membership application in June 1970. The vote was 132 votes to 17, with four votes switching from the 'no' side since 1967. Negotiations with Norway began in earnest after June 1971. However, in June 1970, the EC announced the basis of a Common Fisheries Policy, created without regard to the interests of the four applicant states, all of which had fishing interests and resources. Of the four, Norway's fishermen were most vocal in opposing the new EC scheme and when negotiators struck a deal with the EC in January 1972 it was immediately repudiated by the Norwegian fishermen's organizations and the Fisheries Minister resigned (Archer and Sogner 1998: 32).

Even before then, the negotiations had brought a larger political casualty. In March 1971 the centre-right government, riven with disagreement as the prospect of real negotiations neared, resigned and the Labour Party formed a minority government (Allen 1979: 109–13). The EC's Hague Summit in December 1969 and the British negotiations had started to arouse anti-membership feeling within Norway and in August 1970 the People's Movement against Norwegian Membership of the Common Market was formed with representatives from all the political parties and from a variety of social movements (Bjørklund 1982: 105–16). This motley crew was nevertheless able to muster a variety of arguments in its counter-report (Folkebevegelsen 1972) to the government's White Paper on membership (*Stortingsmelding* 50, 1972). In particular it picked out the dangers of Norwegians losing control over their economy to Brussels and having to suffer free-market policies and greater social injustice (Folkebevegelsen 1972: 7–17, 31–46, 188–204). For the opponents of membership, autonomy was the key for Norway; they had little faith that as an EC member Norway would have much influence on decisions that would then directly affect the country. This attitude was reflected particularly in the Centre Party. Their leader, the Prime Minister, Per Borten, indiscreetly leaked a document about the EC, and took the opportunity to end what was an increasingly fractious coalition as membership loomed (Bjørklund 1982: 311–16).

The outcome

The new Labour government had opponents within its own ranks but was certainly more united on the membership issue than the outgoing coalition (Bergh 1987: 496–503; Lie 1975: 214–39). It was this new government that concluded the negotiations and campaigned for acceptance in the referendum held on 25 September 1972. Though the vote was in theory consultative, in fact all the political parties accepted that the result would be binding and the Labour government of Trygve Bratelli made the matter one of confidence. With a turnout of 79.2 per cent – some 6–7 per cent lower than in general elections at that time – the Norwegian electorate rejected EC membership with 53.5 per cent voting against. The Labour government resigned and the main opponents of membership formed a minority government. Why had a majority of the Norwegian voters defied their government and many leaders of their economic life and voted against membership of an organization that the British and Danes seemed content to join?

The reasons for the strong negative vote can, of course, be sought in the campaign itself. The 'yes' side only managed to start campaigning once the negotiations had finished in January 1972. It was run by industry and the union leadership, by the Labour government and the Conservatives, not used to campaigning together politically. They were not helped by outside events: a few days before the vote, Ferdinand Spaak, the energy director of the EC Commission, announced ideas for a common energy policy that implied that Norway's burgeoning offshore oil and gas discoveries could become a 'Community resource' (*Dagbladet*, 22 September 1972). The outcry in Norway showed that the feeling was that the EC was about to grab Norway's oil as it would do its fish. Furthermore, the relatively low turnout (79 per cent) seemed to suggest that a number of Labour voters, unable to vote against their own party on a matter that their Prime Minister had made one of confidence, stayed at home on their sofas.

The campaign and the result were nevertheless a reflection of some wider divisions within society. The narrative above has described Norway as a nation-state that, certainly until the 1970s, had a strong sense of being Norwegian. The Norwegians – or at least their leadership – had tried to gain sovereignty for their state in 1814 and throughout the nineteenth century had resisted any imposition of rule and institutions from Sweden. When the opportunity again came for the creation of a sovereign state, the enfranchised adult male population had overwhelmingly voted for it. During the Second World War there had been resistance to the enforced introduction of Quisling organizations in professional, work and social life. Well over 90 per cent of the country consisted of Norwegians, with the

Sami and Finnish-speakers in the north making up the only indigenous minority.

Set against this picture of a monolith was the presence of a number of socio-economic cleavages within society that were also reflected in the politics and in organizations and associations representing a variety of groupings. The main divisions, already noted, were religious (secular against fundamentalist Lutherans), linguistic (Riksmål versus Nynorsk), socio-geographic (rural–urban, periphery–centre) and economic (worker against owner-manager, primary sectors against industry, and sheltered versus 'open' industries) (Rokkan 1967: 389). Nevertheless, the Labour Party, dominant in public life since the 1930s, had managed to tap a deep-seated culture of consensus and, working through civil society and with a wide range of instruments of government, had forged a form of national unity.

The question of EC membership shattered this. It opened up the latent divides within society. By its nature, the issue also created fissures in the institutions of civil society. The EC's attractions were different for the various economic sectors. A customs union with most of Norway's main export market was a pleasing prospect for that section of industry – both workers and management – that had modernized after the war and had already benefited from EFTA. However, agriculture would have to give up its very protected position and face competition from farmers who were more efficient and who had a longer growing season than possible in Norway. Norway's sheltered industries also faced a more difficult time. Competition against the EFTA members' industry was just manageable, but opening to German competition, in particular, and adapting to the common external tariff could inflict mortal wounds.

Membership also offered a clear abrogation of autonomy in favour of influence. Those within the EC could affect the policies being made through a wide range of institutions, but, in exchange, they had to implement the outcome of the policy-making process, whether they liked it or not, as law. This was demonstrated in particular in the fishing industry. The industry would gain access to the EC market and would be able to feed into the decision-making of the Common Fisheries Policy. However, the basic outline of the policy had been determined before Norwegian entry and involved eventually opening up what the Norwegian fishermen regarded as their waters to vessels from other EC states and possibly from some non-EC countries. This would have limited the range of tactics that could be applied on the policy-making side.

This trade-off between autonomy and influence was reflected in the divisions over membership within Norway. Those that were closest to the levers of influence – the Labour Party and trade union leadership, those active in business and commerce – were most confident about the benefits of membership. Those that already had some distance from influence even within Norway – voters in the region, the grass roots of the trade unions, those on the far left – as well as those who saw their national influence declining in a wider context – such as teachers, intellectuals, farmers and fishermen – formed the vanguard of the opposition to EC membership. The coalition under the banner of the People's Movement against the Common Market in 1972 resembled, at least in outline, the alliance between urban radicals and country folk that had formed the Liberals ninety years earlier (Bjørklund 1982: 331).[2]

The referendum marked a seminal moment in Norwegian politics and society: over half the voting electorate rebelled against a central plank of the administration's policy and stopped the government in it tracks. Furthermore, the whole campaign split the country as never before, not even on the alcohol and language issues, though many of the fissures were along the same fault lines as experienced in those campaigns. For a consensus-based society and political system, the bitter in-fighting between members of the same families, trade unions and parties came as something of a shock. For Labour, it was the end of its rule as ringmaster of Norwegian society and the Norwegian nation.

Between 1972 and 1994

The international environment

The context within which Norway operated its European policy from the first referendum in September 1972 to the second vote in November 1994 was one of substantial change geo-politically and one that saw the European issue intrude on the Nordic region through the action of an unexpected agent – the Swedish Social Democrats. Their action eventually placed the question of Norwegian membership back on the menu for consideration by Norway's politicians and people.

The period between the two Norwegian referendums saw the context of Norway's external policy change considerably in the strategic field, in the question of the division of resources and in developments within Europe.

From the early 1970s to the 1980s, Norway's strategic importance increased. The country was sandwiched between a growing Soviet naval presence in northern waters and a more responsive US.

By the end of the 1980s, with the new leadership in the Soviet Union, the tension between East and West began to subside, leading to the end of the Cold War and of the Soviet Union. All that Norway, and its NATO allies, had seen as their opponents had disappeared. What did this mean for Norway's security situation? The direct threat perceived from the Soviet Union to Norwegian security disappeared but was replaced by an increase in the general instability of Europe, especially with the onset of the conflict in former Yugoslavia. Norwegian politicians considered that the country had to be involved, preferably through multilateral institutions, in managing regional conflicts in Europe. However, there was also the fear that, as the focus shifted away from northern Europe, Norway would find itself marginalized in the minds of its traditional protectors, the UK and the US.

The start of the first Iraq conflict in 1990, upheavals in the Middle East and the Balkans and civil wars and terrorism around the world certainly led to a more uncertain international environment for small states such as Norway. As shown by subsequent events, it became difficult for a small ally of the US and the UK not to be involved when its coalition leaders require participation.

Within Europe the widening of the EC had taken place on 1 January 1973 with the UK, Denmark and Ireland joining. The EC had also taken on a programme of deepening cooperation with plans for economic and monetary union, though these soon ran into the sand.

After it had signed a free trade agreement with the EC in 1973, Norway was part of a trade network that had developed in Western Europe. At its heart was the EC with its nine members – the original six plus the UK, Ireland and Denmark. Like the spokes of a wheel, each of the remaining EFTA states – Portugal, Switzerland, Austria, Sweden, Norway and Finland (Iceland and Liechtenstein joined later) – were linked to the EC by free trade agreements that were substantially the same and which achieved industrial free trade by 1977. The EFTA countries had already created industrial free trade between themselves. Contacts between EFTA and the EC remained at the technical level, with other aspects of cooperation being dealt with on a bilateral basis between the EC and the individual EFTA states. After a debate in the Storting in 1979, it was agreed that Norway should extend its cooperation with the EC, and regular, formal meetings with the Commission and the President of the Council of Ministers were set up during 1981 (Frydenlund 1982: 78–91).

Two sets of events made a consideration of the EFTA–EC relationship more important by the end of the 1980s. First, there was the enlargement of the EC to include three Mediterranean members, Greece in 1981 and Portugal and Spain in 1986. Second, the 1985 Milan European Council agreed to the White Paper on the Single European Market which led to the Single European Act of 1986. These events widened and deepened the EC, making it more attractive and more costly to be outside. For Norway two other elements were becoming more important in its relations with the EC. Closer ties had been established with the European Political Cooperation of the EC states, stressing the foreign and security element in talks (Frydenlund 1982: 78–84), perhaps reflecting some of the uncertainties of the period. Also the EC had become an important recipient of Norwegian oil, helping to free it from substantial dependence on Middle Eastern sources and increasing the share of Norway's total exports going to the EC from about 47 per cent in 1973 to 70 per cent in 1980 (Sæter 1985: 177).

The state in a time of crisis

If global developments during the *détente* years set up a number of issues on the international 'menu', the opportunities represented by the domestic political environment provided some constraints.

The referendum day of 25 September 1972 was not the end of the affair. There followed, in a period of international crisis, an earthquake in Norwegian politics that damaged the dominant position of the Labour Party. After the referendum, the Labour government resigned and was replaced by a minority centrist coalition consisting of that part of the Liberal Party that had opposed membership, the Christian Democrats and the Centre Party. The limited mandate of the government was to negotiate an industrial free trade agreement with the EC, and this was signed in April 1973 and came into force in July 1973.

The general election of September 1973 reflected the change in Norwegian politics. The Socialist People's Party linked up with many in the Labour Party who had opposed membership and formed the Socialist Electoral Alliance which emerged from the election with a stunning sixteen seats. A new anti-tax party, the Anders Lange Party (which was eventually to become the Progress Party) gained four seats. The Liberal Party split into two, the anti-membership Liberals were reduced to two seats and the pro-membership breakaway failed to be represented in the new Storting. The Labour Party suffered a sizeable rebuke from the electorate, with its share of the vote dropping from 46.5 per cent in 1969 to 35.3 per cent in 1973. Despite this poor result, the Labour Party, assured of the general support of the Socialist Electoral Alliance members in the Storting, came back into power until 1981 (Julsrud and Malmø 2002: 7–9).

Nevertheless, it was a chastened party, not only much reduced and aware of being outflanked by the new party to its left, but one that had emerged from an internecine battle not seen since the 1920s. Its task in government was not just to heal itself but also to heal the country. This meant that the whole question of Norway's relations with the EC had to be taken out of party politics and run on a strictly technical non-partisan basis. This effectively removed the question of a renewed Norwegian application for EC membership from the agenda for ten to fifteen years.

Furthermore, after the referendum in 1972 the party leadership was in a weakened position on international matters – it had already been challenged once and lost; could it perhaps happen again on, for example, nuclear matters? This thought encouraged a wider range of party activists to broaden their agenda. Also the generation change was to have consequences on foreign policy, as noted by the then Labour Foreign Minister. Those influenced by the wartime were being gradually replaced by 'a generation that had got its impression from the Vietnam War' (Frydenlund 1982: 10).

Norwegian politics in the fifteen years before the second referendum was prosaic after the poetry of 1972. A succession of relatively weak governments wrestled with economic issues, largely determined from outside. The rise of the oil economy, normally a bonus for any Norwegian government from the late 1970s, was adversely affected by a fall in petroleum prices, as in 1985–86. The Conservative administration from 1981 to 1983 and the Labour government of Gro Harlem Brundtland, in power from 1986, seemed to choose the economic virtues of a sound currency and price stability over full employment, though a premium had to be paid to hold fast the value of the krone (Moses and Tranøy 1995: 113). With its dependence on the oil sector of the economy and with the liberalization of its credit market, Norway's domestic economic policies were becoming increasingly dependent on the international situation. It was no longer possible to carry out a policy of 'tax and spend' in the conditions of the 1980s as the Labour Party had done ten years earlier.

While such a choice was appreciated internationally, it was not always understood by the average Labour voter. The Labour Party lost five percentage points and ten seats in the 1989 election and the Conservatives and centrist parties again came into office to face a bank crisis in Norway.

As unemployment escalated in 1989 through to 1991, the new centre-right government, followed by a minority Labour administration, found that they had fewer economic levers in their own hands. Monetary and fiscal policy was increasingly being seen in an international context, and a trading country such as Norway could not afford to lose its competitive advantage. Instead wages had to be kept down and the labour market flexible. The Labour government encouraged a 'Solidarity Alternative', a shadow of earlier corporate deals, whereby the major trade unions moderated wage demands in an effort to maintain low unemployment.

The economy continued to open up to the world in the early 1990s, sometimes with difficult consequences. The effective coupling of the Norwegian krone to the German Mark after 1986 meant that interest rates in the country were being determined in Frankfurt (Moses and Tranøy 1995: 117–18). Then Norway tied its currency to the EC's Exchange Rate Mechanism and European Monetary System which collapsed in autumn 1992. Thereafter the decision to allow the krone to float meant that it shadowed the German Mark. Nevertheless, the economy was again partly sheltered from many of the harsh realities of the early 1990s by its offshore petroleum activity.

In effect, the Norwegian state was becoming increasingly penetrated during this period as its economy became more internationalized. The state monolith created by the Labour Party in the immediate post-war period was chipped away internally as the party wrestled with divisive international issues, and was obliged to lower its defences externally as the Western economies became more open. Still, the influx of oil money – and deliberate political choice – meant that the Norwegian state was able to maintain the welfare society, albeit in a period of change.

A society in flux

The period from 1972 to 1995 can be termed the 'oil years' during which this product increasingly affected the basis of economic life. The country became less dependent on the primary products of agriculture, forestry and fisheries, and the tertiary service sector continued to burgeon. Norway became a more urbanized country and the population profile started to age. By the end of the period Norway was also becoming a destination for a rising number of immigrants and asylum-seekers from outside the EU area. By 1995 the country looked quite different from the Norway of 1972 – the past was indeed a foreign country. It had come to resemble much of the rest of Western Europe in socio-economic terms, with one main difference. It was richer.

For Norway, as many other West European countries, the 1970s represented a period of considerable socio-economic change. However, the country emerged from the decade stronger than many of its neighbours, thanks mainly to the presence of oil and gas offshore. In the period from the 'no' vote until the early 1980s, Norway experienced a tremendous outburst of public spending and investment. Money was in particular being invested in developing the offshore oil and gas activity, especially after the oil price increases in 1973/4.

After losing seats and votes in the 1973 election (see p. 51), the Labour government went on a spending spree. It started to pay back its core voters by putting money into health, old age and family welfare. With an international recession after 1974, the rate of unemployment increased throughout the late 1970s, as did the bill for benefits. The welfare state had been entrenched at a time before the oil and gas industry was making a significant contribution to the economy.

At the time of the referendum on EU membership, the Norwegian economy, thanks to the revival of oil and gas prices, had 'managed to avoid the recession experienced by its European neighbours' (Economist Intelligence Unit 1994: 16), building starts had begun to rise, inflation was low, the current account balance of payments surplus was expanding and even unemployment was beginning to fall from its high of 6.1 per cent of the work force to under 5 per cent (ibid.: 16–19).

The social changes that had taken place between the two referendums were mainly continuations of those experienced in the 1960s. Norway increasingly became a tertiary economy with more people working in offices than in industry or agriculture. Especially from the 1970s a greater proportion of women went to work and found jobs, particularly in the public sector. The proportion of people working and living in urban regions increased: the percentage of the population resident in densely populated areas increased from 65.9 per cent in 1970 to 72.4 per cent in 1990. Unemployment remained comparatively low, closer to the US figure than the other, higher, West European rates.

One change from 1972 was that Norway was becoming a country of immigration. Having seen a quarter of a million people leave the country from 1900 to 1930, and stability from 1930 to 1970 when there was a net exodus of only 800 people, 190,000 more people settled than left from 1970 to 2000 (Statistisk sentralbyrå 2000). The attraction of the Norwegian economy was one magnet for immigrants. By the end of 1994 a sizeable number of refugees had entered Norway from former Yugoslavia, Somalia, Sri Lanka and from the Kurdish area of Iraq, fleeing from the conflict in those areas (Statistics Norway 1995: 73–4). Events in the outside world were affecting society in a fairly direct manner.

The immigrants and refugees represented a source of working-age people. From an economic perspective, they were a welcome addition to an otherwise ageing population. Immigration was also one way of filling a growing shortage of skilled persons and to help staff some of the lower-paid services.

In summary, from the first to the second application, Norway had become a richer, older, more urban society and was beginning to experience significant numbers of immigrants in its larger cities. The working population was more involved in service industries and, while unemployment had increased, it was still lower than in most other West European states. The traditional unions that had supported Labour were weakened, and the party, when in power, found it difficult to uphold the notion of the 'Solidarity Alternative' very much based on the union–employer agreements of earlier years. The economy had become more open to outside influence, especially after controls on capital had been loosened. The exploitation of offshore oil had dominated Norway's economic situation during this period and had meant that the country had managed to ride many of the economic storms suffered by other West European states. It also allowed Norway to maintain its standard of living and welfare state, albeit with a greater distance between rich and poor than before. However, the levers of control over the economy that had been in the hands of the Norwegian governments of the 1950s and 1960s were slipping away from their grip especially as other countries – the US, the UK, then the states in the EU – developed more liberal economic policies against which advanced economies were measured.

A nation awoken

The grip that the labour movement, with the Labour Party in the vanguard, had exercised over state and society in the post-war period was already weakening by 1972 and had been challenged further by the first referendum on EC entry. This undermined the Labour hegemony, with alternative voices claiming to speak for the 'soul' of the nation emerging in 1972. The definition of nationhood had been separated from that advanced by Labour and which involved unity (behind the government), solidarity (with the welfare state) and international involvement (in the UN, NATO and other institutions). The counter-view, such as that expressed by opponents in the 1972 referendum, did not dispute the general themes, just their operationalization. The unity was to be behind the flag, a higher and more exclusive symbol than any offered by Labour; solidarity was needed to protect the welfare state but was against threats from outside; and international involvement was to be with the Third World and was sceptical about the West. In other words, it was based on certain fears: of those who would replace the flag with another (the European one, for instance), of those who would undermine the Norwegian way of doing things in both society and the economy, and of those who threatened the peace and environment of the world.

The Norwegian nation changed in the twenty-two years between the two referendums so that these appeals were no longer so telling, though others became more attractive. The increased internationalization of the economy matched by a substantial rise in wealth meant that the outside world was more familiar than in 1972 and certainly the European part could not easily be used as the 'bogey-man'. Many of the problems that were arising – terrorism, mass migration, diseases – were not ones that Norway could deal with alone, and the Third World was no longer seen as just a place to be helped but also the source of many of the threats and uncertainties.

However, Norway's oil wealth and its increased materialism meant that the debate about the nation was more along the materialist/post-materialist divide (Inglehart 1990). A more materialist view would see Norway as one of the world's richest countries in *per capita* terms, where the market reigns and international commercial culture has become more dominant, as has the English language. The post-materialist view looks at the alternatives to this story and places the emphasis on quality of life and environmental protection, values that have a resonance in the Norwegian nation. These would involve ecological issues, gender equality and solidarity with underprivileged groups. This divide can be seen in the political parties with perhaps the Progress Party and the Conservatives being the most 'materialist' and the Centre Party and the Socialist Left the most 'post-materialist'. It also divides the elements of civil society, with the unions tending to be more materialist and the environmental organizations, such as Bellona, more post-materialist. While the Labour Party can be seen as a traditional materialist party, there is a sizeable group within the party, especially the youth organization, that has espoused an alternative way. The party continues to be split, but along new lines.

Voting 'no' (2) A rational choice?

The application

In 1984 EFTA and EC Ministers agreed on a 'European Economic Space' to link the two organizations, though its content remained somewhat vague. The enlargement of the EC and the move to a single market also led the Norwegian Foreign Ministry to consider the country's relations with the EC in a 1987 report entitled *Norway, the EC and European Co-operation* which stressed the EC–EFTA link as a form of improving relations between the two sides. When the question was discussed by the Storting in June 1988, the government policy, based on this report, proved relatively uncontroversial. Nevertheless, the Conservatives called for Norwegian EC membership and the Centre Party warned against adjustments to the EC that Norway had already made (*Stortingstidende* 1988: 3880–923). Perhaps they had good reason: already in 1988 the Prime Minister had circulated all civil servants asking that any future changes in existing laws and regulations should be compared with EU legislation and any deviation would have to be explained. This suggests a 'pace-setting' tactic in the making, at least allowing Norway to be 'on the inside' should it become more intimately involved in the Single European Market.

Negotiations started between the EFTA states and the EC in June 1990 over a European Economic Area (EEA) agreement. The aim was to extend the Single European Market to the EFTA members on a reciprocal basis. By October 1990 this proposal had intruded on Norwegian politics. The Centre Party refused to accept the European Commission's rejection of an exemption from EC regulations for Norway to allow it to favour Norwegian business over foreign investors. In the eyes of the Commission, granting such a request would have undermined the very basis of the single market. For the Centre Party, a foreign take-over of Norwegian resources was also unacceptable and a betrayal of national policies going back to the early days of independence (see p. 28). The party resigned from the centre-right government which then fell from office and the Labour Party took back the reins of power.

It took until October 1991 to reach an agreement on the EEA but the whole package was unravelled by a ruling from the European Court of Justice and it was February 1992 before a revised treaty was ready. In October 1992 the Storting considered EEA membership under paragraph 93 of the constitution that stipulated the need for a three-quarters majority of the Storting in the case of a delegation of sovereignty to an international organization. An attempt by the Centre and Socialist Left parties to have a referendum on the EEA agreement was voted down by Labour and the Conservatives. In the end the government had the necessary majority with 130 votes in favour of the EEA and thirty-five against. The opposition consisted of the combined forces of the Centre Party and the

Socialist Left, three from the Christian Democrats, two from the Progress Party and two from Labour (*Stortingstidende* 1992: 179). The EEA came into force from 1 January 1994 (see Chapter 4).

Membership of the EEA had clear benefits for Norway, opening up the larger EC market for its exports. However, it meant a further loss of autonomy on a range of key market matters. For the Labour government it provided an opportunity to ease the country into acceptance of the more important goal, that of full EC membership. It seems that the Labour leadership had originally hoped that the EEA would be brought in from 1 January 1993 and, after a few years of 'socialization' in the single market the public would come more easily to accept full membership of the EC, or the European Union (EU) as it would be by then (Archer and Sogner 1998: 49). However, these hopes were dashed when the Swedish Social Democrat government, followed by the Finns, submitted applications for full membership in 1991. By April 1992 the Norwegian Prime Minister, Gro Harlem Brundtland, announced that it had been decided to apply for full EC membership.

By the end of 1992 EU membership was placed before the Storting and 104 of the representatives voted in favour of a membership application, with fifty-five against. The opponents included all eleven of the Centre Party and all seventeen of the Socialist Left Party, twelve of the fourteen Christian Democrats and fifteen of the sixty-three Labour members. The Conservatives' thirty-seven members and the rest of the Labour Party and most of the Progress Party's twenty-two members made up those in favour (*Stortingstidende* 1992: 341). It is worth noting that the number against membership exceeded that required to prevent membership under paragraph 93 of the constitution.

The result

The final referendum result of 52.2 per cent against membership and 47.8 per cent for, with a turnout of 89 per cent, showed a pattern similar to that seen in the 1972 result. The urban administrative centre and south-east of Norway tended to vote in favour, while the rural peripheral west and north tended to be more against membership. On the whole the left was more opposed to the EU and the right more in favour. Workers were antipathetic, leading officials were for. Two important changes from 1972 could be noted in the figures. The first was that a majority of women in 1994 voted 'no': 57 per cent of women voted against membership, but 52 per cent of men voted 'yes' (Bjørklund 1994: 3). The gender difference in the 1972 figure had been very small. Second, in 1972 there was some indication that employees in the private sector had been more opposed to membership than those in the public sector. By 1994 the private sector's employees had become supporters of membership, while those in the public sector opposed it. Furthermore, those working in the public sector had grown in number since 1972. Only 65 per cent of Labour voters voted 'yes' to the proposition advanced by their government (Archer and Sogner 1998: 78–9).

The referendum result had scarcely altered from 1972. However, the outcome was different. The Labour government had not made the issue one of confidence and thus did not resign. In fact, it had been tolerant of opponents within its own ranks, and did not have to face any splits as in 1972–3. Furthermore, Norway was already a member of the EEA so did not have to negotiate a supplementary treaty with the expanded EU. The choice in 1994 was more about the appropriate relationship Norway should have with the EU rather than, as it appeared in 1972, that of turning the Norwegian world upside down. Nevertheless, Norway was left as part of the depleted EFTA side of the EEA: Austria, Finland and Sweden had defected to the EU and the Swiss people had rejected the EEA, preferring their own agreement with the EU. Thus Norway was left to face the expanded EU in the context of the EEA, with only Iceland and the miniature principality of Liechtenstein at its side.

The reasons why: state, society and nation

Why did a majority of the voting electorate say 'no' to Norwegian membership of the EU in 1994? The answers reflect the interaction of the primacy of politics, of interest groups and of ideas and identity, as outlined in Chapter 1.

One explanation is that the government lost the vote. It did so by making a number of strategic and tactical mistakes. The first was probably one it could not avoid – starting the 'yes' campaign so late. The opponents of membership had started to construct their organization in 1989 when the first hints of renewed consideration of EC membership were coming from the Conservatives and the leadership of the Labour Party. On the other hand, the proponents had to wait until the end of membership negotiations with the EC (from November 1993 the European Union, EU) before being able to sell their package to the voters. Second, its campaign was too nebulous and failed to unite around one decisive theme. At one stage it seemed that the Prime Minister wanted to use security as a major reason for membership but this was not at all salient among the population, who considered that NATO membership dealt with that issue (Brundtland 1994b). Finally, the government probably missed an opportunity by not declaring the vote one of confidence. This had had the likely effect in 1972 of keeping at home a few percent of anti-membership Labour voters, thereby undermining the final 'no' vote. Opinion polls showed about 40 per cent of Labour voters in favour of membership, 36 per cent opposed and 25 per cent undecided (Archer and Sogner 1998: 71). If a similar effect had been seen in 1994, the result might have been a slim 'yes'. However, Mrs Brundtland was not prepared to split her party permanently and possibly lose power, and a repeat of the 1972 threat would have been seen as an act of arrogance by Labour. Also, given the decline in party loyalty, fewer anti-EU Labour voters would probably have stayed at home than was apparent in 1972.

Blaming the result on the government might have had some credibility if there had been a majority for membership in the polls before the campaign and this had been dissipated by the government's handling of its own case (as happened in the 2000 Danish referendum on joining the EMU). In the case of the 1994 Norwegian referendum, there was no indication of an innate majority in favour of membership at any time in the years and months before the referendum (Aardal and Jenssen 1995: 31–43).

A second explanation is to stress the role played by the socio-economic groups. The result reflected the economic interests of the country. This argument was made by Raimo Väyrynen concerning Finnish EU membership, which he saw as a result of a 'kind of loose elite bargain' (1993: 44). It is broadly supported by Tor Bjørklund in the context of the three Nordic states that applied for EU membership in the early 1990s, though he notes that the economic arguments were by no means crystal-clear and could have been satisfied by EEA membership (1996: 33). The view is most cogently portrayed by Christine Ingebritsen:

> the political influence of leading sectors (Norwegian oil, Swedish manufacturing, Finnish manufacturing and forestry, Danish agriculture and industry, and Icelandic fisheries) is a systematic way to understanding the politics (and economics) underlying the discourse about European integration ... Nordic constructions of the EC ... reflect the preferences of prominent, well-organized groups within each society.
>
> (Ingebritsen 1998: 43)

Ingebritsen (1998: 43) tempers this opinion by two other factors: '[s]ecurity imperatives may override the political and economic influence of sectors' and the 'sectors are caught in a two-level game', meaning that between the inter-state and the domestic political levels. The first element has more relevance to the case of Finland than to that of Norway.

Ingebritsen (1998: 143) claims in the case of Norway that '[a]s a consequence of societal resistance, the state was unable to join the EC in 1995, as the government had hoped'. This societal triumph was a response to the requirements of the leading economic sectors. According to Ingebritsen (1998: 119) this was because the oil and gas sector had its own 'opt-out' from the single market and the state-subsidized sectors of agriculture, coastal fisheries and small manufacturers 'mobilized against governmental cooperation with the EC ... As a petroleum exporter free riding on an open European energy market, Norway found its subsidized traditional sectors a major obstacle to accession'. In relation to EC membership, oil gave Norway 'the economic capacity for society to wait' (ibid.: 139).

Clearly the opposition by key elements of Norwegian economic life assisted the campaign against EU membership. Indeed, the Norwegian Farmers' Union (Norges Bondelag) helped substantially to bankroll the 'No to the EU' (Nei til EU) campaign. However, the EEA, which represented an equal challenge to the economic groups – and was opposed by them – attracted neither the parliamentary nor the public opposition that full membership did. A poll in August 1992 (Opinion for *Aftenposten*, cited in Ingebritsen 1998: 179–80) showed over 58 per cent of those asked to be in favour of EEA membership, a height never scaled by the 'yes' side in the EU membership campaign.

The key element in the defeat of Norwegian EU membership was the referendum itself. What the socio-economic explanations fail to provide is a 'cause and effect' link between the lead sectors and the voters. Indeed, a detailed examination of the arguments advanced in the 1994 referendum – which might provide some hint of the link – shows how varied both the 'pro' and the 'con' causes were, with economic factors not being the most important element, supranationality taking first place (Rugdal 1995: 45–64).

The third type of explanation looks more to identity. This can be seen especially in the works of Ivar Neumann (2001, 2002a) who looks at the Norwegian discourse over EU membership which he claims 'played itself out in, and therefore on, the nay-sayers' own terms. That went particularly for the two terms "state" and "nation", but also for the terms "people" (*folket*) and "Europe"' (Neumann 2002a: 90). Neumann traces the rise of these terms in Norwegian public discourse, in particular how the parliament, the Storting, was portrayed as the link between the nation and the people, whereas the representatives of the state, the civil service (*embetsmenn*), had no such coupling. He claims that the success of the 'no' side, both in 1972 and in 1994, was its ability to portray Rokkan's notion of the cleavage between 'a centrally placed bureaucracy and a peripherally dispersed people' as a key strand in Norwegian history (ibid.: 124–5). This positioned the 'no' side – as with 'the 143' in 1961 – as heirs to those who had drawn up the 1814 constitution, won the battle for responsible government in 1884, pressed for independence before 1905 and vowed to fight on in April 1940. In so far as this discourse ties 'Norway' 'with the people and "the EU" with bureaucracy, Norway may be represented as a political project which is incompatible with Europe' (ibid.: 125). The no-sayers won the argument in 1994, as they had done in 1972, and it scarcely mattered who won the vote.

This is a powerful interpretation of Norway's relations with the process of European integration, and one that finds some sympathy here. It views the results of the 1972 and 1994 referendums as not yet just the result of government mismanagement of the campaign or as reflections of sectoral interests, but as echoes of the deeper discourse about Europe (and Norway). Even if the Norwegian electorate voted for EU membership in a future referendum, the conflict would remain unless challenged by material pressures over time (Neumann 2002a: 125).

Yet this is not the complete story. Indeed, as Neumann recognizes elsewhere (2001: 141–5), the dominance of the Labour Party from 1935 to the 1960s saw a fusing of state and society. The Labour movement had, from 1935, undertaken the care and maintenance of the nation (and had certainly portrayed itself in that role) and had done so both through the instruments of the state (especially central and local government) and through the agents of civil society. Especially from 1945, the Labour Party presided over and partly orchestrated extensive socio-economic change in the country that masked many of the 'traditional' cleavages. Had Norway, together with the UK, Denmark and Ireland, had the option of EEC membership in 1963, the Labour government would probably have been able to persuade a majority of voters to agree to membership. Of course, what was on offer then was more like a trading bloc, especially if one listened to the British Ministers, as Oslo tended to do. A necessary precondition would have been Einar Gerhardsen, then Labour Prime Minister, supporting membership. The capture of the agents of society by the state works both ways – representatives from agriculture and the trade unions might have persuaded a sceptical Gerhardsen that Norway should stay out.

Between 1963 and 1972 the grip of Labour over the nation weakened. The 1961 election, in 1963 when the government lost power in the summer months, and the 1965 election etched away first at Labour's parliamentary position, then at its hold on government. The gaps between the centre and the counter-culture started to reappear, not least over external policy issues such as defence and Europe. Associations such as those representing fisheries and agriculture started to distance themselves from a party no longer in government and with a European policy inimical to their basic requirements.

In 1972 it might have appeared possible to return to the heady days of 1945–61. After all, Labour had won 46.5 per cent of the vote in the 1969 election. Turning the referendum into a vote of confidence faced the country with a 'Labour or chaos' alternative that the voters failed to heed. The discourse on Europe may have been dominated by those who linked the people and Norway against the bureaucracy and Europe partly because Labour's alternative cry of 'the party and the people' no longer rang true.

By 1994 the hegemony of Labour over the Norwegian state and society had been further eroded. Though the oil economy had placed useful economic instruments in the hands of government, these tended just to underpin the reliance of societal groups – state employees, welfare recipients as well as farmers and coastal fishermen – on the *Norwegian* state rather than the EU. These groups had undertaken a partial capture of the state in the period of weakened government after 1972. The discourse in the EU debate of 1994 among the public, if not the politicians, was more varied than in 1972 (Ringdal 1995: 52–7) and tended to be about the specific question of whether membership was the right form of link with the EU and about self-interest, rather than primarily about issues of national identity.

Conclusions

This chapter has shown how Norway was swept along with the British flotilla towards European integration in the 1960s. However, between the first British application in 1961 and the Norwegian referendum in September 1972, Norway underwent both considerable social and economic change and political development, with the Labour Party losing its grip on power. Furthermore, a different image of the nation was arising that challenged that which the Labour hegemony had created since 1945. The referendum opened up latent divisions in society. It showed that a majority of the electorate were prepared to forswear the influence offered by the membership to keep their country's autonomy in certain key areas.

Both internationally and internally, Norway experienced extensive change from 1972 to 1994. It became an oil-rich, mostly post-industrial society in post-Cold War Europe. It had to face a world torn by ideological and economic rifts and riven with conflict. The EC had become the EU of the fifteen, ready to expand to twenty-five by mid-2004. Norway participated in the Single European Market through the EEA and in the Schengen agreement. Norwegian politics, meanwhile, had become more fragmented, with the Labour Party merely *primus inter pares* in a time of turbulence in the economy as well as in political life.

The referendum vote in 1994 seemed a reflection of the one in 1972, though that probably did not reflect what could have been a stronger 'no' vote in 1972 had the Labour government not made the matter one of confidence. The negative result can be dismissed as a result of poor government tactics. A more substantial case has been made for it reflecting sectoral interests but there is also the notion that the division demonstrated by the vote reflected a longer-lasting divide in Norwegian identity, with the opponents of membership taking up the cause of 'the people' and 'the nation' against the state and Europe.

An interest-based explanation of Norwegian popular opposition to aspects of European integration would deal with 'the benefits of increased cooperation and the drawbacks of reduced national autonomy' (Petersen 1998: 43). However, to make such an evaluation, the electorate (let alone the interest groups) must have had a concept of what their own country could mean for them as well as of European integration. For those against membership, Norway was better not just in material terms, but also in terms of values. For example, in 1992 the Norwegian Farmers' Union saw Norwegian agriculture as a business but also 'part of our history and cultural heritage' (*Stortingsmelding* 40 1994: 470). The Labour opponents of membership placed their stress on the contrast between Norwegian society and that represented by the Maastricht Treaty, which they saw as 'colder', more competitive and with higher unemployment and crime (Gerhardsen *et al.* 1994: 3).

An 'interest group plus security' approach may explain why certain groups of Norwegian voters and politicians resisted (or were in favour of) particular types of European integration. But it does not necessarily explain why the electorate did not have the same level of enthusiasm for particular types of integration (especially the political) as did many Norwegian politicians and some interest groups. Thus people's beliefs about the values imbued in the Norwegian nation were not well represented by politicians, who were seen to adopt an increased adaptive acquiescence towards the EU. Under certain circumstances, the identity of a section of the electorate triumphed over what the state defined as interests. In the first referendum, those interest groups – agriculture and fisheries – that thought they would suffer from EC membership were able to capture an important part of the national discourse. In the second referendum this was less necessary, as a sufficient section of the population could be persuaded to vote 'no' for the sake of *their* interests (their public service jobs, their welfare benefits, their standard of living).

The need for dialogue between the interest and identity explanations has been recognized by Christine Ingebritsen (2003; also Ingebritsen and Larsen 1997) and can be seen in the works of Sieglinde Gstöhl (2002: 13, italics in original), who considers that 'both material and ideational factors must be considered'. She argues that '*the lower the economic incentives and the higher the political impediments to integration are, the more reluctant a country's integration policy will be*...' and that in these conditions 'the more important will be the maintenance of operational sovereignty relative to the acquisition of international voice opportunities'. When the economic elites favour integration, the economic incentives are high; when the political elites favour it, the political impediments are lower (ibid.: 14).

The crucial question is about the interaction of identity and interests. This chapter has traced the way that the arbiter of Norwegian interests and the focus of identity in the immediate post-war period, the Labour Party, lost its hegemonic grip from the first round of applications in 1961–2 to the crucial year of decision in 1972. With a state in favour of EC membership and interests divided, the answer to Gstöhl's calculation was tipped by 1972 through the anti-membership interests coopting aspects of the national identity that demanded the maintenance of autonomy and the rejection of influence. By 1994 the government was again in favour of membership, the interest groups were even more divided and the traditional opponents were willing to play the same national tune as in 1972.

However, it seems to have had less resonance, with a straightforward calculation of *personal* interest tipping the balance in this case.

As outlined in Chapter 1, the outcome of a momentous policy decision for a country – such as whether to join the EU – is affected not just by external elements but also by a mixture of interests, identity and interests shaped by identity. In turn, an appeal to a particular identity is made easier if it has been embedded in the country's culture and institutions.

4 Norway and the EEA

> If Finland, Sweden and Austria become members of the EU, and Norway stays outside ... [t]he value of the [EEA] agreement ... will be reduced as the possibility of us exercising influence and affecting the shaping of rules is weakened.
>
> (*Stortingsmelding* 40 1994: 77, author's translation)

From the beginning of 1994, Norway's commercial relationship with the European Union has been based on the European Economic Area (EEA) agreement. From 1 January 1995, the EFTA side of the EEA was severely reduced by the move of Austria, Finland and Sweden into EU membership. This chapter will examine how Norway has interacted with the EEA. It will look at the external events that have impacted on Norway during this period, and will outline the EEA agreement and how its institutions have worked. In considering the process of Europeanization brought about by EEA membership, special attention will be given to the response of the Norwegian parliament, government, administration and civil society. The forms of adaptation necessitated by EEA membership will be considered.

Developments after 1994

International events since the establishment of the EEA provide the external environment (see Figure 1.1) for Norway's relationship with the EU. Developments in the state, society and nation of Norway from 1 January 1994 have both reflected and affected the interests, identity, culture and institutions of the country. These have helped determine the activities of the government within the EEA framework.

International developments

In the latter part of the 1990s, the process known as globalization continued apace and has had important consequences for Norway's relations with the EU. This process has been defined as that 'of increasing interconnectedness between societies such that events in one part of the world more and more have effects on peoples and societies far away' (Smith and Baylis 2001: 7). It covers a variety of complex phenomena and it is not the intention here to deal with its many-faceted aspects. However, the novelty and extent of globalization have been questioned (Hirst and Thompson 2000). One way of trying to manage some of the effects of globalization on a universal basis has been through the World Trade Organization (WTO) which started work on 1 January 1995. This organization, to which the EU and its member states and Norway belong, provides a framework for world trade in goods and services and for such matters as intellectual property rights. It also has its own system for the settlement of disputes. It is thus an organization of supreme importance for the future of trading groups such as the EU and EEA and it seems 'likely to see further consolidation, development and evolution' (Wilkinson 2000: 137).

The link between globalization and European integration is complex. Globalization is certainly a process that has taken place parallel to and separate from that of European integration. It has benefited from global rules such as those instituted in the WTO system and what has been called their internationalization in national policy-making (McMichael 1996: 39), to which can be added EU policy-making. European integration is often seen, in part, as a response to globalization, whereby the capacity to make national policies in a wide range of areas is lost. Ross (1998: 176, 179) challenges this view and sees the decisions by particular European actors in the 1980s who 'decided to accelerate integration rather than to continue [their] discrete national strategies' of the 1970s as being key contributory factors towards the elaboration of the globalization regime of the 1990s. Nevertheless, the effects of globalization in Europe, whether facilitated by European integration or not, have often been distinct. 'Global cultures involve promoting lifestyle, consumption, products and identities', according to Kellner (1998: 28) and many of these values and products are US-based rather than 'European'. The general expectation would thus be that these forces would weaken separate feelings of identity within states and would undermine distinct cultural and institutional elements (see Figure 1.1).

From the start of 1994 the EU spent much time and effort on the Enlargement Saga. Once it had decided that the Central and East European states (plus Cyprus and Malta) could become full members, the questions of who could join, when and on what conditions seized the EU of the Fifteen. Furthermore, the EU had to make its own internal adjustments in the Amsterdam and Nice treaties and in the attempt at a constitutional treaty, so that its institutions could function reasonably well after enlargement.

The move from an EU of fifteen to the EU of twenty-five by 1 May 2004 had a number of consequences for the EEA and Norway. Apart from the direct effect on the EEA agreement, there were broader consequences. The new EU started to resemble more closely the map of

Europe, with common policies in not just trade and commerce and associated policies but also justice and home affairs and the foreign and security arena, eventually effective from Madeira to Estonia and from Malta to the Western Isles of Scotland. This certainly changed the balance within the EEA between the EU members and the EFTA ones.

The Amsterdam and Nice treaties, and European Council decisions, also altered the Union's approach to decision-making. Allowance was made for a group of member states to go forward with policy not accepted by all, and the Lisbon Strategy, aiming at creating a more competitive EU, encouraged members to achieve this by means of 'benchmarking' rather than Brussels directives and copying best practice rather than following legislation. The 'open method of coordination' shifted emphasis away from the Community method of legislation to it acting as a framework for more voluntary action.

More broadly, the international environment since 1994 saw a rise in turbulence and turmoil, with an effort being made by some states, led by the US, to manage new threats and uncertainties by a range of diplomatic and military instruments, exercised sometimes unilaterally but more often multilaterally, including through 'coalitions of the willing'. Events such as the conflict in former Yugoslavia, the Israel–Palestine dispute, what became known as 'the war against terrorism' and the military actions in Afghanistan and Iraq, faced small rich European states such as Norway with the dilemma of whether, and how, to be involved in these areas. Such countries have also had to consider their involvement in international negotiations about the environment and such questions as the establishment of an International Criminal Court.

Norway the state

The main domestic political event that dominated Norway during 1994 was the referendum on EU membership, covered in Chapter 3. The reasons mentioned there (p. 58) – the issue was not made one of confidence by the Brundtland government and Norway already had EEA membership – meant that the 1994 'no' vote caused less turbulence in Norwegian politics than in 1972.

Nevertheless, it had some effect on the political scene. The Labour government was particularly concerned, as it had made clear during the referendum campaign, about Norway being marginalized should the other EFTA applicants join the EU and Norway stay outside. The government realized that the influence of the EFTA side of the EEA would drop dramatically, and that Norway would have to accept policies determined by the enlarged Union. Furthermore, there were concerns about the security aspect (see Chapter 6). The government therefore undertook a deliberate policy of keeping Norway's profile high internationally and of confirming the country's links with the EU (Godal 1997).

After the heat of the referendum, the 'Europe issue' soon went off the boil politically, especially as other concerns came to the fore. The September 1995 local elections showed Labour in decline, and the Centre Party receding from its 1993 gains, with its leader Anne Enger Lahnstein, the 'No Queen', having sung her best songs during the referendum campaign. Labour continued in government first under Gro Harlem Brundtland and, from October 1996, under Thorbjørn Jagland, who took the party to defeat in the September 1997 election. Three centrist parties – the Christian Democrats, the Centre Party and the small Liberals – then formed a minority government with Kjell Magne Bondevik as Prime Minister. In turn, this government was ousted by a vote of no confidence in March 2000 and the Labour Party, led by Jens Stoltenberg, took over government until the September 2001 election. After Labour declined to a record low vote since the Second World War, Mr Stoltenberg resigned as Prime Minister and handed the office back to Mr Bondevik, this time as head of a 'cooperation government' consisting of the Conservatives, the Christian Democrats and the Liberals. To gain a majority, these parties often needed the support of the populist Progress Party, which was prepared to share its favours only at a price.

Norwegian politics became fragmented and lost what ideological edge it previously had. Voters became more like consumers, chosing from what to them appeared to be similar parties. The opinion polls showed large swings of opinion, sometimes within a few months. Voter loyalty decreased and the politicians floundered, trying to find a replacement for ideology. Labour collapsed as a mass party and seemed to be competing with the Conservatives, the Socialist Left and the Progress Party to get a few points above the twenty-five per cent mark. The Norwegian political scene looked to the outsider like the fragmented systems of continental Europe. The hegemony of the Labour Party of the 25 years after 1945 seemed a distant dream.

The question of Europe slipped down the political agenda from 1994, as was clear from the decline in the Centre Party vote. While the Conservatives and the Labour Party could always muster a majority for European issues in the 1997 to 2001 Storting, and were often joined by the Christian Democrats and the Progress Party, they lost this majority after the 2001 election. Neither during the 1997 to 2001 Storting nor since the 2001 election was there any enthusiasm within parliament to take up the issue of EU membership. The exception was Mr Jagland, who had other problems to deal with when Prime Minister but had some influence when Foreign Minister from March 2000 to October 2001.

Norway: society and economy

The picture given in Chapter 3 of Norway's economy in the lead up to the second referendum was one that had survived quite well the more general market uncertainties of the late 1980s and early 1990s. It was becoming not only more integrated into the European economy, especially that represented by the EU, but also into the emerging world economy. The main distinction was that Norway, compared with other European states, was buttressed by its exports of offshore oil and gas. This pattern broadly held since the 1994 Norwegian 'no' to EU membership.

There were few signs that Norway suffered economically from remaining outside the EU, though the economic benefits of EEA membership were hard to calculate.

The economy managed to weather the economic downturn of the early new century.[1] Employment in the service sector accounted for 76 per cent of total employment in 2002, of which the public sector made up 41.2 per cent.[2] The state still has some direct involvement in the economy. During early 2001 the Labour government decided partially to privatize Statoil, the state-owned oil industry, and 17.5 per cent of its shares was sold in June 2001. The remaining state-owned oilfields are run by a new state-owned company, Petoro.

The socio-economic trends of the early 1990s continued into the late 1990s and early 2000s. In particular, small settlements suffered as the industrial sector continued to decline and government-subsidized services were pared back. One of the most noticeable trends was that of continued immigration to Norway. By 2003 the total immigrant population – which included those born in Norway but of parents not born in Norway – was 332,800, that is, 7.3 per cent of the population. This was a 72 per cent increase over the previous ten years, with those from Eastern Europe trebling and those from Asia, Africa and South America doubling. This latter group tended to be concentrated in the large cities, especially in particular quarters of Oslo. As mentioned in Chapter 3, the new immigrants fulfilled a market role by taking on less well paid jobs and also offered a potential short-term solution for Norway's ageing work force and the need for personnel in the health and old-age care sectors. The larger cities had come to resemble other European cities, with quarters containing a noticeable non-European population. Referring to this increase in immigration, a publication by the Ministry of Local Government and Regional Development (2002: 4) stated that 'Norway today is in many ways different from the Norway of ten or twenty years ago'.

Norway: culture and identity

Indeed, one of the effects of a more global market was to make Norway seem more like other Western countries. Again, the main difference was that Norway was better-off. In both 2001 and 2002 Norway topped the UN's Human Development Index which purports to measure life expectancy, education and *per capita* income (UN Development Programme 2002). The rise in access to the internet and satellite television stations, the increased number of immigrants and asylum-seekers, and the intrusion of events such as the terrorist attack on the US of 11 September 2001 and the subsequent war in Afghanistan, brought the world closer to Norwegians. In a number of ways Norwegians started to behave more like continental Europeans: wine sales increased from 1995 to 2001 by 79 per cent (*Dagens Næringsliv* 2002: 20).

The imposition of EEA rules and the open borders of the Schengen arrangement have faced Norwegians with the reality that they have less control of what – or who – comes into their country than ever before. Their finance has been internationalized and each trouble spot in the world brings a new tide of humanity to their shores. It is becoming less easy to divide Norway and the Norwegians from the rest of the world. Concepts of autonomy are breaking down and strategies of adaptation – either on a personal, institutional or a governmental level – are becoming more complex.

The next section will examine how the EEA institutions have worked since its inception and will then consider to what extent the EEA has represented an adaptation, successful or not, to new conditions.

The EEA agreement

The background to the EEA

Norwegian membership of the EEA was part of a more general settlement between the EC and the EFTA states (see pp. 56–7). The aim was to extend the planned Single European Market of the European Communities (EC) to EFTA states. Thus the EC–EFTA area would benefit from the EC's four economic freedoms of movement of goods, services, labour and capital. The EFTA states would not, however, have to adopt either the Common External Tariff or the Common Agricultural Policy of the EC, though there would be agreement on certain other policies that complemented the Single European Market (see Box 5.2).

The EC and EFTA had agreed the basis for negotiations in December 1989 and these had started in June 1990. By October 1990 the Norwegian centre-right government had resigned because of disagreement about the extent to which it could accept an end to favouring Norwegian over foreign businesses in Norway. The argument was one over the balance between internal needs and external demands, with the Centre Party being intransigent and placing the emphasis on the former while the Conservatives were more acquiescent, trying to adapt to the latter. It was two years before the incoming Labour government could bring the EEA agreement before the Storting, and much had happened in that time. By October 1992 four of the EFTA states – including Norway – had decided to apply for full membership of the EU. This changed for them the nature of the EEA from being an end in itself to a staging post on the way to EU membership. Furthermore, the EEA agreement had been renegotiated after the European Court of Justice had struck down key clauses of the original agreement, perhaps giving an indication of things to come. Nevertheless, the Storting accepted the EEA agreement. The Socialist Left and Centre parties took a strong position on Norway's autonomy, preferring not to be inveigled into the spreading market arrangements of the EU-to-be. The other parties – the Conservatives and an overwhelming part of the Labour Party, the Christian Democrats and the Progress Party – chose both the economic access and the implied political influence offered by the agreement (Inns.S. nr 248 1992: 20–30). They must have hoped, in Rosenau's and Petersen's terms (see pp. 14–16), to maintain a preservative mode of adaptation, balancing internal and external factors. The Centre Party and Socialist Left, from their perspective of intransigence, warned that the settlement would be one of acquiescence, giving preference to the requirements of the EU.

To examine how the agreement worked out, this chapter will outline the institutions that were part of the 1992 agreement. It will then look at the way that the agreement has worked in practice for Norway and in particular the interface between the EEA and Norway at the governmental level. Chapter 5 will examine some particular case studies, especially ones at the core of the treaty, and associated issues on the periphery of the original agreement.

The institutions

The original institutions of the EEA reflected the task expected of the organization. Broadly, this was to extend the Single European Market to the EFTA states. Three points should be noted straight away. First, the Single European Market was on the way to creation when the EEA agreement was being negotiated, and it was to be part of a future European Union rather than the then-existing European Communities with which the EFTA states were negotiating. The EEA Oporto agreement thus refers to the Treaty of Rome rather than to the Maastricht treaty. Second, the EFTA countries were buying into an EC product; they were the *demandeurs*. Nevertheless, though not very large markets, they were rich and, collectively, represented the largest market partner of the EC. Finally, as noted, the agreement was changed after it had been accepted by both sides.

The institutions reflect the expected relationship between the two sides. The basis of the institutions was willingness by the EFTA states to adapt EC legislation on competition law and in exchange the EC would not apply anti-dumping measures to EFTA exports (Regjeringens informasjonsutvalg for Europasaker 1994: 12–13). This was of importance to Norway, which had suffered a number of EC cases against exports from its metal processing industry. Adjustment was also to be made in a number of flanking policies such as research and development, education, environment, social policy and consumer protection. As this represented a swathe of public policy, the institutions seemed to allow some form of discussion as to what might be acceptable to the EFTA states and what not. An EEA Council was to be set up, consisting of one Minister from each of the EFTA and EC governments and a representative of the European Commission, and it was to set guidelines, provide a political will to implement the agreement, assess developments and decide any amendments. It was to meet twice a year and decisions were taken by agreement between the two sides, the EC and EFTA. A Joint Committee, with official representatives of all the EC and EFTA states and the Commission, was to be the active decision-making and processing body, and it was to have a number of subcommittees (Archer 1994a: 183).

On the implementation side, an EFTA Surveillance Authority (ESA) was established to ensure compliance with the agreement's obligations by the EFTA members. The idea was that the ESA, acting together with the Commission on the EU side, would ensure uniform surveillance of implementation and would receive complaints from the EFTA side. In the original agreement, the two sides agreed the establishment of an independent EEA Court and Court of First Instance. However, a complaint by the European Court of Justice (ECJ) led to these institutions being dropped and replaced by an EFTA Court which would hear appeals against the action of the ESA and would deal with disputes involving EFTA states. The ECJ's objection was that an EEA Court would be ruling on the implementation of policy throughout the whole of the Area – including the EU – and would therefore trespass on the ECJ's position as the highest court on EC matters in the member states of the EU. The replacement of the EEA Court by an EFTA Court and the required renegotiating of the EEA agreement already demonstrated the supremacy of the EC legal system in any arrangement and left the judicial authority to examine the activities of one set of EEA members (the EFTA states) with reference to the agreement, while the judicial authority on the other side – the ECJ – would be primarily concerned with the *acquis communautaire*, subordinating the EEA agreement to that (Archer 1994a: 180–3).

An EEA Joint Parliamentary Committee was established, with an equal number of MPs from the EFTA states and the European Parliament, and an EEA Consultative Committee had a membership drawn from the EFTA Consultative Committee and the EU's Economic and Social Committee, representing social partners and civil society (EFTA Secretariat 2003a: 80–1).

By the time they started work on 1 January 1994 the EEA institutions had already changed in nature. First there was the downgrading inflicted by the ECJ. Its ruling showed that any notion of partnership between EFTA and the EU was not possible in legal terms. Second, in November 1993, the Treaty of Maastricht came into force and the European

Communities became enveloped by the European Union. This broadened the range of subjects being covered by the EU members, and not specifically covered by the EEA agreement. Third, after an adverse referendum on the issue, Switzerland pulled out of the agreement. This considerably weakened the EEA side and it received a further blow when the other four larger EFTA states – Austria, Finland, Norway and Sweden – started membership negotiations with the EU. Indeed, it seemed that by 1 January 1994 the main use of the agreement was to extend the single market, and related policy areas, to the EFTA applicants, thereby making negotiations smoother and, in the end, sliding them into the EU in two easy stages. The Norwegian rejection of membership meant that the EEA could continue after 1 January 1995 when Austria, Finland and Sweden left EFTA and joined the EU.

The original intention of the EEA agreement was that there would be a bilateral system with EFTA on one side and the EC/EU on the other. The agreement would involve the EFTA members accepting the *acquis communautaire* – the backlog of EC legislation and rulings – in the areas covered by the agreement. However, the institutions would allow both sides to consider more or less on a case-by-case basis the transposition of further EC legislation to the EFTA states in the field of the single market and related policy areas. The EFTA states could refuse to adopt certain EC legislation, though if the EC felt that this would cost it markets it could impose compensatory tariffs on some imports from the EFTA members of the EEA. This 'two-pillar structure' of the EEA has been challenged by the Commission (EFTA Secretariat 2002: 38). While the introduction of new legislation within the EEA is undertaken through a joint body (the EEA Joint Committee), surveillance would be the task of a two-pillar system. The agreement's implementation is to be monitored by the European Commission on the EC side and by the ESA on the EFTA side, with the two bodies cooperating and consulting each other.

Before the start of the EEA this two-pillar notion may have seemed more of a fig leaf covering the reality of an uneven relationship. The acceptance of the *acquis communautaire* by the EFTA states at one stroke emptied much of the legal archives of the EC on to the EFTA legislators. They were obliged to swallow the whole lot without being able to change a comma, a humiliating task for any assiduous parliamentarian. It could be regarded as a massive dent in the autonomy not just of the individual EFTA member states, but of their parliamentary sovereignty, so much so that the Swiss people rejected it.

However, there were two factors that made the process bearable. If the legislators expected sizeable economic benefits in return, then agreeing to what were mainly either sensible laws or ones with little relevance to Norway may have been seen to be acceptable. It was a one-off dose of pain to gain future benefits, an expectant acquiescence. This seems to have been the line taken by the Christian Democrats and Progress Party in their acceptance of the EEA (*Stortingstidende* 1992: 169–341, especially contributions by Gundersen, Hagen and Marcussen from the Progress Party and Bondevik and Gjønnes from the Christian Democrats). The other rationale was that if EU membership was considered inevitable, then early acceptance of the *acquis communautaire* would merely speed that process. It was therefore not surprising that the EEA agreement was supported by the Labour Party and the Conservatives and rejected by opponents of full Norwegian EU membership such as the Centre Party and the Socialist Left.

By the time the agreement was brought before the Storting in October 1992 it must have been clear that the institutional arrangements for future EEA policies would scarcely be balanced. The agreement bore the fruits of the ECJ's onslaught. Far from being two legal control systems developed 'in parallel' (EFTA Court 2003a), the EC system would develop pretty well independently of the EFTA system, while the EEA EFTA side would be following and trying to replicate as closely as possible the EC output. The structure was not to be one of negotiating between two sides, as had been supposed in 1989, but one whereby the EC/EU would pass on its decisions for the EFTA side to transpose into national law and implement (*Stortingstidende* 1992: 169–341, especially Lahnstein and Jakobsen, Centre Party). The only defence of any EFTA state autonomy was the possibility of a 'veto' being used by the EFTA side in the EEA Joint Committee (ibid., see, for example, Bakke, Labour Party). The substance of that promise will be examined below.

The functioning of the EEA

The EEA agreement has been functioning between the EU and Norway since January 1994. For the first year Norway was negotiating its settlement with the Union and it seemed that the EEA would be superseded by all the main EEA EFTA states joining the EU. The rejection of membership by the Norwegian electorate meant the continuation of the EEA, though with only three non-EU members, Norway, Iceland and Liechtenstein. What, in metaphorical terms, had been seen as two convoys sailing in close order to the same destination (albeit one larger and in tighter formation than the other) had become more of a minnow following every contour of its much larger partner. This section will examine how the institutions and workings of the EEA have developed and what they show about the relationship between Norway and the process of European integration. This will demonstrate the degree of autonomy Norway has left in the areas covered by the EEA and also the influence it has on the formulation of the policy in these areas and in its implementation.

The institutions generally

The institutions of the EEA agreement are supposed to form a two-pillar structure (see above, p. 73). This means that the structure on the EU side of making and taking decisions is reflected on the side of the three EFTA members and that there are joint institutions supported by these two pillars. The whole structure is complicated by the non-membership of the EEA by Switzerland, which found it could get a better deal on its own (Gstöhl 2002; Church 2002; Jervell 2003). As a result, the EU Council is not mirrored on the other side by the EFTA Council, though the European Commission and its services are reflected by an EFTA standing committee (on which Switzerland has observer status) and the EFTA Secretariat. There is no joint body between the ECJ and the EFTA Court, the ECJ having flatly refused to consider such an institution (see above, p. 72), but the EEA Joint Parliamentary Committee and EEA Consultative Committee bring together representatives from equivalent institutions from both sides (see Box 4.1).

Box 4.1 The structure of the EEA agreement

Iceland Liechtenstein Norway	→	EEA Council EU and EFTA EEA Ministers	←	EU Council
EFTA Standing Committee* EFTA Secretariat	→	EEA Joint Committee Commission and EU and EFTA states' officials	←	European Commission
EFTA Surveillance Authority		*cooperation with*		Commission services
EFTA Court		*reference to*		European Court of Justice
Committee of MPs of the EFTA states* EFTA Secretariat	→	EEA Joint Parliamentary Committee*	←	European Parliament and EP Secretariat
EFTA Consultative Committee and EFTA Secretariat	→	EEA Consultative Committee	←	ECOSOC and Secretariat

Key: → Membership. * Switzerland has observer status.

Source: adapted from http://secretariat.efta.int/efta/euroeco/HowEEA.

The EEA Council and Joint Committee

The EEA Council is the highest body of the agreement and it provides the EEA with 'political impetus and guidance for the implementation and development' of the Agreement (EFTA Secretariat 2003a: 42). The original intention of the EFTA Ministers meeting the Ministers of EU states soon faded, as the EEA was seen as relatively unimportant by the members of the EU Council. Instead the EEA EFTA Foreign Ministers have twice-yearly meetings with the Foreign Ministers of the EU presidency and incoming presidency and the Commissioner for External Relations.

The basic work of the EEA is undertaken through the EEA Joint Committee structure. On the decision-making side, 'EFTA experts are consulted on the same basis as EU experts' when legislation is being prepared and, once the legislation has been submitted to the EU Council (see p. 86 below), the EEA EFTA states are consulted (EFTA Secretariat 2003a: 42, 47). EFTA working groups and technical subcommittees, often after informal meetings with the European Commission, prepare material for the EFTA Standing Committee, which meets at ambassadorial level. These meetings allow a single EFTA line to emerge on any issue ahead of the EEA Joint Committee meetings. The EFTA side then speaks with a single voice in its meetings with the European Commission from the EU side in the EEA Joint Committee and its five joint subcommittees (on the free movement of goods, on the free movement of capital and services and company law, on the free movement of persons, on flanking and horizontal policies, and on legal and institutional matters) where the detailed work is undertaken. The EEA Joint Committee takes 'Decisions' that 'integrate EU law into annexes and protocols of the [EEA] Agreement, whereby committing the EEA EFTA States to transpose new rules into their national law' (EFTA Secretariat 2002: 37).

The EFTA Surveillance Authority

A decision to extend EU law to the EEA EFTA states has certain consequences. In EEA terms the law is to be implemented in the European Economic Area but, as it is already EU law, the effect of an EEA decision is to commit the three EFTA countries to transpose these EU laws to their own national law. Supervision of application and implementation in the EU area is anyhow undertaken by the Commission, regardless of the EEA agreement. Its implementation in Norway, Liechtenstein and Iceland is undertaken by those countries' governments and supervision by the EFTA Surveillance Authority (ESA) which, in this area, 'has been given powers corresponding to those of the European Commission' (EFTA Surveillance Authority 2003a). The Authority can investigate infringements on its own initiative or which have been brought to its notice. The EEA EFTA states inform the ESA of the transposition of EEA provisions into their own national law. At that stage the Authority can intervene and require the state to make corrections. If not satisfied, it can start infringement proceedings and, as a last step, take the matter to the EFTA Court. The ESA cooperates closely with the Commission and, if there is a disagreement between the two, can refer the matter to the EEA Joint Committee for solution.

The ESA, located in Brussels, is led by a college of three members, one from each EEA EFTA state, who are appointed by common accord by these governments for a period of four years. The president of the college is appointed in that post for two years by agreement of the governments. The college is independent of its government, and other institutions, and takes decisions by a majority vote. It is assisted by a staff of about fifty and two databases, the Acquis Implementation Database (AIDA) and the General Case Handling database (GENDA). AIDA provides an overview of implementation by the three EEA EFTA states and the state of play for any particular measure in any of the countries. GENDA allows the monitoring of individual cases of non-compliance and the tracing of a record of action by the ESA in each case (EFTA Surveillance Authority 2003b).

The EFTA Court

The EFTA Court is based in Luxembourg (as is the ECJ) and is the highest legal authority for the EEA EFTA states with regard to EEA matters. If an implementation issue concerning an EEA EFTA country has not been resolved by the ESA, the matter then goes to the EFTA Court, just as an implementation question in the EU could end up at the ECJ. The three judges on the court are appointed by accord by the EEA EFTA states for a period of six years, giving them the sort of independence enjoyed by their ECJ colleagues. From their establishment in 1994 until mid-2003, the court had made fifty-nine rulings and had two cases before it at the start of 2004 (EFTA Court 2003b). A number of important EFTA Court cases have impinged directly on Norway. An example that will be covered in Chapter 5 is that of the ruling on the sale of 'alcopops'.

Other institutions

The other two advisory institutions associated with the EEA agreement may not be as vital to its functioning as the Council, Joint Committee, ESA and EFTA Court, but are nevertheless important in allowing the input of civil society to the process.

The EEA Joint Parliamentary Committee engages in a dialogue with the other EEA institutions on the functioning of the EEA and about its previous resolutions which have been forwarded to the EEA Council. It tends to discuss broader subjects such as 'New governance of the EU and its implications for the EEA' and the almost inscrutable subject of 'EC comitology and the EEA' (EFTA Secretariat 2002: 66). The EEA Consultative Committee includes representatives of the social partners from both the EFTA Consultative Committee and the European Economic and Social Committee (EESC), with the European Trade Union Confederation (ETUC) and the Union of Industrial and Employers' Confederations (UNICE) sending observers. The members have established an 'osmosis process' by which EFTA Consultative Committee members can present their views to the EESC. An area of special concern has been the free movement of labour in the context of enlargement, and resolutions on this and other matters are forwarded to the EEA Council (EFTA Secretariat 2002: 65–6).

As the single market touches so many aspects of everyday life, it is important to have the input of those representing social and economic groups. This is a familiar process within Norway, as has been pointed out in Chapters 2 and 3, and one that is well entrenched within the EU's decision-making process. Indeed, both the Confederation of Norwegian Business and Industry (NHO) and the Norwegian Confederation of Trade Unions (LO) have their European offices in Brussels and often these can be 'more up to date than the administration itself' about EU activities, working as they do in the 'committees and corridors' of the EU (Statskonsult 2002: 15, author's translation). Furthermore, the EEA Joint Parliamentary Committee acts as a feedback mechanism for legislators at the national level on the EFTA side and allows the members of the Storting's EEA committee to keep in touch with developments.

There are a number of other organizations that, though not associated with the EEA, can have an input into the EU decision-making process from the viewpoint of civil society. Examples are the Council of European Municipalities and Regions, the Conference of Peripheral Maritime Regions of Europe and the Association of European Regions and Eurocities, which brings together representatives of European cities with populations of over 250,000 inhabitants (*Stortingsmelding* 27 2002: 81).

Europeanization and adaptation

In considering the relationship between Norway and the EEA as outlined above, a little more detail is needed of the interlocutors on the Norwegian side. As seen, the Norwegian government and administration is the dominant actor in most of the institutions of the EEA, with parliamentarians and civil society playing a less central role. The next section will give a brief account of what is meant by the term 'the Norwegian government' and will analyse the way it has responded to the EEA.

Norway's government and parliament

The 'government' of any country can refer to the political leadership of the state and/or to the administrative structure of the state, including the civil service, agencies and local and regional sectors. Here the term will be used to refer to the political leadership chosen, or at least supported, by the Storting to hold ministerial office. The political impetus for Norway's policy towards the EEA has come from the governments in place since 1994. These have all been minority governments, with a Labour government from 1994 to 1997 and March 2000 to October 2001, a centrist coalition from September 1997 to March 2000 and a centre-right coalition from October 2001. The political debates in the Storting on the question of EEA relationship after 1994 provide an indication of how these governments balanced the internal and external factors in their response to EEA issues.

After the rejection of EU membership by the electorate in November 1994, the Labour government's main priority in its European policy was to manage the consequences of three members of EFTA leaving the organization and joining the EU. It had to deal with a number of practical issues that resulted from the change from a trade relationship with these states based on EFTA rules to one based on EEA rules. The government was also concerned about the marginalization of Norway outside the EU and conducted an active foreign policy to compensate (Archer and Sogner 1998: 137–46).

The centrist government contained three parties – the Christian Democrats, the Centre Party and the Liberals – that had been opposed to membership in the 1994 referendum. Indeed, the leader of the Centre Party and a Minister for much of the government's time in office, Anne Enger Lahnstein, had been one of the most outspoken critics of Norwegian membership during the campaign. The government was meticulous in transposing EU legislation into Norwegian law through the EEA and tried to improve Norway's relations with the EU, especially on trade and technical cooperation. However, there were some sticking points, especially those areas of legislation that had been of such importance in the anti-EU campaign in 1994 – regional aid, food additives, fisheries.

The Labour government of Jens Stoltenberg (March 2000 to October 2001) had as Foreign Minister Thorbjørn Jagland, one of the few Norwegian politicians who saw Norway's future in the EU. He was constrained by the general inter-party agreement that the membership issue should not be raised during the 1997 to 2001 parliament, and by his party being in a minority. Nevertheless, the government oversaw the publishing of the report to parliament on 'Norway and Europe at the Dawn of a New Century' (*Stortingsmelding* 12, 2000), which provided an extensive overview of the relationship in the light of the general changes affecting Europe and the specific ones in the EU. It was the opportunity for a report from the Foreign Affairs Committee (Innst.S. nr 239 2001) and for a debate in May 2001 in the Storting (*Stortingstidende* 2001), both of which provided evidence of the political constellation in Norway on the issue of Europe.

The May 2001 debate demonstrated that the three parties that were to form the new minority 'cooperation' government in October 2001 – the Conservatives, the Christian Democrats and the Liberals – had the potential for deep dissent over Europe. The Sem Declaration, which represented the government's platform, deftly placed the subject to one side. One party bringing up the issue of EU membership would free the others of the responsibility of government, the so-called 'suicide clause'. The new government's approach towards the EEA and the EU developed over a period of time and can be seen in a number of documents (see Traavik 2001; UD 2002), including the full report on the working of the EEA that they had promised on coming to office (*Stortingsmelding* 27 2002). During these debates in the Storting, four themes emerged: an evaluation of the EEA, the 'right of veto', exports to East and Central Europe, and membership of the EU.

On the first issue, there was general satisfaction, but the changes within the EEA were noted, as were the areas of concern and the effect on Norway. No party spokesman expressed total dissatisfaction with the agreement. The Centre Party and the Left Socialists did not drop their principled opposition to the agreement – John Dale of the Centre Party complained that the 'greater part of Norwegian legislation, through the EEA, has moved out of the country' (*Stortingstidende* 2001a: 3143, author's translation) – but considered the EEA a reality, and one better than EU membership. The other parties were more positive towards the EEA, with the Progress Party, Christian Democrats and the Liberals considering it more than satisfactory (though open to improvement in a few areas), while the Labour Party and Conservatives, the latter somewhat grudgingly, accepted EEA membership as what the government had to deal with. The views of the individual parties on the 2000 report, sometimes expressed in groups, reflected their stance on both the EU and the EEA. The two parties that had the greatest belief in the EEA were the Christian Democrats and the Liberals – they had originally accepted the idea as having value in itself rather than as a stepping-stone to EU membership. They saw the EEA as 'securing a necessary harmonization of technical rules and trade decisions for the goods and services covered by the agreement in the whole of the EEA area' (Innst.S. nr 239 2001: 5, author's translation). They saw no reason for the agreement to be renegotiated and considered it 'robust' and able to continue in substance.

The party political support for the EEA had not changed from 2000 to October 2001, but, as mentioned, the government had. All three governing parties were satisfied with the EEA – they had all voted for it in 1992 – but the Christian Democrats and Liberals saw it in more positive terms than the Conservatives. State Secretary[3] Kim Traavik (2001) stressed the continuation from the previous government's treatment of European policy with the promise of following 'as least as active' such policy, but with scepticism about Norway's ability to maintain its favoured position with the EU. He recognized, as had his predecessors, the limitations of the EEA agreement in the petroleum and fisheries sector, but also pointed to a reduction in problem areas after Norway had adopted directives on the gas market, food additives, Protocol 3 on regional policy and patents. The one area where the new government hoped to perform better was that of contributing to and influencing EU policies where possible (Traavik 2001).

The government's support for the EEA was spelt out further in its European Policy Platform of 21 February 2002. This was a reflection of a number of political factors: that Norway was not going to be a member of the EU, if at all, for some years; that the EEA was 'the cornerstone' of Norway's relations with the EU (UD 2002: 2), that Norway was the key country in making the EEA work and that a pragmatic and organized approach to the EEA would receive widespread support in Norwegian political life and civil society.

With this in mind, the government embarked on what was an ambitious programme aimed at a more proactive relationship with the EU within the EEA context. Under the heading 'Intensification of efforts in relation to the EEA' it listed thirteen points, six or seven of which were internal to Norway, one was Nordic-related, two involved the new EU members and three or four concerned the EEA itself. The internally oriented aims ranged from an annual report to the Storting on EEA cooperation to Norwegian involvement in the new EU agencies and greater information about the EEA process for the public (UD 2002: section 4.1).

The next step in the 'cooperation' government's policy of engagement with the EEA was the annual report to parliament, issued on 26 April 2002. Given that this was the first of its kind, it looked back. Once again the tone was basic satisfaction but with some concern about the challenges (*Stortingsmelding* 27 2002: 1.2). The agreement was described as 'robust and functional'; it had secured Norwegian industry equal access to the EU market and had created the basis for 'a broad, mutually beneficial cooperation' between the EU countries and the EEA EFTA states (*Stortingsmelding* 27 2002: 1.2).

The 2001 report from the Foreign Affairs Committee noted that the nature of the EEA had changed since its inception in 1992, and not just because of the shift in membership. It pointed to the new activities of the EU outside the rule-base aspects of the four freedoms of action which were the core of the EEA. There was concern that Norway should not lose *influence*, as developments outside the EEA could still affect Norway's competitive position in the single market (Innst.S. nr 239 2001: 4). One area outside the EEA agreement was that of access for Norway's fish exports and it was felt difficult to negotiate a better settlement than the existing one, poor as that was considered (Innst.S. nr 239 2001: 5). Of the committee members, the majority from the Labour Party and the Conservatives, together with two renegade Progress Party members,[4] supported the Labour minority government's line that stressed cooperation with the EU on a range of new issues including justice and home affairs, the CFSP and new methods of economic cooperation (ibid.: 6–8).

The reference point for the minority remarks was the 1994 referendum and the need to respect the people's wish. The Christian Democrats, the Centre Party, the Socialist Left Party and the Liberals wanted any development of European cooperation to be based on mutually binding cooperation between independent states. They called for a 'national, independent and active appraisal of the regulation that follows from the EEA agreement' (Innst.S. nr 239 2001: 5, author's translation). In particular they mentioned the need to maintain strong veterinary controls in Norway and that the EEA agreement should not hinder the Norwegian authorities upholding regulations concerning the monopoly on the distribution of wines and spirits, charging for packaging of drinks and having regional differentiation of employers' social security contributions. The stress was on autonomy rather than the search for influence.

The Christian Democrats and the Liberals pointed to two problem areas, fish and gas. In the case of fish exports, which they noticed had increased strongly to the EU, they considered that a future enlargement of the EU should be accompanied by either an increased tariff-free quota for Norwegian fish exports or lower tariffs (Innst.S. nr 239 2001: 10). In the case of gas, they point out that Norway's strategic position as a gas supplier added weight in any negotiations that the report should stress more strongly (ibid.). These parties considered that Norway had influence within the EEA, which they believed should be exercised at an expert and a political level, and that the democratic process around the EEA should be evaluated with a view to making it more open, accessible and inclusive (Innst.S. nr 239 2001: 5).

This sanguine view of the EEA was offset by the views of the other opposition parties. From the right, the Conservatives accepted the need for such broader involvement in connection with the EEA agreement and Norway's cooperation with the EU, but they saw the EEA as nothing more than a staging post on the way to full EU membership (Innst.S. nr 239 2001: 11). They pointed to the limited influence of the EFTA states in the EEA from the start and the subsequent weakening of the EFTA pillar, with a further shift in power to be expected with another EU enlargement. Their criticism of the report was that it did not analyse the democratic weakness of the EEA and other agreements Norway had with the EU. The Conservatives considered that there was 'less room for the exercise of power with the EEA connection than with [EU] membership' (Innst.S. nr 239 2001: 12, author's translation).

From the centre left, the Centre Party and the Socialist Left Party had other gripes about the EEA. They had, after all, opposed the agreement from the start and, perhaps unsurprisingly, found their original reservations well founded. They cited Trond Nordby and Frode Veggeland (1999), whose thesis was that the Storting was becoming 'a passive recipient of EU laws and regulations' (Innst.S. nr 239 2001: 13, author's translation). They considered that the EEA weakened Norway's regional policy with its ruling on regionally differentiated employers' social security contributions; it led to Norway accepting products that were dangerous to health and the environment and that the agreement had not stopped the EU from taking anti-dumping action against Norwegian salmon exports. Finally, the EU was placing pressure on Norway to accept the Gas Directive through the EEA. Nevertheless, the two parties recognized the difference between the EEA and EU membership. The EEA allowed Norway independent policies in, for example, tax policy, economic and monetary policy, fisheries and agriculture and in foreign policy. Norwegian membership of the EU would mean greater adaptation to its policies. In later debates the two parties' criticisms of the EEA sharpened after the ESA and EFTA Court had handed down rulings against Norway. They considered that the EEA was no longer working as had been predicted in 1992 when, for example, Norwegian Ministers had promised that it would not adversely affect Norway's regional policy (*Stortingstidende* 2002a, Haga; Innst.S. nr 24 2002).

A second issue was the possible use of the 'right of veto' within the EEA structure.[5] In the 2001 report from the Foreign Affairs Committee, the Centre and Socialist Left parties berated the government for its lack of will to use this right, especially against health and environmental legislation, describing the report as 'needlessly defensive' in its stance on Norway's position in negotiations that would result from further enlargement of the EU. Indeed, the two parties wanted another institutional settlement than the EEA – they wanted a bilateral link with the EU similar to that gained by Switzerland (Innst.S. nr 239 2001: 13). For the Centre Party and the Socialist Left this was a means of maintaining a certain amount of autonomy within the EEA agreement. The three centrist parties had even wanted this right of reservation to be used in the case of the EU's directive on food additives being accepted into Norwegian law (*Stortingstidende* 2001a: 3149). The Progress Party was dismissive of the 'right of veto', the Labour deputy leader of the Foreign Affairs Committee, Marit Nybakk, was sceptical about the centrist parties' line (*Stortingstidende* 2001a: 3153–4), while the Conservatives considered that the problem was Norway's lack of influence in the EU's decision-making process (*Stortingstidende* 2001a: 3154, Siri Frost Sterri). In later debates the Centre Party in particular criticized the 'cooperation' government for failing to use the right of reservation especially against the food additives and children's food directives. Their representative, Åslaug Haga, noted that there had been opposition to directives on health, safety and environmental matters within the EU membership and, had Norway entered a reservation against these directives in the EEA, the EU would have had difficulty in introducing retaliation (*Stortingstidende* 2002, Haga).

The third question that arose was what might happen to Norwegian interests, especially fish exports to Central and Eastern Europe, after countries there became part of the EU. Norway seemed likely to lose out, as a tariff would replace free trade in these products. Members of the Centre Party and the Socialist Left wanted Norway to press for compensation and even to take up the issue in the World Trade Organization, a line that was mocked by the Labour spokesman, who wondered whether they would do the same to get free trade in food across frontiers (*Stortingstidende* 2001a: 3136, Haakon Blankenborg). Again, the Labour emphasized negotiating a settlement rather than using threats.

The last issue was that of full membership of the EU. The May 2001 debate allowed the 'no' parties – the Centre Party, the Socialist Left, the Christian Democrats and the Liberals – to reiterate their opposition to such membership and to attempt to force a statement by the Labour government that it would not pursue membership. Labour speakers refused to be tied down and tried to steer the argument away from the EU back to the EEA. Carl I. Hagen of the Progress Party seemed to entrench his party's growing scepticism about the EU and clearly thought that the whole issue should be postponed for another parliamentary period. He considered that, as opinion had not changed since the 1994 referendum, a new debate on the subject would merely split the nation. The party would allow its representatives a free choice to work for either the 'yes' or 'no' side but the party would vote together for whatever decision the people made in an eventual new referendum (*Stortingstidende* 2001a: 3145). However, the party advanced a proposal (which was defeated by fifty-eight votes to forty-nine) that 'Norway should not seek membership of the EU in the next Storting period' (*Stortingstidende* 2001a: 3184). When pressed, Mr Hagen did admit to being in two minds on EU membership and having swung from being more in favour to being 'fifty-fifty' (*Stortingstidende* 2001a: 3146). The Storting debate showed a path dependence on the EEA–EU membership was only really mentioned to force Petrine denials from the Labour government (*Stortingstidende* 2001a: 3135–40, especially Blankenborg).

As mentioned, the Sem declaration that established the 'cooperation' government made the issue taboo. This tied the Conservatives into a possible four-year period of EU chastity, ironically what the Progress Party had tried to impose in the May 2001 debate. However, Conservative speakers in Storting debates after coming to power were willing to support full membership, even if the Foreign Minister, from the Conservative Party, did not mention it (see, for example, *Stortingstidende* 2002a, especially contributions by Christiansen, Lønning and Petersen). The membership issue had been taken off the political agenda.

The interface with the EEA

The above section has outlined some of the major political debates within Norway about the EEA relationship. The political composition of the Storting and of the governments was a key factor in how governments played the hand that had been dealt them from the European integration pack. External events, such as the progress of EMU, the ESDP or enlargement, set the opportunities, but the political groups showed a greater or lesser willingness to adapt, one way or another, according to the interests they represented and also their vision of Norway and Europe, as shaped through their understanding of the culture and institutions of both (see Figure 1.1).

Nevertheless, much of the interface between Norway and the EU, especially through the EEA, did not trouble most politicians. It was conducted by the civil service and by elements of civil society, especially those representing economic and social interests within Norway. It is not the intention to cover this aspect in detail, as that has been done extensively elsewhere.[6] However, a brief overview of the relationship between Norway's administration and civil society and the EEA will be given before an analysis is made of its meaning for Norway's adaptation to the EU. The involvement of civil society is covered in the next section (pp. 91–2).

The EEA agreement institutionalized certain relationships between the country and the EU; it also created its own EEA institutions that impinge on the running of Norway (see above, pp. 75–8).

The first level is the political level, including the Ministers, as outlined above, and the EEA Committee of the Storting. The second is that of the high administrative level and the Coordination Committee and the technical level in the departments (Ministries) and specialist committees (Statsministerens kontor 2001: 7).

Important issues in relation to the EU and EEA are dealt with by the government at ministerial level. Government conferences (*regjeringskonferenser*), meeting about twice a week, may discuss issues relating to the EEA or European integration more widely. A Minister raising a matter at this meeting will prepare a two- to three-page government memorandum. Any conclusions arising from the meeting are placed in a protocol. Formal decisions are taken either in particular government departments with the competence to do so or by the King in Council (Statsministerens kontor 2003: 6–7). Memorandums on matters dealt with by the EEA Committee or issues being decided in the EEA process itself are normally prepared by the Ministry of Foreign Affairs (MFA) or relevant government department, such as the agriculture or environment ministries. All issues with economic consequences for Norway have to be dealt with by the Finance Ministry. There can also be an input into this process from meetings of Nordic ministers (Statsministerens kontor 2001: 7–8).[7]

The senior civil servants provide the second level at which government policy is coordinated. They meet about once a month just before the meeting of the Storting's EEA Committee. This Coordination Committee is led and serviced by the Ministry of Foreign Affairs and can also cover WTO issues. It deals with issues not sorted out at a lower level and passes on for political decision either important issues or those where agreement between departments has not been reached (Statsministerens kontor 2001: 8). As a former minister remarked about tendencies in recent governments in Norway, 'Ministers must have support in the government. That has become more difficult, especially in coalition governments. Frighteningly many questions, including purely technical issues, must go up to the government' (Statskonsult 2003c: 15–16, author's translation).

Much of the interface between the administration and the EU is at the technical and expert level. Norway, as a signatory of the EEA agreement, is allowed the possibility of access to European Commission working groups and committees in the preparation phase of the EU's decision-making process, according to Articles 99, 100 and 101 of the EEA Oporto agreement (Statskonsult 2001a: 4). Article 99 states that 'the EC Commission shall informally seek advice from experts of the EFTA States in the same way as it seeks advice from experts of the EC Member States' and Article 100 provides that the EC Commission 'shall refer to experts of the EFTA States on the same basis as it refers to experts of the EC Member States' in the case of the committees where the Commission has delegated powers, the comitology committees. There are also working groups that prepare issues for the comitology committees. It is estimated that Norway participates in about 200 committees, which meet between two and twelve times a year (Statskonsult 2001a: 4).[8] According to Article 101, in other committees 'experts from EFTA States shall be associated with the work when this is called for by the good functioning of this Agreement'. While Norwegians sitting on these committees and working groups are there as a result of their expertise, they also see themselves as representatives of Norway. Though some feel that they are 'second-class' members by virtue of Norway not being an EU member, they also feel that respect is won by expertise (Statskonsult 2001a: 10). There is a tension between being an expert and the political role that such a representative can play, even at the most technical level, and this is reflected in the relationship with the sponsoring department with its mixture of the formal and informal, control and decentralization, technical and political (Statskonsult 2001a: 15–16).

Since 1994 the Norwegian government administration itself has had a system of special committees to coordinate the work related to the EEA agreement at the technical level.[9] There are twenty-two such committees covering the areas of the EEA agreement (UD 2003b). Each committee is led and serviced by the Ministry most involved in its area, and the Prime Minister's Office, the Ministry of Foreign Affairs and the Finance Ministry have membership of all the committees, with other ministries being members of those in which they have a functional interest (Statskonsult 2001a: 17).

The responsible department prepares 'framework notes' for the special committees under its wing. These notes, structured by the Prime Minister's Office's guidelines, are the basis for working out Norway's stance for the various stages of the EU decision-making process, and contain reference to the Commission's document, an outline of the purpose and contents of the case, an account of the Norwegian legislation in the area, an evaluation of the effect on Norwegian interests and a recommendation on the Norwegian position (Statskonsult 2001a: 17).

Once EU legislation has been accepted, the question arises concerning its acceptance by the EEA EFTA states (see pp. 76–7). When the EEA Joint Committee has made a decision, it enters into force 'on the first day of the second month following the last notification' (EEA agreement, Article 103.1). However, if a contracting party such as Norway has informed the other contracting parties that constitutional requirements have to be fulfilled, there is in effect a six-month period for such a process. Otherwise the Joint Committee's decision can be implemented provisionally pending such fulfilment (EEA agreement, Article 103.2).

An EEA decision that needs the Storting's consent has to be agreed by the Storting either as a law or as a decision within six months of the EEA Joint Committee's decision. This requires a certain amount of choreographing on the Norwegian side. In certain cases, such as EEA EFTA states' participation in EU programmes, a Storting decision can be made before that of the Joint Committee, though this is exceptional (Statsministerens kontor 2001: 11). The normal process is that the Ministry of Foreign Affairs (MFA), after a decision has been made by an EEA subcommittee, prepares a resolution concerning the Norwegian adoption of that decision by the Joint Committee about a week before the committee meets. The relevant government department then prepares a proposition for the Storting. The MFA informs the EEA Joint Committee when the legislation has become law in Norway. A decision that does not require the Storting's consent can be placed before the king in council for a resolution in advance of a Joint Committee meeting (ibid.: 12).

From the Norwegian side, the process involves the Storting's EEA Committee (EØS-utvalget). This is in fact the Foreign Affairs Committee constituted with the Norwegian members of the Parliamentary Committee of the EEA (Article 13a, the Storting's rules of procedure, at http://www.stortinget.no/om_stortinget/lover_regler/forretningsorden.html). It deals with EEA matters in two ways. First, the daily ration of most EEA decisions is sent to the committee with a note as to whether they are proposals, decisions or have been adopted by a subcommittee. Commentary on these is agreed by the MFA and the relevant lead ministry. The list is then cleared by the senior civil servants' Coordination Committee for sending to the Storting for acceptance (Statsministerens kontor 2001:

13–14). Second, the committee debates proposals that are of special importance or are contentious, and its reports to the Storting reflect party divisions that are often seen again in the plenary debate. Examples can be found in the some of the debates cited above and in Chapter 5.

Once EEA decisions are turned into Norwegian law, then implementation is a matter for the agencies that enforce Norwegian laws generally. However, there is a difference between traditional Norwegian laws and those that are EU-based. The Norwegian tradition of rule-making, being Nordic, is based 'on relatively brief laws and regulations' in contrast to 'the [EEA] Agreements' requirements of detail and prescription' (OECD 2003a: 18). There is the added complication that should the Norwegian government either act in a way or introduce legislation that seems contrary to the EEA agreement, the ESA can start discussions to reverse that action or, finally, can take Norway to the EFTA Court.

Europeanization

The structure built up by the EEA states and Norway to deal with EEA legislation since 1994, and the response of Norwegian governments to that legislation tells us something about the processes of Europeanization and adaptation in relation to the EEA and Norway.

As far as Europeanization is concerned, there are clear indications that the quickening, though uneven, pace of European integration since the Maastricht treaty has impacted on the 'political structures and processes' (Börzel 2002: 193) of Norway. The process has clearly affected the *content* of Norwegian policy, as by 1994 a whole raft of EU legislation had been transposed into Norwegian law and, since then, a steady stream of EEA decisions have been placed on the Norwegian statute book in areas including animal welfare, transport, small and medium-sized businesses, public procurement, state aid, financial services, education, consumer policy and the environment. There has also been a noted effect on decision-making in Norway, with a 'fifth column' of detailed legislation being accepted by a process of participation in EU and EEA committees and what in effect has been a 'rubber-stamping' by the Storting. For those political parties and interest groups that supported Norwegian membership of the EEA, this approach of least resistance has been a necessary price to pay for access to the Single European Market.

What has been the effect on the decision-making processes and its participants? Much depends on the salience of areas for Norway (Miles 2001) but also on their functional nature. Patently some areas, such as technical barriers to trade, with its thirty-five committees of the European Commission, demand a greater Norwegian input than others. Nevertheless, there has been a general effect on the Norwegian government administration and on Norwegians working on EU committees.

Andersen (2000: 5) has pointed to the distinction between the formal and informal influence of EU decision-making on Norway. The former concerns the committees and working groups mentioned above, to which Norway has access through the Oporto agreement. This is limited to access to the Commission in the early stages of decision-making (important as that is) but once issues are sent from the European Commission to the EU Council of Ministers they 'disappear into a "black hole"' as far as Norway is concerned (Statskonsult 2001a: 25, author's translation). To have influence there, Norway needs to call on its contacts in the EU Nordic countries, in other member states and in the European Parliament. This reflects more the informal aspect of the general partnership implied by the EEA agreement and seems not always to have been fully exploited (Statskonsult 2001a: 37–45).

Andersen notes that there has been a bifurcation in the treatment of the EEA by the Storting and the administration. The former has seen it as a foreign policy issue, with its EEA Committee being, in effect, the Foreign Affairs Committee. He claims that parliament has 'voluntarily abdicated its legislative authority within the framework of the four freedoms' (Andersen 2000: 8). However, the national administration has incorporated EEA issues within its own structure and regards them as part of national policy-making (Veggeland 1999b), though this adaptation is less prominent than in the Nordic EU members (Lægreid 1999). Trondal and Veggeland (1999: 3) note that while the Storting and the MFA do not have formal interlocutors within the EEA system, the directorates and functional departments within the civil service do, thanks to Articles 99 to 101 of the EEA agreement.

Trondal (1998: 23) finds that the sectoral dynamics within the Commission, through Norway's EEA involvement, have indeed strengthened a vertical sector dynamic in the national administration. In his study of Danish, Norwegian and Swedish government officials attending EU committees, he also finds ambiguity in the effect of the sectoral approach underpinning Commission expert committees. It means that the MFA is 'largely bypassed as a vital coordinating unit at the domestic level'.[10] However, this effect of 'sectoralism' may be 'filtered and modified to some extent' if the MFA is perceived as a 'central coordinating body as far as domestic EU politics and policies are concerned', and the Council of Ministers' activities contribute to this role (Trondal 1999: 2). Nevertheless, responses to integration are 'filtered – even conditioned – by a prior state of affairs' (Spanou 1998: 469, cited in Trondal 1999: 2). Trondal also suggests that, in looking at Europeanization of domestic institutions and politics, it is important to focus on the match between the institutional dynamics in the EU and those domestically, as well as the domestic mechanisms that promote institutional robustness and inertia (1998: i).

The problem is that the domestic mechanisms have an ambiguity. The Norwegian political system has been one in which the individual ministers and ministries have enjoyed a certain strength and independence, not least in times of coalition government (Statskonsult 2003c: 201–17), and the MFA has itself always had a strong position in coordinating and running external affairs. Trondal's work identifies the conditions under which both these elements may be reinforced. This and other work by Trondal and Veggeland and the Statskonsult (2001a) study demonstrate that there has been a differential effect. While the MFA continues its *general* coordinating role, especially in relation to dealings with the intergovernmental-based Council, on the all-important *sectoral* issues this role has been taken over by the functional ministries, especially when dealing with the Commission.

These studies of the effect of Norwegian participation in the EU and EEA committees bring out important points. First, there is potential tension between the participants in Commission committees acting as experts and as representatives of Norway. They are open to socialization by participation in the Brussels system, and the forms of control by the national administration are irregular and weak (Veggeland 1999a: 22–4). There is the suggestion that these participants can 'go native' and undertake what has been called 'technocratic collusion' at the EU level (Trondal 1999: 1). Participation in committees can also be restrained by other factors. Norwegian input is seen as 'short and sweet'. Norwegian participation is valued for its high level of expertise, but there is agreement from both the Norwegian side and from other participants that, in general, the Norwegian members of committees and expert groups are rather taciturn and not always community-oriented (Statskonsult 2001a: 23, 36–8).

The reasons for this reticence reflect the nature of the relationship between Norway and the EU. First, Norway is not a member state and therefore has observer status in the comitology committees, and the Norwegian participants seem well aware of that. However, Article 99 of the EEA agreement allows that the Commission shall seek advice from Norway 'in the same way as it seeks advice from experts of the EC Member States' in the case of the expert committees. This has not stopped the Norwegians on such committees from either being treated differently from member states and/or feeling that they have a different status than members from the EU states, though there is often stress on value being attached to those who are expert and well informed rather than to their status.

Thus there can be both an institutional and, sometimes, a perceptual restraint on Norwegian input. There are other organizational factors: Norwegian representatives may be of lower standing in their departments and they may be rotated more frequently in their job than those from the member states. Nevertheless, cultural difference is an important factor in limiting Norwegian effectiveness in the range of committees in Brussels. In such meetings consensus is king and it is reached by an understanding of the different position of other states and through informal contacts and building alliances. In a number of cases, Norwegians may feel their country is ahead of the rest of Europe in its standards (for example, in animal health, consumer protection and, more generally, the environment), so why compromise? (Statskonsult 2001a: 38–9). Furthermore, the cultural differences between the typically shy and laconic Scandinavian and the more outgoing Mediterranean participant seems to work against Norwegians when networking and alliance-building are required (ibid.: 37). Norwegians are having to learn to 'do lunch'.

These factors are of importance for two reasons. First, the EEA EFTA states have a special position in the decision-making process of the EU. The EEA in reality is a means of translating the laws of one party (the EU) into the legislative stock of another party (the EEA EFTA states). What has been described above is a process whereby the latter party can have a direct input into the decision-making process of the former. The strengths and shortcomings of the Norwegian input are therefore of some importance.

The second point concerns the long-term effect of participation on the Norwegian side. It has blurred the difference between domestic policy and foreign policy, as the process is, in effect, one of making domestic laws for Norway in Brussels. However, it is a special form of legislative process, one in which the Storting's committees and full meeting have a position reminiscent more of that of the king than of an active parliament. It is, in Claes's words, neither democracy nor diplomacy (2001: 23). However, the process seems to have been accepted and internalized into the Norwegian system. When issues seen to be inimical to Norwegian interests arise there is a fluttering in the parliamentary dovecotes, but the will of most of the parties and a majority of the parliamentarians prevails and all is quiet again. Such a democratic process, alien to Norwegian tradition, together with the capturing of some Norwegian legislative powers by an outside body and the intrusion of a Norwegian input into decision-making by that body is bound to have a long-term effect on Norwegian institutions (especially the political ones) and the culture and identity of at least the political elite.

As well as the involvement of government with the decision-making processes of the EU and EEA, *civil society* can also have its input. Again this can be formal, for example through the consumers', employers' or trade union representation on the relevant committees (see p. 78) or it can be more informal, through input into the work of experts on the EU committees and expert groups. Local authorities are learning to act transnationally and relate with EU bodies separately from the government in Oslo (Holm-Hansen 2000: 82–3). There are signs of increased engagement by civil society in the activities of the EU, for example in the EU programmes. This involves a wide spectrum of Norwegian organizations, ranging from health professionals to the universities and the Research Council of Norway (Statskonsult 2003b). However, while it is the case that economic and social life has been increasingly affected by EU regulations transposed into Norwegian law though the EEA, the organizations representing those affected (such as trade unions and consumer groups) still act at the national level with only a part of their activity geared towards Europe. Also the extent to which organizations 'bypass' rather than 'go through' national institutions to gain access to the EU is still unclear, but probably quite limited (Pedersen and Pedersen 2000; Myrjord 2003).

Adaptation

What has been described above is a process of Europeanization whereby European integration, in the form of the EU and through the EEA, has impacted on what Börzel (2002: 193) describes as the 'political structures and processes' (and, one might add, culture and identity) of Norway. This section will examine how Norway has adapted to the process in the first decade of the life of the EEA.

Chapter 1 described how decision-makers could try to balance domestic expectations and external requirements in their adaptation strategies. Of the four modes of adaptation outlined there (pp. 14–17), that of *acquiescence* seems to fit the policy behaviour of Norway in its general approach to the EEA. Andersen (2000: 5) considers that 'EU adaptation has taken place with little active [Norwegian] involvement except in a few areas of confrontation' such as salmon exports and oil and gas. The exceptions were in areas where Norway had considerable resources at stake, where these were of some importance to the EU countries and where they were either not covered by the Single European Market arrangements of the EEA (fish) or were part of a more complicated market arrangement (energy) (see Chapter 5). In other words, the exceptions were areas where Norway had a greater opportunity for political action at the inter-state as well as Community level, and where there was a greater domestic willingness to show *intransigence*.

However, the situation is by no means as simple as 'acquiescence but with a little bit of intransigence over gas and fish'. The process outlined above shows that Norway, as an EEA EFTA state, has a privileged position at one stage of EU decision-making. The accounts in the Statskonsult report (2001a) and in Veggeland (1999) and Trondal (1999) seem to suggest that there is a good deal of Norwegian *quiescence* in committees and expert groups (often taken as acquiescence), to such an extent that the silence causes remarks from other committee members and Commission officials. In certain cases, the high adaptation costs to Norway of new EU rules – for example, veterinary and food safety matters – would suggest an *intransigent* approach in these committees. However, this is circumscribed by Norway being an observer and thus without a vote (Veggeland 1999: 10), but also by weaknesses in control and coordination from Oslo (ibid.: 17) as well as a socialization process that places the emphasis on consensus (ibid.: 12–16). In the end, Norwegian representatives are more likely to move to a preservative, balanced approach, finding a *via media* between home requirements and what is on offer from the Commission. Over time, this seems a more likely outcome for even the more difficult issues, particularly if the Norwegian participants in the committees experience what one described as 'a Europeanizing of the soul' (cited in Veggeland 1999: 16, author's translation).

The extent of Norwegian adaptation of administrative practices to fit into the EEA relationship has to be viewed in the light of the range of policies covered. The EEA is more limited in scope than membership of the EU, though, as noted above (p. 88), it still covers a wide spectrum of policies. Furthermore, that Norway has an opportunity to affect EU policy as it is made. Knill (2001: 46–7) suggests a number of factors that may determine a state's ability to affect the EU. These are: the 'fit' of existing structures (is there a need to change much?), the institutional embeddedness of the challenged sectoral arrangements, and the national capacity for administrative reform. In the case of Norway, the difference of its law-making style from that of the EU has already been noted (p. 88). The institutional embeddedness is likely to be stronger in those areas with a long history of a close relationship with the functional sector 'managed' by the ministry, such as agriculture and fisheries. The OECD has questioned Norway's capacity for administrative reform in the area of regulation, describing it as 'a *reluctant reformer* of the boundaries between state and market', with '*no immediate sense of urgency* for regulatory reform' and with social and political demands increasing the complexity and rigidity of the structure without improving its ability to deliver (OECD 2003a: 5–6, emphasis in original). However, Norway has introduced regulatory reforms, often in response to EEA obligations, and the structure of coordination committees established throughout the civil service when the country was expected to join the EU has been continued to cope with EEA coordination. Furthermore, the centre-right government that came into office in October 2001 introduced a raft of administrative reforms, mainly aimed at making the public sector more 'user-friendly, efficient and simple' (OECD 2003a: 9) and, while the pace of reform was slow, these brought Norway more in line with the changes in EU decision-making favouring a less interventionist, more example-driven process.

It should be noted that Norway has been remarkably successful in transposing EU regulations into domestic law, and by May 2002 the transposition deficit – the EEA internal market directives still waiting to be placed on the Norwegian statute book – was down to 0.5 per cent. Furthermore, the 'framework' format of existing Norwegian laws has meant that EU regulations 'can be accommodated through adjustments in existing regulations' without involving the Storting. Indeed, only about 5–10 per cent of amendments to laws passed by the Storting result from EU regulations (OECD 2003a: 17). This does not indicate the share of Norwegian regulation that has its source in the EU, merely that a small amount of it needs to pass through parliamentary procedures.

Conclusions

Ten years after the coming into force of the EEA agreement, the arrangement has fulfilled the hopes of the original treaty in extending the Single European Market, together with other aspects of EU policy, to the EEA EFTA states on a reciprocal basis. However, the structure of the EEA is different from that originally perceived, with the EFTA members attracting little attention from the institutions of the EU. The ten years from 1994 have also seen Norway becoming more like other EEA states (including those of the EU) in a number of ways, including important societal elements such as increased immigration. However, Norway remains richer than its neighbours to the south and it has only partial access to the EU institutions through the EEA.

The effect of EEA membership on society and the political system has been varied. The effect on the economy and those employed in it is direct, though it is not part of this study to estimate that outcome (*Stortingsmelding* 27 2002). A much clearer outcome can be seen in government but, again, the pattern is uneven.

The most obvious point is that a section of legislation, formerly carried out by the Storting, now *de facto* comes from the EU. That weakens the role of parliament in Norway, especially as what oversight is given treats the process as an element of foreign policy rather than as a new part of the legislative system. It seems that parliamentarians have been content for much of the interface between Norway and the EU on EEA matters to be dealt with by the government administration.

Second, there has been a Europeanization of this central administration especially with a steady presence of civil servants and experts on EU committees. However, the involvement of various parts of the administration is uneven, with some, such as parts of the Ministry of Trade and Industry, being more frequently and earnestly engaged in Brussels and other sections having practically no involvement. Thus Europeanization, the impact on the 'political structures and processes' of the administration, is partial and limited. The general effect of this is, nevertheless, to strengthen the hand of the administration as against ministers and parliament. It can also strengthen the position of individual ministries as against the Ministry of Foreign Affairs (MFA), though the MFA still has the key role in overall relations with the EU through the EEA, especially with the intergovernmental element.

Third, it would seem that the general pattern of Norwegian behaviour in the Commission-based committees is one of quiescence, sometimes acquiescence. This is sometimes offset by the respect paid to Norwegian expertise in particular areas (aquaculture is often mentioned) and an amount of intransigence in key areas for Norway that do not fit easily into the central framework of the EEA (energy and fisheries). The reasons for this reticent Norwegian response are partly institutional and partly cultural.

Finally, the broader process of Europeanization, with an effect on Norwegian laws, and on society as well as on the state administration, may change both the balance of interests in favour of full membership as well as the national feeling towards the EU.

Particular societal, interest-based, attitudes will depend on their perception of a cost–benefit analysis of membership as opposed to the current situation. Having a relatively limited input into the formulation of EEA legislation that directly affects them may persuade interest groups that full membership would be better. There have been indications that some groups are rethinking their position along these lines (Economist Intelligence Unit 2003b: 16). The effect on national feeling is harder to gauge, though opinion polls give some indication. The response of the nation to the EEA 'cuckoo in the nest' may be to stiffen the elements of autonomy and the resolve against EU intrusion, as seen in the case of the Centre Party and the Nei til EU (No to the EU) campaign. Or it may be to accept full EU membership in the hope that Norway will have greater influence in the decision-making and implementation process of the Union than is at present afforded by the EEA arrangement.

Looking at Figure 1.1, had the cultural and institutional factors from the period until 1965 endured, the emphasis of the Labour Party and other parties would have been on protecting key perceived Norwegian interests such as the welfare state, ownership of natural resources and national autonomy in areas such as fisheries, agriculture, district policy and alcohol policy. Indeed, these are just the key elements stressed in the EEA ratification debate, especially by Labour and Christian Democrat speakers (*Stortingstidende* 1992: 169–341, especially Bakke, Olsen and Schiøtt-Pedersen of Labour and Bondevik of the Christian Democrats). The expectation of the institutions would be that they should be intergovernmental, with a Norwegian veto being available against anything inimical to Norwegian interests. The Ministry of Foreign Affairs would be expected to lead on such matters and to show a certain intransigence in key areas, as was done in Nordic negotiations and in EFTA over matters such as fish fillets. The 1994 vote could be expected to stiffen such intransigence. However, external events, not least the strengthening of the EU, and the unwillingness of the Norwegian political parties to jeopardize the EEA agreement by intransigence over particular interests, has led to a different outcome. Structurally, the EEA's functioning has weighted the balance against the EEA EFTA states, in effect removing from them the opportunity to use their 'right of reservation'.

The next chapter will examine how the above institutions have worked in policy terms. In particular it will look at how Norway has fared in particular cases within the EEA and the adaptive responses that it employed, at least up to the point of the enlargement of EU membership in May 2004.

5 The EEA in action

> To accept the Gas Market Directive is banana republic politics.
> (Åslaug Haga, Centre Party, *Nationen*, 6 May 2002)

The European Economic Area (EEA) has, since 1994, given Norway access to the EU's Single European Market. This chapter will examine how the EEA agreement has worked and whether Norway has opted for autonomy or influence in its dealings with the EU, when the opportunities have been available. The four case studies – alcopops, the Gas Directive, fisheries and regional aid – have been chosen for their salience within Norway and to provide evidence of Norway's response to EEA requirements.

The working of the agreement

This section will consider those areas related to the single market aspects of the EEA. EFTA and the EU themselves have produced a good deal of material on the working of the agreement, as have the institutions associated with it, notably the ESA and EFTA Court. In 2001 the Norwegian Storting requested a report on the EEA and this document, actually covering the period from 1994 until 2001 inclusive, was presented in 2002 (*Stortingsmelding* 27 2002: 81). It thus provides much raw material for any appreciation of Norway's position within the EEA. It will be used to provide a fairly descriptive overview of that relationship, divided into sections to reflect the four freedoms and other matters, which will then be evaluated.

Free movement of goods

This element of the EEA had already been partially achieved by the 1974 free trade agreement between Norway and the EC which removed most trade barriers on industrial goods. In this area the Single European Market represented a tidying-up process and also one that dealt with the more stubborn non-trade barriers. Of course, the greatest barrier to trade flowing within the EEA area as if it were within one country has been the existence of different national currencies, and from 1 January 2002 this element was removed in twelve of the EU states by the creation of a single European currency, the euro. The three EEA EFTA states were not part of this venture, neither were the UK, Denmark or Sweden within the EU. Much of the EEA's activities in freeing trade between the member states has been aimed at dismantling technical barriers to trade, simplifying legislation, harmonizing product legislation, transposing EEA legislation into national legislation as quickly as possible and improving the business environment.

The *trade in processed agricultural products* was precisely the sort of borderline issue made to create problems. Whether processed cheeses or tomato purée, such products are a negotiator's nightmare and a lawyer's dream. At what stage does a tomato stop being agricultural and start to be industrial? As the three EEA EFTA states were not part of the Common Agricultural Policy, it was clear that they would not be part of the EU's internal agricultural market. However, if agricultural products were produced under different market conditions in an EFTA state than in the EU (Norway's agricultural products are even more subsidized than those of the EU), this would affect the trade conditions for processed agricultural goods produced from farm products from either EU or EEA EFTA states. Protocol 3 of the EEA agreement dealt with such products and set them out in a table. The idea was that price measures would be taken for these goods that would compensate for the cost differences of the agricultural raw materials. However, the list was suspended when the EEA came into force in 1994, as there was disagreement over the price compensation system (EFTA Secretariat 2002: 42). Indeed, these products – the ones that had received different treatment within EFTA than in the EU – caused some problems when three EFTA states joined the EU in 1995. In particular, they were the subject of a spat between Norway and Sweden over the likes of pizza toppings (Economist Intelligence Unit 1995a: 13). An agreement between the EEA EFTA states and the Commission was held up by the opposition of some EU states but a new Protocol 3 was instituted in July 2001. This committed both sides to eliminate the non-agricultural side of the customs duties on Protocol 3 products, ending them by 1 July 2004 (EFTA Secretariat 2002: 42).

This episode perhaps foreshadowed what was to happen with the 2004 enlargement, in so far as free trade agreements have been replaced by new tariff barriers. In this case, lack of clarity over the new arrangements – after all, Norway had been expected to join the EU with Austria, Finland and Sweden – could only be cleared up once its former EFTA colleagues were EU members and Norway remained outside. This placed Norway at a disadvantage in the decision-making process, as Sweden, in particular, was in a position to be intransigent and block any agreement between Norway and the Commission until the Swedish fish quota for the North

Sea was settled (Veggeland 1999c: 233). In the end, Norway had to adopt a more acquiescent approach which, with some quiet diplomacy aimed at Sweden, allowed a fairly swift solution to the question.

One of the areas of some concern for Norway has been developments under Annex 1 to the EEA agreement on *veterinary and phytosanitary matters*. In the 1972 Norwegian referendum on EC membership, veterinarians were one group that spoke out against membership for fear that Norway might have to give up its strict control of animal health for looser EC standards. It also provided the opponents of membership with the metaphor of pure Norway being infected by continental Europe.

From the early 1990s, Norwegian governments were under pressure from fish exporters to adopt EU veterinary legislation set out in Chapter 1 of Annex 1 to the EEA agreement, which Norway had set aside on the basis of protecting animal health. Adopting the EU regulations would mean that inspections at border inspection posts with third countries (Russia, as far as Norway's land frontier is concerned) would have to be in line with the procedures required by the European Commission and ESA, internal inspections would have to fulfil EU rules, and products coming from the rest of the EEA could not normally be stopped at the border. The arrangement for Norway to be part of this system was agreed in 1996, but it was the centrist government that was obliged to introduce the legislation. Indeed, the Centre Party, although in government, voted against the agreement, which was accepted in the Storting by a large majority (Veggeland 1999c: 237–8). Better information, and the responsibilities of government, persuaded others, such as the Christian Democrats, to change their mind on the issue (Veggeland 1999c: 246), moving from a position of intransigence to acquiescence in less than a year. The agreement has led to a major reform of the way that Norway manages veterinary control, and has brought it into line with the EU in an area that was once a totem for the opponents of membership.

Box 5.1 Protocol 4 of the EEA agreement

Protocol 4 deals with Customs Matters and Rules of Origin. The EU had attached origin protocols to the free trade agreements that it had signed with the Central and East European applicant states. In January 1997 these were harmonized in the pan-European cumulation system covering thirty states which allowed the same rules of origin for all partners, including the EEA EFTA states. Since then the Working Group on Customs Matters has cooperated with the Central and East European states to simplify these rules of origin and to spread the system to Mediterranean partners. A harmonized system was agreed for 1 January 2002.

In the area of veterinary and plant health matters, the EEA adopted 995 EU directives, regulations and decisions in 2001, by far the largest for any of the twenty-two EEA annexes (*Stortingsmelding* 27 2002: 29).

Free movement of services and capital

These two sections of the four freedoms of movement of the Single European Market can be drawn together, as the agents involved in moving capital – banks and other financial services – are themselves important parts of the service industry. Attempts by the European Commission to facilitate and regulate financial services have been controversial and extensive. It is an area where the EEA EFTA states have had an input: experts from these countries took part in meetings of Commission working groups preparing proposals for directives and observed at meetings of the Banking Advisory Committee, the Insurance Committee and the European Regulators Committee. They have also participated in meetings of the Forum of European Securities Commissions, the Committee of European Securities Supervisors, Groupe de Contact (banking supervisors) and the Conference of Insurance Supervisors of the European Union (EFTA Secretariat 2002: 48). During 2001 six new Acts on financial services were integrated into the EEA agreement. These were part of the thirty-four new Acts that the EEA's Subcommittee II on the Free Movement of Capital and Services identified as being ready to incorporate into the agreement. In the end thirty-two Acts were integrated into the agreement by EEA Joint Committee decisions. Many of these were in the area of transport (EFTA Secretariat 2002: 48–51).

Article 40 of the EEA agreement on the *movement of capital* within the Area conflicted with some precious Norwegian beliefs. It required Norway to change its laws on ownership and concession laws concerning property and the purchase of shares in various operations. This included ownership of and concessions in property, waterfalls, petroleum, minerals and mining, and fisheries, finance and transport businesses. As mentioned in Chapter 2 foreign ownership of Norwegian land and resources was a political issue and since 1905 its control was accepted by most political parties. In preparation for EEA membership such discrimination that, for example, allowed Norwegian but not foreign ownership of resources was prevented by changes introduced by the government in the 1991–2 parliamentary session (*Stortingsproposisjon* 100 1992). This changed the basis of ownership of financial institutions, for example, in which previously foreign owners could have no more than a third share of the ownership. New regulations meant that no one, Norwegian or foreign, could own more than 10 per cent of shares in a financial institution (*Stortingsmelding* 27 2002: 38–9).

Given the extensive nature of this area of the EEA agreement and the pre-existing Norwegian regulations, the prospect of conflict was present.

Indeed, there was a raft of exchanges between the Norwegian authorities and the ESA, but none came to the EFTA Court, partly because of this dialogue and partly because of other changes. These were the developments in the economic and social field covered above (pp. 51–2). It became increasingly difficult for Norway to enter into the wider world economy and to maintain control of its own resources. Part of the game was the attraction of foreign direct investment (FDI) to Norway to do the work that Norwegian capital was unable or unwilling to do. However, most of the political parties were ambiguous about this: they naturally wanted the investment but on their terms. So throughout the late 1990s and early 2000s there have been a number of cases, normally involving showcase companies such as banks, telecoms and transport, where Norwegian governments have worked to frustrate take-overs by foreign companies of Norwegian-owned assets. In these cases, the ESA has kept an eagle eye on Norwegian governmental activities and has felt it necessary to comment on some, such as the Norwegian law on the ownership of financial institutions (EFTA Surveillance Authority 2000: PR(00)23; EFTA Surveillance Authority 2001b: PR(01)19).

An example of ESA involvement is the restrictions on the acquisition of waterfalls in Norway. These restrictions can be found originally in the 1909 Concession Laws (see p. 28) that limited foreign ownership of waterfalls. A 1917 Act made the acquisition of waterfalls by anyone except the state subject to a concession which could be granted for a period of up to sixty years. After that period, all installations had to be returned to the state without compensation. However, the law did not apply to local authorities or state-owned enterprises – including limited companies of which the state owned two-thirds or more – which had the right to unlimited concessions. This was seen by the ESA as favouring undertakings of Norwegian nationality, and thereby contrary to Article 31 of the EEA agreement. It was also contrary to the free movement of capital under Article 40, as the limited nature of the concessions for private undertakings could deter investors from acquiring shares in them. The ESA did not consider that Norway had provided 'objective reasons' for the restrictions and decided to send a formal letter questioning its compliance with EEA rules (EFTA Surveillance Authority 2001a). In its letter of 20 February 2002 the ESA stated its disagreement with the Norwegian view and gave Norway a last chance to comply, threatening to bring the matter before the EFTA Court (EFTA Surveillance Authority 2002: PR(02)02). Meanwhile the Ministry of Petroleum and Energy had evaluated the energy market within the country and had concluded that the concession system was not optimal with regard to competition and effectiveness in the sector. As a result the centre-right government decided to reform the concession regulations as between private and public owners. Such a change would alter the basis of the ESA's case on waterfalls, which was thus not pressed to the EFTA Court (*Stortingsmelding* 27 2002: para. 2.3.3).

Free movement of persons

The aim of this freedom is to create a common labour market within the EEA. This is to be achieved by allowing free movement within the Area of those who wish to work and means free access to work in Norway on the same basis as Norwegians for those from other EEA states. It also meant deeper involvement of the EU-based system of controlling those desiring access to most EU states, the Schengen agreement (see Chapter 7). This has meant not just an easing of controls on those entering Norway from EEA states but also steps being taken on an EEA-wide basis to make it easier to move from one EEA country to another. To this end the EEA EFTA states have participated in MISSOC, the system of mutual exchange of information on social protection in the EU, and EURES, the database of job vacancies and living and working conditions in EEA states; the EEA Joint Committee has also made progress on the mutual recognition of professional qualifications and diplomas with the Area (EFTA Secretariat 2002: 53–4).

The free movement of persons under the EEA agreement was not a political issue within Norway until the 2004 enlargement. Indeed, in many areas of expertise Norway has welcomed those coming from EU and other EFTA states and has actively tried to recruit them for the health service, for example (Economist Intelligence Unit 2003a: 13). It has been the non-EEA migrants that have been the cause of political debate and these issues are tied in to the Schengen debate (see Chapter 7).

Flanking and horizontal policies

This heading included policies that relate to the 'horizontal provisions of the EEA Agreement' which are relevant to the four freedoms, as well as cooperation outside those four freedoms (flanking policies). (See Box 5.2 for further details.)

Implementing the market

The extension of the Single European Market to the non-EU EEA states was aimed at creating a market within which goods and services could be traded under the same conditions throughout the area, and capital and labour could move as freely between the member states as within them. That was the aspiration but, as seen, there are some barriers that have yet to be removed – the single currency covers only twelve EU states and the movement of labour is constrained by many cultural as well as economic conditions.

Nevertheless, there has been a welter of EU legislation that can be classified as what Knill and Lehmkull (1999: 3) describe as 'negative integration', which is deregulatory and alters the opportunities and

Box 5.2 Flanking and horizontal policies

A range of policies are included under this heading, which are dealt with by Subcommittee IV of the EEA Joint Committee. In 2001 this subcommittee identified sixty-five new Acts to be incorporated into the EEA agreement and prepared sixty Acts for inclusion. During the year fifty-one Acts were actually integrated into the agreement under this heading. The main areas of interest are:

- *Research and development.* The EEA EFTA states contribute to and participate in the management committees of the seven programmes of the Fifth Framework Programme for Research, Technological Development and Demonstration Activities, 1999–2002 (and its successor, the Sixth Framework Programme, 2003–6).
- *Environment.* The EEA Joint Committee in 2001 incorporated into the EEA agreement legal Acts concerning waste, eco-labelling, air quality, drinking water and genetically modified organisms (GMOs). The EEA EFTA states decided to participate in a marine pollution programme. In an effort to shape decisions the EEA Working Group on the Environment discussed policy documents and new legislative proposals with the Commission.
- *Education training and youth.* The EEA EFTA states participate in a wide range of programmes, such as Socrates and Leonardo da Vinci, and have consulted the Commission on issues such as lifelong learning and education through sport.
- *Gender equality and family policy.* A number of working groups are involved in work on anti-discrimination and programmes on fighting violence against children, young people and women (Daphne programme) and a new Gender Equality Programme.
- *Labour law.* Preparation was made for the incorporation of the extension of the working time directive. A number of health and safety directives were adopted, including those concerned with worker exposure to chemical and biological agents. The EEA EFTA states were involved in the EU Workshop on Health and Safety and were closely involved in a range of expert groups.
- *Consumer protection.* There was close following by the Joint Committee of EC directives on, for example, the distance marketing of consumer financial services and on consumer credit.

Source: EFTA Secretariat 2002: 54–9.

constraints for producers and consumers. Much of this EU legislation has to be transposed into national law and, in the case of the EEA, first has to be accepted by the EEA EFTA states in the joint committees (see p. 76).

As can be seen in the case of the Gas Directive below, this allows the EEA EFTA states the opportunity to ask for a transition period from the European Commission, a request normally met with stiff resistance. Transposition also allows EFTA states the chance to foot-drag in an effort to maintain some autonomy. However, Norway, like its Nordic EU members, has prided itself on rapid and full implementation, pushing it to near the top of the EEA league table on that issue. EFTA reported that in the league table of laws not transposed into national legislation (as a percentage of total directives)

> Norway maintains the second lowest implementation deficit of the eighteen EEA States with a transposition deficit of 0.5 per cent. Only Denmark has implemented a higher proportion of the *acquis communautaire*. Iceland now ranks as No. 4 (up from 8) with 1.0 per cent, and Liechtenstein is keeping its fifth place with a 1.1 per cent deficit. It is worth mentioning that in May 2002 Norway and Iceland stood at a record 0.5 per cent and 0.8 per cent transposition deficits, respectively.
>
> (EFTA Surveillance Authority 2004: 5, italics in original)

In this vital area, Norway has indeed been the pace-setter. This has not always been the case in either the making or the implementation of EEA-related policy. The case studies are chosen for their importance in Norwegian culture and identity (alcohol policy, fisheries and regional policies), and in the country's economy (regional policy, gas and fisheries).

Case study 1: alcopops

One case concerning the free movement of goods that was brought before the EFTA Court is worth examining here because it displays a clash of values, not only of groups within Norway but also between the Norwegian state and the views of the European Commission about the limitations on the free movement of goods. In the alcopops case (E-9/00), these foreign-produced soft drinks pre-mixed with alcohol were prevented from going on general sale and were restricted to the state retail monopoly shops, Vinmonopolet, and were also forbidden to be served in bars on the same basis as beer. However, beer, mainly Norwegian-produced and with the same percentage of alcohol, was allowed to be sold in general stores and served at bars. The ESA considered this to be discriminatory treatment of foreign as opposed to Norwegian products and brought the case to the Court. The ESA cited case law of the ECJ that national measures contrary to Article 16 of the EEA agreement (on state monopolies)[1] cannot be justified on grounds of public health. Furthermore, the European Commission's argument against Norway was supported by the ESA and both sides cited the same ECJ case (Keck and Mithouard), leaving the EFTA Court to decide on its interpretation (EFTA Court 2002, E-9/00: 15). The Norwegian government's case was twofold. First, it claimed that beer and alcopops were not substantially in competition and therefore placing alcopops on more general sale would add to the market. Second, the government's action was aimed at preventing alcopops from being readily available to young people (at whom they were aimed), thereby limiting the damage done to them by freer access to alcohol. This was part of the government's strategy under the Norwegian Alcohol Act, and is, in the words of the Court, a comprehensive strategy whose aim is to 'curb to the greatest possible extent the harm to society and the individual that may result from the consumption of alcoholic beverages'. There is differential treatment of beer, spirits and wines included in the Act (EFTA Court 2002, E-9/00: 7–8). The Norwegian government referred to World Health Organization studies and to a draft EC proposal on 'Drinking of Alcohol by Children and Adolescents'.

The Court found against Norway. It noted the seriousness of Norway's alcohol policy and that there was nothing in the EEA agreement to prevent Norway from implementing a strict alcohol policy, though it must be implemented so as not to impede the free movement of goods within the EEA. It considered that the core question was whether there was a competitive relationship between beer and alcopops and thought that they represented 'at least partially and potentially, alternative choices for certain groups of consumers' (ibid.: 12). Furthermore, social and health aspects offered 'no direct basis for derogations from Article 16 EEA' (ibid.: 10). Norway had failed to comply with Article 16 of the EEA agreement.

The value that triumphed in this case was that of the overriding importance of the free movement of goods and it is one supported by the European Commission as well as political groups within Norway that could be seen in the Conservative Party and the Progress Party. These domestic political groups in Norway stress free choice by the individual, fewer government restrictions on trade generally and a more 'Continental' approach to alcohol, meaning fewer restrictions on its sale.

The value represented by the Norwegian government was one that can be seen in the country's alcohol policy since the inception of the state. The dangers of alcohol are weighed and restrictions placed, especially to protect vulnerable groups such as young people. This is done not just for their sake but also for the sake of society which otherwise has to bear the cost of alcohol misuse. This view is held especially by church groups, the Christian Democrats, some members of the Centre Party and some in the medical profession. However, as witnessed by the continuation of a stringent alcohol policy, it is tacitly accepted by a wider section of public opinion, not least by many in the Labour Party.

The issue of alcopops in Norway was defined as one of alcohol policy – how to prevent young people from drinking more, getting hooked on alcohol and drinking at a younger age. There is little indication that the restrictions on alcopops were seen in trade and competition terms, except by those who wished to market the product. In the end the judgement on whether this should be a social policy issue or a commercial one was taken out of the hands of the Norwegian authorities and decided by a court that gave greater weight to Commission arguments.

It can be argued that alcopops represented but a minuscule part of the Norwegian drinks market and that they are anyhow a passing phase. Likewise it could be argued that the Court clearly knew little about alcopops. Very few beer drinkers would regard them as an alternative choice; the most likely consumers would be young and possibly under-age drinkers whose powers of discrimination have perhaps not fully developed. The drinks were marketed to a teen market, and especially young girls, a discriminatory argument that the Court was not asked to consider. Nevertheless, the argument as to the merits of the case is not the main issue. It is that an interpretation of a key piece of Norwegian social legislation – and one with political implications – was decided by the EFTA Court with its mind on the EEA agreement, its ear tuned to Commission advice and its eye on ECJ precedent. Norway's autonomy to interpret that piece of legislation had been lost, though the free market in alcopops in Norway had been given a boost.

The case could be seen, in dramatic terms, as a blow against the Norway represented by the opponents of EU membership. Indeed, the party that represents that element of the counter-culture, the Christian Democrats, has been obliged to accept worse. In December 2002, Mr Bondevik's party had to swallow a reduction in the duty on alcohol to get the centre-right government's budget accepted by the Progress Party and thus have a majority in parliament (Economist Intelligence Unit 2003b: 14–15). However, this was done within the Norwegian political system, not imposed from outside. A later compromise won by the Christian Democrats led to the duty on spirits-based alcopops being increased more than wine-based ones, possibly lining Norway up for another trip to the EFTA Court (*Aftenposten*, 14 June 2003).

The Court's alcopops decision is just one indicator among many that, in this area of culture as in others, Norway is becoming more like other European states. While of little economic consequence, such changes erode the notion of Norway as a different, special country.

Case study 2: the Gas Directive

The Gas Directive provides an example of Norway having to accept new EU legislation that was of economic importance to it. Norway is blessed with an abundance of power. It generates 30 per cent of Europe's hydro-power, and has 45 per cent of the continent's gas reserves and 75 per cent of its oil (Brinchmann 2000: 16). As seen in Chapter 3, Norway became a major oil and gas producer during the last quarter of the twentieth century. By 1994 Norway was producing some 130 million tonnes (mt) of crude oil and 31.2 million tons of oil equivalent (toe) of natural gas, and was vying with the UK for the position of Europe's largest oil producer (Economist Intelligence Unit 1995b: 19–20). By 2002 the Norwegian oil output was at 157.4 mt, after peaking at 162.2 mt in 2001, and gas production was at a record high of 58.9 million toe (Economist Intelligence Unit 2003c: 54). By 2002 Norway had become the world's third-largest petroleum exporter, with oil and gas making up some 42 per cent of the country's total export revenue, up from the 1999 figure of 32.7 per cent, mainly as a result of the rise in petroleum prices. Norwegian petroleum production doubled from 1990 to 2002, and is expected gradually to decline after reaching its peak just before 2010. However, this downturn is likely to be partially offset by an increase in natural gas production (Archer 2003: 506–7).

Norway had become a net exporter of petroleum by 1975 and two years later it was supplying the UK and continental Europe with natural gas through pipelines. By 1994 the main export markets were the UK, which took about 35 per cent of the total value of oil exports and 12 per cent of gas exports; France (8 per cent and 23 per cent respectively), Germany (7 per cent and 33 per cent), the Netherlands (14 per cent and 11 per cent) and Belgium (3 per cent and 12 per cent) (Statistics Norway 1995: table 285). By 1998 Norway was providing 33 per cent of Belgian gas, 29 per cent for France, 21 per cent of Germany's, and 17 per cent of Spain's (*Statoil Magazine* 2000: 45–7).

From the beginning the Norwegian state had an important direct and indirect stake in the offshore sector. In 1972 Statoil, a state-owned company, was set up to provide exploration and exploitation resources and it has handed over to the government almost a third of its post-tax operating profits. In June 2001 almost a fifth of Statoil's shares were sold by the government. The government part-owns another offshore concern, Norsk Hydro. Also the State Direct Financial Interest (SDFI), established in 1985, owned some 40 per cent of Norway's oil and gas fields, though these were managed by Statoil. In 2001 part of the SDFI was sold off to Statoil and some to Norsk Hydro and foreign concerns. The rest of the SDFI's offshore activity was organized into a new state-owned oil company, Petoro, and an equivalent gas company, Gassco (Innst.S. nr 267 2002: 3; Economist Intelligence Unit 2003c: 29). The SDFI's regulatory functions were then taken up by the government. The state also had involvement in the gas market with its Gas Negotiating Committee (GNC) taking on the task of concluding contracts for the sale of Norwegian offshore gas. Most of the contracts negotiated were with preferred buyers and were long-term, providing an element of stability as well as profitability (Akselsen 2000: 11). However, by the time the Gas Directive was being considered by the Commission, this whole structure was creaking. The SDFI and Statoil link was under fire; the constrictions on the market caused by the GNC's activities were apparent, with the danger that they could fall foul of the EEA agreement. Furthermore, the whole issue of energy law reform in Norway in the first half of the 1990s became tied into, and affected by, a similar process in the UK and the discussion of reform in the EU (Claes and Eikeland 1999: 167–71).

Given Norway's dominant position in the ownership of European energy and its growing importance in the Continental gas market, coupled with the intrusive position of the Norwegian government in Norwegian offshore oil and gas business, Norway should have had a strong position in any negotiations with the EU on natural gas. Until the late 1990s the EU had not managed fully to liberalize the gas market, and its Gas Market Directive of 22 June 1998 represented a major thrust in this direction. It covered the member states' transmission, distribution, supply and storing of natural gas and regulated the gas sector's organization and function.

Norway's position on such all-encompassing legislation and its possible transmission into EEA legislation could be surmised from its position in the European gas market – it would at least want to have a say in the making of the legislation. In other words, it could quite reasonably expect to be a 'pace-setter' in such discussions. This can be seen in the Norwegian application for membership in 1994. In dealing with the energy sector, the government's White Paper made out a strong case:

> For Norway it will be important to participate in the shaping of rules in the energy field that also take account of the environment in a satisfactory manner ... As a member [of the EU] Norway will be able to achieve great influence on the shaping of the future energy policy in the EU.
>
> (*Stortingsmelding* 40 1994: 190, author's translation)

The government had negotiated Protocol 4 of the membership agreement, concerning the energy sector in Norway, and this seemed to confirm Norwegian jurisdiction over its petroleum resources and the Norwegian state's right to own them and the national monopoly of management, including the extent of the role of the SDFI.

The Gas Directive started its stately progression through the EU decision-making process in 1997 and was adopted in summer 1998 with implementation planned for August 2000. By the autumn of 1998 the EEA EFTA states had been invited to adopt it. The response of the then Labour petroleum and energy Minister, Olav Akselsen, showed that its contents were not exactly to the liking of even a pro-EU government:

> it is not entirely clear today what the directive will mean for us.
>
> The Norwegian government is prepared to incorporate the directive in the EEA provided an acceptable solution for resource management can be secured.
>
> Norway also needs a transitional arrangement for adopting the directive into its legal system, and we are currently engaged in a dialogue with the Commission on these issues.
>
> (Akselsen 2000: 11)

The Labour government accepted the directive in the EEA committee in the dying days of its administration in October 2001 and on 18 June 2002 it came before the Storting, where it was accepted into Norwegian law, with twenty members of the Socialist Left and Centre parties voting against (*Stortingstidende* 2002b).

Was the directive such a problem for Norway? There is evidence that the centrist administration of Kjell Magne Bondevik, in government from October 1997 until March 2000, had tried to get British support in revising it. That the remaining version was not to Norway's liking is reflected in Akselsen's lukewarm statement above and by his appreciation of the effect of the directive:

> the market [in gas] – which has so far been based for Norway on long-term sales contracts which ensure that developments are profitable – will become more short-term. That could increase the level of risk associated with developing new fields and pipelines, and a lot of this risk could be transferred to the seller.
>
> (Akselsen 2000: 11)

As this was in answer to a question about the consequences of the directive for Norway as one of Europe's leading gas exporters, it is reasonable to assume that the then Minister of Petroleum and Energy saw an increase in the risk burden borne by Norway as a major consequence of the directive. The account of EEA cooperation provided for the centre-right government that took over from Labour after the September 2001 election was not complementary about the directive, which it declared had been 'controversial among EU member states' (*Stortingsmelding* 27 2002: 56). Noting that it had been adopted after long-drawn-out processes between the EU member states, it remarked that the EEA agreement did not give the EFTA states the possibility to take part in such deliberative discussions. Norway had been active among key member states and the Commission before the directive's adoption but its request for a transition period for the national implementation of the directive was not granted (*Stortingsmelding* 27 2002: 56).

In summer 2001 the European Commission sent a 'Statement of Objections' for breaking the rules of competition to all the companies that sold gas from the Norwegian offshore. This was a direct challenge to the policy of the Norwegian government, especially that of supporting the GNC (*Stortingsmelding* 27 2002: 56). It came at the end of a period during which the Commission and the ESA had been increasingly aware of the cartel nature of Norwegian gas sales. Under heavy pressure, the GNC ceased its activities from 1 January 2002 and the Commission dropped its case against Norwegian gas companies (Claes 2003: 23). In June 2002 the Storting transposed the Gas Directive into Norwegian law. Some seven years after Norway had failed to join the EU, its government had accepted lock, stock and barrel EU regulations on one of its major export industries and a central part of its economy. In this crucial area of policy-making, foot-dragging (at least by Norway and its gas companies) had proved impossible, and reluctance in implementation had bought it at the maximum only a couple of years' respite compared with EU member states. Indeed, this could be seen as a reasonable time in which such a major piece of legislation could be translated into EEA law. It seems that in such an important activity Norway had exercised very little influence (compared with the potential muscle provided by such gas resources) and had lost a great deal of autonomy to market forces and to the EU as their regulator.

Norway's seeming subjection to the EU's will can be seen as a reflection of the comparative power of the EU and Norway, but this brushes aside the fairly dominant position of Norway in the European gas market. It could have been an expectant acquiescence on Norway's behalf, with the hope of making gains elsewhere, though there is little evidence of that.

During the debate about acceptance of the directive in the Storting, those supporting the resolution – the Conservatives, Labour, the Progress Party, the Liberals and the Christian Democrats – advanced a number of arguments. Their basic reasoning was one of adaptation, with the aim of defending core principles. They saw the directive as a further stage in creating an internal market for natural gas and opening it up to competition based on non-discrimination, a process continuing with the Barcelona European Council in March 2002. In relation to the effect on the 'upstream sector' of the market, they pointed to the changes Norway had already made to the SDFI and the establishment of Petoro and Gassco which allowed gas from the Norwegian continental shelf to be sold on an individual basis rather than just through long-term contracts. This would allow Norwegian gas production 'to adapt to the structural changes that are now taking place in the European gas market' (Innst.St. nr 267 2002: 2–3, author's translation) but to do so in keeping with the main principle that had always formed the basis of Norwegian petroleum policy, that the oil and gas resources should be managed to benefit all of Norwegian society.

The Centre Party and the Socialist Left advanced the opposing viewpoints that the issue reflected clashing interests between the EU and Norway and that these needed a political solution (Innst.St. nr 267

Box 5.3 The Gas Directive

Having regard to the Treaty establishing the European Community, and in particular Articles 57(2), 66 and 100a thereof...

Acting in accordance with the procedure laid down in Article 189b of the Treaty,

1 Whereas, according to Article 7a of the Treaty, the internal market shall comprise an area without internal frontiers in which the free movement of goods, persons, services and capital is ensured; whereas it is important to adopt measures to continue the completion of the internal market;

...

3 Whereas the establishment of a competitive natural gas market is an important element of the completion of the internal energy market;

4 Whereas Council Directive 91/296/EEC of 31 May 1991 on the transit of natural gas through grids ... and Council Directive 90/377/EEC of 29 June 1990 [concerning gas and electricity prices] ... constitute a first phase of the completion of the internal market in natural gas;

5 Whereas it is now necessary to take further measures with a view to establishing the internal market in natural gas;

...

9 Whereas a certain number of common rules should be established for the organisation and operation of the natural gas sector;... these rules are no more than general principles providing for a framework, the detailed implementation of which should be left to Member States...

10 Whereas the external supply of natural gas is of particular importance for the purchase of natural gas in Member States highly dependent on gas imports;

11 Whereas, as a general rule, undertakings in the natural gas sector should be able to operate without being discriminated against;

12 Whereas for some Member States the imposition of public service obligations may be necessary to ensure security of supply and consumer and environmental protection, which, in their view, free competition, left to itself, cannot necessarily guarantee;

13 Whereas long-term planning may be one means of carrying out those public service obligations...

...

continued

Box 5.3 Continued

15 ... Member States need not apply Article 4, in particular, to their distribution infrastructure in order not to obstruct in law or in fact the fulfilment of obligations of general economic interest imposed on gas undertakings;

16 Whereas, when imposing public service obligations on undertakings of the natural gas sector, Member States must therefore respect the relevant rules of the Treaty as interpreted by the Court of Justice of the European Communities;

...

22 Whereas the accounts of all integrated natural gas undertakings should provide for a high degree of transparency; whereas the accounts should be separate for different activities when this is necessary in order to avoid discrimination, cross-subsidisation and other distortions of competition...

...

25 Whereas, in order to achieve a competitive market in natural gas, provision should be made for access to upstream pipeline networks; whereas separate treatment is required as respects such access to upstream pipeline networks, having regard, in particular, to the special economic, technical and operational characteristics relating to such networks; whereas the provisions of this Directive do not in any event affect national taxation rules;

...

32 Whereas this Directive constitutes a further phase of liberalization; whereas, once it has been put into effect, some obstacles to trade in natural gas between Member States will nevertheless remain in place; whereas proposals for improving the operation of the internal market in natural gas should be made in the light of experience; whereas the Commission should therefore report to the European Parliament and the Council on the application of this Directive...

Source: Directive 98/30/EC of the European Parliament and the Council of 22 June 1998 concerning common rules for the internal market in natural gas, *Official Journal L 204*, 21 July 1998 P.0001-0012.

2002: 4). Indeed, they saw the directive as a result of a struggle between Energy Commissioner de Palacio, who wanted a stable supply of Norwegian gas, and Competition Commissioner Monti, whose emphasis was on a more competitive market for gas. They agreed with the majority view that the directive was part of the EU's liberalization project, but saw an imbalance between the liberalization of the upstream part of the gas sector (in Norway) and the lack of change in the downstream market, where Commission efforts had been resisted by France and Germany (ibid.: 3). They recognized that any change in the gas regime involved a number of issues such as the market balance between the EU and Norway, the division of ground rent between the two, the need for long-term investment, security of supply and an overall energy and environment policy (ibid.). As the EU would have conflicting as well as common interests with Norway in these matters, they wanted Norway, with its unique position as a large exporter of gas to the EU and as an EEA member, to take a holistic approach to the substance, balance and tempo of the liberalization process (ibid.: 3–4). In other words, they were still interested in the policy formulation process. They recognized that Norway could no longer sit outside the process, clinging to its autonomy, but was part of the development of a European gas market. Given the country's strength in that market, it had to act as a pace-setter, promoting its version of a good outcome. On the contrary, the majority seemed to have conceded the struggle over the policy-making and were adopting a policy of quick and thorough implementation in order to win influence in the further development of gas market regulation.

The majority group, in swallowing the Gas Directive whole, accepted its path-dependent nature. The directive was a logical step in developing the single market and in its regulation by the EU. Indeed, the preliminaries to the directive provide the signposts that point towards its inception (see Box 5.3, points 1, 3, 4 and 5). However, that is not the whole story. There was clearly an awareness, tutored by those within the EU that had offshore operations – the British, the Danes and the Dutch – that these could not just be treated as part of one gigantic European gas market. Thus special aspects of the case were referred to in the preliminaries, covering a number of the points to which the Centre and Socialist Left parties referred (see Box 5.3, points 12, 13, 15 and 16). In other words, there was not just one narrow path pointing to liberalization, but a broad way of moving towards a number of goals. In reality much of what the Centre and Socialist Left parties were wanting – negotiations between the gas producer Norway and the Commission – had already been undertaken by the UK (and to a lesser extent Denmark) and was reflected in the final directive. It may not have spoken to particular Norwegian concerns about, for example, foreign ownership of its resources or the existence of the GNC, but neither was it a march towards a totally free market.

One aspect of the importance of the Gas Directive can be seen in the light of Norway's history and also the outcome of the 1994 referendum. As mentioned (see Chapters 2 and 3), the control of Norwegian natural resources was an important political issue for its leaders when the kingdom was established and remained a sacred cow for much of the twentieth century. It was utilized as an issue during both referendums, with stress being placed on the dangers of foreign ownership of Norway's natural resources and also on foreign (EC/EU) *control* of those resources, especially the gems of fisheries, hydro-electric power and oil and gas.

Janne Haaland Matlary (1993: 57) made the point that 'for the next 20–40 years there will be sufficient influx of oil revenue in order for exposure to the competition in the European marketplace to be deferred'. The same could have been said of gas revenue. Given that the twenty years are now that much closer, the Norwegian exposure is a little more apparent. Nevertheless, Christine Ingebritsen (1998: 130–1) took up the importance of the petroleum industry in writing on the 1994 referendum. She made the point that:

> European importers of petroleum rely heavily on exports from the continental shelf. Norwegian petroleum companies reap the same economic benefits, regardless of whether the state is in EFTA, the EEA, or the EC. The European energy policy regime is relatively underdeveloped compared to regimes in agriculture or fisheries.
>
> (Ingebritsen 1998: 130–1)

For Ingebritsen (1998: 139) the importance of the petroleum industry in Norway provided 'the economic capacity for the society to wait' instead of 'rushing' into the EU. Indeed, when the EU tried to regulate the energy sector in the early 1990s, and 'the Norwegian national petroleum regime ran into conflict with the requirements of Europeanization, the state came to the defense of the industry in the negotiations' (Ingebritsen 1998: 140).

The Gas Directive has changed this calculation. It means that the regulations for an important part of the energy market come from – and will continue to emanate from – Brussels and not Oslo. At least the gas part of the energy industry in Norway must take this into account, and this seems, according to Ingebritsen's explanation of acceptance or rejection of EU membership, to help swing the balance of reasons for full participation in the EU towards the 'yes' side.

This move also should affect the wider national perception of the EU. The Gas Directive is no longer the Norwegian nightmare of foreigners grabbing Norway's resources. It is about market regulation. The notion that Norway can regulate this market by national legislation is one that has been considerably undermined by the ups and downs of the world market and by the decisions of the multinational oil companies themselves – they will just not invest in an over-regulated area – as well as Norwegian governments in the late 1980s and early 1990s. There was every indication that Norwegian ministers found it difficult to keep a handle on the large energy companies dominant in its continental shelf, despite state ownership (Claes 2003: 20). EU regulation offers a balance between consumer and producer and even between industry and the environment. It therefore offers an alternative framework, and quite an attractive one in terms of the points made by both sides in the Storting debate, for the development of Norway's offshore gas to both national regulation and the free market. The question is then less one of 'selling off Norway' than of participation or not in the future development of the regime. This supports the conclusion of Claes and Eikeland (1999: 172) that Norway 'can be *served* by a liberalizing of the European gas market' (author's translation, italics in original). How well it is served and which firms are best served will depend not just on the utilization of the present laws but also on Norway's ability to affect the formulation of future legislation.

Case study 3: fisheries

The area of fisheries has been described as being 'the most complicated and conflictual in the connection between Norway and the EU' (Hoel 1999: 209, author's translation). The fisheries industry has been of vital importance to the economy and has in particular formed the underpinning of the local economy of settlements along the Norwegian coast (see Chapters 2 and 3). Although fishing was often mixed with farming and forestry, it was nevertheless essential both to supply food for the community and for trade. Norway's Exclusive Economic Zone (EEZ) is some 1.2 million km^2 (even without the Svalbard zone), equalling about a quarter of the total zones of the EU member states. By 1999 Norway's catch was 43 per cent of that of the EU and Norway was the world's largest fish exporter (Foss *et al.* 2003: 35; Economist Intelligence Unit 2003c: 35–6).

The fishing industry played an important role in the 1972 referendum (see above, p. 46). It formed one of the key economic interests that fought membership, and the imagery often created of Norwegian resources – the fish caught offshore – being plundered by EC states was one that stuck in the minds even of those distant from fishing areas. The adoption of the Common Fisheries Policy (CFP) by the EC of the Six just before negotiations started with the four fishing states of Denmark, Ireland, Norway and the UK in 1970 did little to lighten this image, neither did the resignation of the Labour Minister of Fisheries at the time of Norway's membership negotiations (Allen 1979: 127). The fishing industry had built a close relationship with central government that seemed to suit both well; membership of the EC would have interfered with that. In terms of Figure 1.1, cultural and institutional factors, a sense of identity and raw interests all led to a cry of 'No to the EC' in the case of fisheries policy in 1972.

Fisheries and the EEA

From 1 January 1977, the EC states that had coastlines declared Exclusive Economic Zones, most of up to 200 nautical miles from their coast baselines. Despite talk of a 'Community sea', the CFP that had been decided for the EC of ten members by 1983 contained a number of compromises that detracted from the idea that EC vessels would be able to fish in any part of the 'Community sea'. Access to fishing within member states' 12nm coastal zone was to be limited to vessels from the adjacent region, and access was further limited in particular sea areas. Most important, the right to fish was limited to those vessels with quotas and the principle of relative stability was used to allocate these between the member states. Total Allowable Catches (TACs) were to be calculated for different fish stocks, based mainly on scientific evidence on the sustainability of the stocks, and the quotas for the member states reflected relative stability based on historical fish catches, loss of catches in non-EC areas and the special needs of areas most dependent on fishing.

In 1983 relative stability meant that the allocation of fish quotas more or less mirrored the catches by member states from 1973 to 1978 (Hauksson 2000: 9). Also technical measures, such as limiting the mesh size of nets, were adopted to help conserve stocks. Another issue has been that of the ownership of fishing vessels. According to Article 12 (ex 6) of the EC treaty, all discrimination on the grounds of nationality is prohibited and Article 43 (ex 52) allows freedom of establishment throughout the EC area on a non-discriminatory basis. This should allow any national of an EC/EU state to own a vessel in any other state and has led to 'quota hopping' whereby, say, Spanish fishermen who cannot obtain a quota from Spain buy British vessels and their quotas. This has contrasted with Norwegian law that allows only Norwegians to own Norwegian-registered fishing vessels (Foss *et al.* 2003: 26–8).

As part of the CFP, the EC negotiated agreements with other fishing states which dealt mainly with annual quotas for fishing in each other's waters. Norway and the EC signed just such an agreement in 1980, with part of the aim to reach a balance in this quota exchange. In 1976 the EC states were taking some 550,000 tonnes of fish from the Norwegian zone, while Norwegian vessels took 330,000 tonnes from the EC zone; by 1992 a greater balance had been achieved: EC vessels took 262,700 tonnes from Norway, Norwegian fishermen 275,000 tonnes from the EC zone (Innst.S. nr 15 1993).

By the time the EEA agreement was finalized in 1993 Norway had just over 25,000 fishermen aboard 8,829 decked vessels and 7,573 open ones (Statistics Norway 1995: 258). Fishing accounted for 0.7 per cent of both GDP and employment, with fish and fish products providing almost 7 per cent of merchandise exports (Economist Intelligence Unit 1995b: 17). However, this belied the political strength both of fishing communities and of Norway's position compared with that of the EC. As from 1 January 1977 Norway has forbidden fishing within its economic zone, except by agreement with neighbours, such as Russia, and third parties, such as the EC. The extension of fisheries jurisdiction led to a number of conflicts with neighbouring states, not least Iceland, which on the whole were settled diplomatically (Henriksen 2003: 112–34). Norway's offshore empire made it a powerful factor in any calculation concerning Europe's fisheries.

The EEA agreement had a protocol appended (Protocol 9) on fisheries which dealt with tariffs and market access. White fish was allowed tariff-free access. Tariffs on other fresh fish were up to 18 per cent, while those on processed fish products were 25 per cent. However, of direct importance to Norway was the exchange of letters of 2 May 1992 that set the EC fishing quota, specifically of Arctic cod, in Norwegian waters. EC fishermen's quota of Arctic cod in the Norwegian economic zone north of 62° latitude was to increase from 2.14 per cent in 1991 to 2.9 per cent in 1993 of the largest catch allowed. The EC would receive an extra quota of some 7,250 tonnes of cod in 1994, rising to 11,000 tonnes in 1997, though this was to be reciprocated by quotas of other fish being provided for Norwegian fishermen in the EC's fisheries zone (Regjeringens informasjonsutvalg for Europasaker 1994: 16–17).

The parties supporting the EEA stressed that this deal was not part of the EEA agreement and in particular was not tied to the market access for Norwegian (and other EFTA states') fish found in Protocol 9 of the Oporto agreement (Innst.S. nr 15 1993). However, this view was challenged by the opponents of the EEA, the Centre Party and Socialist Left Party, who pointed out that the EC side was quite happy to link the two elements. They saw the agreement as a serious weakening of the principle that the coastal communities of Norway should have exclusive right to fish resources (Innst.S. nr 15 1993). Nevertheless, this principle had already been somewhat weakened by the exchange of quotas under the 1980 agreement. More specifically, the complaint, made by Peter Angelsen of the Centre Party, was that the EC had been given treaty rights within Norway's northern zone and the Barents Sea, something that would undermine the work of defendable resource management (*Stortingstidende* 1992, Angelsen). What was seen as an economic exchange by the pro-EEA parties (though one that, merely by coincidence, was taking place at the same time as the EEA agreement) was seen by others as the start of the give-away of Norwegian resources to the careless forces to the south.

The negotiations of the 1994 terms of entry to the EU were thus conducted against a different background from those in 1971–2. The Norwegian grip on offshore resources was stronger but a deal already existed with the EC which could be used as a basis for the starting point of give-and-take. This meant that the 1994 negotiations could be seen less a matter of principle than in 1972 – though the opponents of membership wanted to make it such – and more a question of detailed conditions. Any deal had to be compared with what Norway would have under the EEA agreement rather than with no settlement at all.

The final agreement would indeed have given Norwegian fish exporters better access to the EU market than under the EEA agreement (*Stortingsmelding* 40 1994: 47), though at the cost of some fish more for EU fishermen. Furthermore, the whole issue of the control of Norway's offshore resources was left for future decision, with disagreement between the two factions within Norway as to what that meant. The pro-membership side saw it as a victory for Norwegian fish management techniques, whereas the opponents of membership considered it to be an abdication to the wiles of the CFP and the eventual inclusion of 'Norwegian' fish as a 'Community resource' (*Nordlys*, 22 July 1994).

Fisheries issues since 1995

Norway's failure to join the EU meant that the EEA agreement, with the associated deal on fisheries, continued in train. However, a number of issues have arisen from this agreement and the change in market conditions since its inception.

One major development within the EU has been the reform of the CFP introduced from 1 January 2003 and in force until 2012. In effect, these changes reflected the failure of the CFP which, according to the Commission, was:

> Not effective enough in doing what it had been created to do, that is, to conserve fish, protect the marine environment, ensure the economic viability of the European fleets and provide good quality food to consumers.
>
> (European Commission 2003)

Such an admission of failure was a vindication of those within Norway who had opposed EU membership partly on the grounds of the iniquities of the CFP. Nevertheless, the reforms introduced in 2003 have addressed a number of issues: conservation, control and enforcement of such measures, the structure of the industry and relations with third countries. In doing so, the EU has adopted a number of policies that are close to Norway's: a multi-annual approach to fisheries, a precautionary approach in calculating TACs, conservation measures by member states within the 12 nm limits, a voice for fishermen in Regional Advisory Councils, the phasing out of state aid for new vessels and better enforcement measures (Foss *et al.* 2003: 18).

A major issue at stake between the EU and Norway has been that of *salmon*. Norway is the world's leading exporter of farmed salmon and the greater part of these exports are to EU states, though here it has had to compete with Irish and Scottish salmon exporters. In the rest of the world the output of Chilean salmon (with some help from Norwegian investment) grew rapidly throughout the 1990s to challenge Norway's dominance.

In keeping with the general tenor of Protocol 9, fresh Norwegian salmon has faced a much lower tariff wall than processed fish. However, it also faced competition from aggressive Scottish and Irish producers within the EU tariff wall, who were prepared to do battle with Norway to retain their market position. Already by 1996 the Scottish salmon producers had reported their Norwegian counterparts to the Commission for dumping and accepting subsidies that undermined competition (*Stortingsmelding* 12 2000: 17). During 1996 Norwegian salmon exports to the EU were showing a strong increase despite efforts by the Labour Minister of Fisheries, Jan Henry Olsen, to limit salmon production by introducing feed quotas (Economist Intelligence Unit 1996: 12). The subsequent investigation by the European Commission found that Norwegian producers had been selling their goods to the EU at less than the cost of production and had been paid unfair state aid, leading the Commission to recommend punitive duties on Norwegian salmon imports. The EU Anti-dumping Committee that discussed the report failed to agree on how to deal with the case. While the British and Irish representatives urged a strong response, Denmark and Sweden wanted a negotiated resolution with their Nordic neighbour (Economist Intelligence Unit 1997a: 12). As a result, a five-year agreement was reached between the EU and Norway on salmon exports, containing the following points:

- The Norwegian government would limit the increase in salmon exports to the EU by 12 per cent in 1997 and 10 per cent per annum between 1998 and 2002.
- Individual Norwegian salmon producers would sign a five-year agreement with the Commission to limit their exports to the EU and accept a minimum price, thereby becoming exempt from a 14 per cent anti-dumping duty which would otherwise be imposed on such exports.
- The tariff on Norwegian salmon would increase from 0.75 percent to 3 per cent. Half the income raised by this increase would be spent on generic marketing of Atlantic salmon, while the other half would be devoted to marketing Norwegian salmon.
- Trilateral cooperation between the Norwegian, Scottish and Irish producers would continue.
- The Commission would continue its consultation with all parties.
- The question of whether Norwegian regional aid, from which many salmon producers benefited, was legal under EEA rules was left unresolved (*Stortingsmelding* 27 2002: 54; KPMG 2002: 14; Economist Intelligence Unit 1997b: 13).

Otto Gregussen, the Labour Minister of Fisheries, met criticism of the Salmon Agreement in May 2001 by reminding critics that the agreement was made not through Norway's choice but because the Commission was threatening Norway with an anti-dumping tariff. He doubted whether Norwegian salmon producers would have been so successful in the EU market had they faced a 14 per cent tariff (*Stortingstidende* 2001: 3170).

The agreement was valid until September 2002. In the first years after the agreement the strong pound sterling and disease in the Scottish farms led to a boom in Norwegian production. However, by the autumn of 2001 the salmon market in the EU had become flooded with produce from the Faroe Islands and Chile as well as from the three traditional producers of Ireland, Scotland and Norway. A weaker pound and a stronger Norwegian krone led to a dramatic fall in prices and by November 2001 the Norwegian Fish-farming Association (Norske Fiskeoppdretteres Forening) was complaining that, as the minimum price fixed for Norwegian salmon on the EU market was well over the market price, Norwegian exporters were being priced out of the market. The new centre-right government in Oslo was in constant discussions with the Commission over the practical implications for the Salmon Agreement (*Stortingsmelding* 27 2002: 54). The Commission's response was to undertake a review of the Norwegian industry during the second half of 2002. This resulted in a Council regulation on 26 May 2003 that lifted the anti-dumping and anti-subsidy measures imposed in 1997, leaving Norwegian salmon free to compete in the EU market (*Dagens Næringsliv*, 27 May 2003: 16). By early 2004 market conditions had led to a further threat by the Commission of limiting Norwegian salmon imports, though this time the Commission opened a dialogue with Norway on the issue (*Dagens Næringsliv*, 6–7 March 2004: 9).

This case illuminates a number of elements in the Norwegian relationship with the EU that are not readily seen in other areas. It is a special case for a number of reasons. First, there is the institutional point: fisheries were not covered by the four freedoms of movement that are the core of the EEA agreement; they were covered separately in a protocol. It is thus not the case that CFP regulations have to be adopted by Norway. This places Norway in a stronger position in any negotiations, even compared with the case of gas. Second, Norway is not a small power when it comes to fish. It has enormous resources and these are sought after by EU consumers. Of course, the relationship cuts both ways: Norway is dependent on the European market to sell its fish, not least salmon exports, which are up against stiff competition from both within and outside the EU. Third, though there are some environmental issues involved in the fishing industry, the prime nature of the relationship between Norway and the EU on the salmon issue has been commercial and thus the state of the market has been the important factor. While the question of EU interference in that market has been crucial for Norway, external changes in the market (increased consumer demand, the value of the krone, the rising Chilean salmon market share) have all affected Norway's hold on the Continental market, especially for its salmon. These three factors have given Norway greater leeway in its dealings with the Commission on the treatment of salmon exports, allowing it to be pace-setting in the policy-making (or, rather, regulation) as well as in any implementation of agreements. Clearly, Norway's market position and its bilateral relationship with the Commission on this issue have allowed it much greater influence than in other trade matters. From within Norway, the position of Norwegian Fish-farming Association has acted as a spur to government action, and this has been underpinned by the privileged position given to the Norwegian salmon producers and their trilateral link with the Scottish and Irish producers in the Salmon Agreement.

Wider fisheries policy questions also reflect the strength of Norway's position both as a country with a vast offshore domain and the non-inclusion of fisheries policy in the main EEA agreement. However, these issues are not solely market-led, just involving the EU as a market regulator at the point of sale. The whole debate between Norway and the EU has been at its testiest over the issue of regulating fishing and Norway's sovereign right to do so in its waters. It was mainly on this issue that the fisheries organizations opposed the Labour government's membership agreement with the EU in 1994, and since then governments in Oslo have attempted to keep the issue separate from market access. In this they have had some considerable success: after all, access to Norwegian waters was kept within bounds already agreed and the salmon agreement did not involve any trading of rights to fish in Norwegian waters for market position. Such an exchange would have been politically difficult, as it would have meant taking from the fresh fish producers to satisfy the fish farmers.

The question remaining for Norway is whether it wishes to have any say not just in the development of the EU's attempts to regulate the fish markets of some of Norway's major customers but also in the formulation of rules concerning how, where and when fish are caught. Norway can, within international agreements, decide on such matters itself, though it still has to come to joint management agreements with its neighbours – including the EU – for stocks that have little respect for maritime borders. As the EU has been reconsidering its own fisheries management policies, and as a number of the reforms already undertaken came closer than before to Norwegian practice (Hoel 1999: 223), there might be some purpose in being on the inside of decision-making at a time when changes are still being worked out. However, the CFP reforms do not go as far as Norwegian and Icelandic practice in a number of areas (Foss *et al.* 2003: 18–19) and, for many within Norwegian fishing, greater EU access to Norwegian waters will be seen as too high a price to pay for tutoring EU fisheries in best practice. This is even more the case as Norway seems to be able to negotiate with the EU on a more equal basis than in other areas, and the benefits of a Norwegian-type conservation strategy are available for the EU to see without Norwegian participation in the CFP.

However, once again the calculations about Norway, fisheries and the EU have changed over the EEA years. Within Norway, the emphasis has moved away from control of catches towards supply of fish-processing factories and from sea-based fishing to fish farming. The need for market access has been underlined by the salmon issue. The CFP reforms mean that there is no longer such a strong contrast in conservation, links between fishing and local communities, and structural changes, between EU policy and that in Norway. Fishing organizations in Norway, though still strongly sceptical, are no longer automatically opposed to EU membership (Tande 2002). There has been a weakening of the factors that made it easy in 1972 and even in 1994 to contrast the CFP with Norway's fisheries policy and to make acceptance of the EU policy almost connivance with European pillaging of Norwegian natural resources. This seems to be affecting the interests' views of the acceptance of the CFP, but may also be changing the identification of control of fisheries as a key indicator of Norwegian autonomy.

Case study 4: regional aid

Regional policy has been of importance not just for social and economic reasons but also as a recognition of the need to keep the framework of the country functioning. Its geographical elements – a long coastline with a number of small settlements, backed by a mountain range with dales and fjords – and its arctic and sub-arctic climate have always meant that settlement and economic activity in Norway have been precarious, except outside the main cities. In the Cold War, the need to maintain a settlement pattern in the north of the country was seen as vital for maintaining sovereignty and control over that region. As shown in Chapter 2, there was also a close connection between town and the countryside, and this has been reflected in Norwegian politics, where at key stages parties such as the Liberals and Labour relied on coalitions of urban and rural voters.

Especially since British, Irish and Danish membership from 1973, the EC, and then the EU, has developed a regional policy of its own. The Treaty of Amsterdam's Article 158 states its purpose: 'the Community shall aim at reducing disparities between the levels of development of the various regions and the backwardness of the least favoured regions or islands, including rural areas'. The establishment of a meaningful regional policy from the 1970s through the 1980s was a constant battle between national governments and the Commission (Bache 1998: 136). The whole thrust of the EC and then the EU was to create a single market among the member states, and this would certainly involve the abolition of state aid (including regional aid) that interfered with the market. However, another aim was that of solidarity, expressed in Article 158 cited above, whereby some of the main social and economic disparities between, in this case, regions were to be addressed by state and EU assistance. The bulk of any regional aid has always been national. The EC/EU's role has been twofold: first, to ensure that regional assistance and other aid packages (such as social funding) is not discriminatory in so far as it unfairly subsidizes business activity in one region; second, it has added to national efforts through its own structural funds such as the European Regional Development Fund.

The two may seem contradictory policy aims and indeed there is tension between them. Nevertheless, the market conditions for the production of goods and services is rarely a 'level playing field' and one of the factors that causes unevenness is geography: one factory may be more remote from the market than another and therefore have to pay higher transport costs, but it may also have greater difficulty attracting labour and providing basic services for its workers. State aid in providing better transport and services for a distant region may thus be justified even in a market-type economic model.

As we have seen (see p. 43), regional policy was one of the instruments used by the Norwegian state to pursue its own objective of solidarity. Together with other policies (for example, on agriculture) regional policy was aimed at ensuring that a chasm did not develop between city dwellers and those in the countryside. It was also meant to make sure that north Norway did not become depopulated in such a way as to threaten the very security of the state. As one commentator noted: 'the equalization at the regional level was brought about by subsidies and transfers both from the state and between one authority and another' (Grønlie 1995: 400). However, by the 1990s this policy had become less generous, with all government 'subsidies' coming under political scrutiny.

The EEA agreement under Part 2 on State Aid contained Article 61 which defined what was acceptable as state aid (see Box 5.4). Furthermore, according to Article 62, all 'existing systems of State aid in the territory of the Contracting Parties, as well as any plans to grant or alter State aid, shall be subject to constant review as to their compatibility with Article 61' and this review was to be carried out 'as regards the EFTA States, by the EFTA Surveillance Authority', the Authority cooperating with the Commission to assure uniform surveillance throughout the EEA. Annex XV set out the specific provisions on state aid, including those on shipbuilding, aid to employment and for training, that had been adopted by the EC, and Article 64 established the process that would be followed to assure uniformity, including consultation in the EFTA Joint Committee. This in effect plugged Norway into the EC/EU system of reviewing state aid, though it certainly did not rule out such assistance.

During the negotiations for Norwegian membership of the EU in 1994 the issue of regional aid was a matter of contention between the Nordic applicants and the EU. The idea of EU regional funding going to some of

Box 5.4 The EEA's Article 61 on state aid

2 The following shall be compatible with the functioning of this Agreement:
   a aid having a social character, granted to individual consumers, provided that such aid is granted without discrimination related to the origin of the products concerned;
   b aid to make good the damage caused by natural disasters or exceptional occurrences;

...

3 The following may be considered to be compatible with the functioning of this Agreement:
   a aid to promote the economic development of areas where the standard of living is abnormally low or where there is serious underemployment;
   b aid to promote the execution of an important project of common European interest or to remedy a serious disturbance in the economy of an EC Member State or an EFTA State;
   c aid to facilitate the development of certain economic activities or of certain economic areas, where such aid does not adversely affect trading conditions to an extent contrary to the common interest;
   d such other categories of aid as may be specified by the EEA Joint Committee in accordance with Part VII.

Source: EFTA Secretariat, *Agreement on the European Economic Area*, 2003b.

the richest countries in the Union to provide aid to areas that were far better-off than many regions to the south was not popular with the twelve member states. However, it was recognized that the areas in northern Norway, Sweden and Finland were relatively deprived compared with the rest of their own countries, and had particular problems in terms of their remote situation, low population density and harsh climatic conditions (*Stortingsmelding* 40 1994: 50). It was also recognized that to curtail existing national grants would not help in the referendums that all three countries were holding. Indeed, even with the continuation of regional aid schemes, the creation of a new Objective 6 that allowed the northern counties of Norway to receive EU regional grants and the acceptance of the notion of 'arctic agriculture' (Archer and Sogner 1998: 62–3), it was these areas that produced the strongest 'no' votes in the November 1994 referendum (Pesonen *et al.* 1998: 21).

One issue that was unresolved both by the EEA and the EU negotiations was that of the form of national support for regional policy. In the Norwegian White Paper on EU membership, two forms of support were specifically mentioned: it was claimed that new EU regulations meant that the existing basis of Norwegian regional policy could be maintained and that this would allow the continuation of support for regional transport and reduced employer social security payments for priority areas (*Stortingsmelding* 40 1994: 50). Support for regional transport could certainly be seen as a way of making up for businesses being in remote areas, but selective social security payments could be seen as subsidizing jobs and therefore adversely affecting the conditions of competition.

In the English résumé of the 2002 White Paper that provided an overview of EEA cooperation from 1994 to 2001 there was little hint of anything but a transitional problem in the section on the effects on municipalities and districts:

> Given that most of Norway's export industries are located in the districts, the EEA Agreement has helped to safeguard the economic base and maintain settlement patterns in these parts of the country. The extensive harmonization of legislation resulting from the EEA Agreement may have caused some adaptation problems for a number of companies and industries. It has however been fully possible for Norway to continue to implement the main features of its regional policy.
>
> (*Stortingsmelding* 27 2002)

However, the more extensive Norwegian version gave more than a hint of a worm in the apple:

> The Norwegian arrangement with differentiated employers' [social security] payment has been a particular problem. The EFTA Court considered that the employers' payment was contrary to the rules on state aid.
>
> (*Stortingsmelding* 27 2002: 9, author's translation)

Indeed, the EFTA Court had done just that on two occasions. In the Employers' Payment case (E-6/98) the Court had been asked to adjudicate by Norway on the ruling made against it by the ESA in 1998.

The first hearing was about giving Norway a stay of execution, but nevertheless the substance of the issues was aired. In 1975 Norway had introduced a system of regionally differentiated tax rates for employers, including social security contributions paid by employers that varied according to five tax zones.[2] In a letter of 16 June 1995 to the Norwegian government, the ESA enquired about 'the compatibility of the system with Article 61 of the EEA Agreement' (EFTA Court 1998). After an extended period of discussions and meetings, the ESA concluded that the scheme was contrary to the meaning of Article 61(1) that could not be upheld under Article 61(3) EEA (see Box 5.4), and on 14 May 1997 the ESA proposed measures that Norway might take. However, these were not adopted by the Norwegian government, and on 2 July 1998 the ESA found Norway to be in breach of the agreement. In its ruling, the ESA proposed how the Norwegian system might be made compatible with the regional transport aid, which could be allowed. This assistance would have to be open and limited.

In 1998 Norway took the ESA to the EFTA Court to have the implementation of the ESA Decision suspended until the full court case had been heard. The ESA argued that '[t]he system of regional differentiation of employers' social security contributions in Norway is incompatible with the EEA Agreement', and it listed a number of conditions that Norway would need to adopt to make the provisions compatible 'with the rules on regional transport aid as reflected in the Authority's State Aid Guidelines' (EFTA Court 1998). The restriction of these rules and the emphasis on supporting regional transport were scarcely a match with the Norwegian wide-sweeping tax break. Furthermore, the ESA wanted the Norwegian authorities to stop any benefits not consistent with the ESA rules from 31 December 1998. It was on this rush to judgement that Norway appealed to the Court, claiming not only that its regulations were compatible with the EEA but that the changes demanded by the ESA were so wide-ranging that they could not reasonably be introduced in the period demanded. In upholding Norway's request to suspend the ESA's decision until it had ruled on the substance, the Court used common sense: the decision could have far-reaching consequences and, since the Norwegian scheme had been in place since 1975, and given the complexity of the case, enforcement could wait a little longer (EFTA Court 1998). Norway had effectively dragged its heels on implementation, but the stay of execution was to be overturned by the Court's judgement on substance.

The Court ruled on the actual case on 20 May 1999 and it was a blow for Norway. The substance of the Norwegian case was that the measures were so general – 'neutral as to the type of industry, company size, occupation and form of ownership and location of the enterprise' – as not to affect specific export industries. Furthermore, Norway claimed that the ESA had overreached its authority in its interpretation of state aid under Article 61(1) of the EEA. The Norwegian scheme was a tax measure, which by its nature discriminates between different sectors of the economy, and tax measures were not covered by the EEA (EFTA Court 1999, point 25). Norway also accused the ESA of failing to consider its employment policy and claimed that:

> maintaining settlement patterns, income equalization and employment equalization throughout the country must be viewed as *legitimate aims*

> capable of justifying the fact that the effect of the scheme may differ from one undertaking to another. This is so because of the special problems Norway faces, *inter alia* on the labour market, because of its geographical location, long distances, climate, population and settlement patterns.
>
> (EFTA Court 1999: point 29, italics in original)

The complaint was that the ESA was meddling in an area of Norwegian policy not covered by the EEA and, furthermore, the policy involved was desirable and apt:

> the Norwegian scheme is purposeful, effective and proportionate when assessed in relation to its objectives. It is also easy to apply and administer and it does not constitute any danger as regards the objectives of the EEA Agreement.
>
> (EFTA Court 1999: point 30)

The ESA disagreed. It had commissioned an independent study of the economic effects of the scheme, which it considered to be state aid benefiting certain enterprises and distorting (or threatening) competition within the EEA. However, it was prepared to allow transport aid for certain areas but not for certain sectors or for enterprises that had no alternative location (EFTA Court 1999: points 25, 6 and 7). For a system of regionally differentiated social security employers' contributions to be compatible with the rules on regional transport aid, it would have to be adapted to comply with a number of conditions. It would have to be time-limited, require annual reports, be transparent and not allow over-compensation (EFTA Court 1999: point 9).

The Court agreed with the ESA that the Norwegian system was a breach of the limitations on state aid found in Article 61(1) of the EEA. While the Court agreed with the Norwegian government that 'as a general rule' the tax system of EEA/EFTA states was not covered by the agreement, it *was* a matter for concern if it had the effect of a state aid. It was not decisive that regulations were based on certain legitimate policy considerations. Indeed, this seemed to strengthen the case against the Norwegian government as those policy considerations could be achieved under the scheme advanced by the ESA (EFTA Court 1999: points 34–9). The Court also dismissed the Norwegian contention that the differentiated social security contributions did not affect trade and therefore stood outside the scope of Article 61(1). It pointed to the ESA's argument that the undertakings benefiting from the lower rates in zones 2 to 5 were in competition with producers in zone 1 of Norway and producers in other EEA states. Indeed, it was not necessary for the benefiting undertaking to export its products – after all, the effect might be that of cutting the opportunity of a firm from another EEA state exporting to Norway

(EFTA Court 1999: point 59). The Court did find that certain activities could benefit from regional transport aid and noted that the ESA had not 'fully considered the effect of harsh weather conditions' or other conditions that could justify the lowering of labour costs in the regions and that these factors should be taken into account by the ESA in evaluating any revised system of regional aid (EFTA Court 1999: point 70).

The Court's decision ran counter to Norwegian regional policy and to an aspect in use since 1975. However, the door was left open to regional support based on limited criteria mainly associated with overcoming the extra transport costs suffered by enterprises in such regions. Furthermore, a hint had been dropped to the ESA that it should look kindly on schemes that took into account the physical problems of the regions.

In response to the Court's new judgement, the centrist government introduced new regionally differentiated social security contributions. This time there were four zones with the rate varying from 14.1 per cent in zone 1 to 0 per cent in zone 5, but a statement was made as to which activities could not benefit from the lower rates, being those mentioned by the ESA in its earlier submission to the Court. In the list were hydro-power production, mining, gas and oil production, shipbuilding, financial services and freight transport. The scheme was time-limited (to 31 December 2003) and Norway was to make regular reports and help the monitoring of the proposal. The ESA decided not to challenge this scheme (EFTA Surveillance Authority 1999).

This was not the end of the matter. The parties that had opposed the EEA – the Socialist Left Party and the Centre Party – chastized the other parties for believing that the system of regionally differentiated social security contributions would not be covered by the EEA and, with the support of all the other parties, advanced a resolution that requested the government to clarify the long-term effect of the Court's decision and to prepare the work for maintaining geographic differentiation and support in regional policy after 2003 (*Stortingstidende* 2001b).

In 2002, the ESA enquired what would happen on 1 January 2004, when the time period for the measures that it had sanctioned ended, and it required the Norwegian authorities (by then the centre-right government) to state how it would eliminate the state aid element in the social security tax or make it compatible with Article 61 of the EEA agreement. By 2003 the Norwegian government was considering a direct transport aid scheme which again attracted a certain amount of ESA attention (EFTA Surveillance Authority 2003c). In July 2003 the ESA decided to open a formal investigation into the transition period for the regionally differentiated social security contributions and the direct transport aid. In the transitional arrangements, the government proposed phasing out the scheme in zones 3 and 4 by 2007, saying that abolition by 2004 would 'raise very serious difficulties for the areas'. Furthermore, the new transport aid was to be given to four municipalities outside the regional aid map approved for Norway in 1999 (EFTA Surveillance Authority 2003d). In the end the ESA broadly accepted the Norwegian case, providing the government with some respite. The ESA closed its investigation into the contributions (though maintained that into the transport aid schemes) and allowed Norway a three-year period from 1 January 2004 within which to phase out the differentiated payments in zones 3 and 4. No transition period having been asked for zone 2 or for zone 5, 'the EFTA States decided by common accord in [*sic*] the continuation of the zero tax rate' (EFTA Surveillance Authority 2003e: 1). This deal secured the status of the northernmost counties (zone 5) and had a significant meaning for the larger firms in zones 3 and 4 (Foss 2003).

The compromise confirmed the dominance of EU legislation in a policy area of great importance not just economically but socially to Norway. However, it showed that the EFTA states and the ESA were prepared to give ground in the face of some truculence by the Norwegian government. The Norwegian authorities battled away over implementation, trying to postpone the day when their system of support was brought in line and gained a couple of important concessions. Given the need of the governments involved for political support in the benefiting regions, there was little incentive to go quietly into the night.

The nature of the relationship: adaptation and Europeanization

Looking at the relationship between Norway and the EU under the umbrella of the EEA, the first point is that it has been remarkably successful for Norway in general economic terms. The EEA has provided access to the EU's single market at a time when the size of the market has grown with the addition of the three EFTA states. It is, however, very difficult to calculate how Norway has fared economically compared with how it might have done had it been a full member of the EU.

The main advantage of the EEA compared with the EU has not been so much in macro-economic terms as in terms of the autonomy allowed for the control or regulation of certain sectors of the economy, namely agriculture and fisheries. In the case of agriculture, the case can be made that the consumers and taxpayers have had to pay more than even those within the EU who underwrite the expensive Common Agricultural Policy. However, the producers continue to benefit from Norway's system of agricultural support and so do the rural areas and regions. This last point, which is somewhat debatable, at least seems to be accepted, or not hotly contested, by the political parties in Norway outside the Progress Party and the Conservatives. The case for self-regulation of fisheries rests on the need for conservation of stocks, an area where the CFP has been seen to be a miserable failure, even on the Commission's own admission.

The major disadvantage of the EEA has been in the lack (or very limited amount) of influence on policy-making and in the undermining of parliamentary authority by the 'take it or leave it' nature of the legislation. This is clearly contrary to the long democratic tradition of a country such as Norway, but there is not much that either the government or the parliament can do about it. There is the possibility of greater scrutiny of legislation from the Norwegian side and a more active role in the information and expert side of implementation, but little more.

The case studies, and other cases mentioned in this chapter, demonstrate where Norway has been able to exercise some autonomy and some influence, and where not, and which tactics have been used by Norway (see Table 1.3 in Chapter 1). Table 5.1 portrays the most dominant of those tactics in both policy-making and implementation.

Five factors account for Norway's success or failure in trying to obtain influence or maintain influence in these cases: allies, identity, interest, institutions and salience. The first indicates whether Norway had powerful allies within the Commission or in the EU's Council of Ministers. The second indicates the extent to which the issue is one of importance for Norwegian identity politics. The third reflects the strength of Norwegian interest in the question, especially when weighed against interest in the rest of the EU. The fourth point involves the institutional framework within which Norway has dealt with the EU over particular issues. Finally, salience refers to the importance of the issue to the people, interest groups and government of Norway.

In the case of the Gas Directive, Norway had some important allies within the Council of Ministers, not least the UK and Denmark. This

Table 5.1 Tactics used by Norway in cases mentioned

Tactic	*Policy-making*	*Implementation*
Pace-setting	**Salmon 2002**	***Gas Directive*** Pizza topping
Foot-dragging	Gas Directive	***Waterfalls(>2002)*** Alcopops ***Regional Aids***
Fence-sitting	Salmon 1996	**Salmon 1997–2002**
Least resistance	**[Most SEM legislation]**	**[Most SEM legislation]**

Key to cases
Salmon 1997 Salmon Agreement between Norway and EU. *Gas Directive* Directive 98/30/EC. *Pizza topping* Trade in processed agricultural goods. *Waterfalls* Norwegian legislation on the ownership of waterfalls. *Alcopops* Alcopops case (E-9/00) before the EFTA Court. *Regional aids* Case before ESA and European Court on regionally differentiated social security contributions in Norway. *SEM* Single European Market.

Key to outcomes
Normal typeface: unsuccessful. **Bold** typeface: some success. In [brackets]: too extensive to determine. *Italic* typeface: not yet determined.

helped to take some of the sting out of the directive, but in the end neither the British nor the Danes were prepared to fight for Norwegian interests. To a certain extent, the Scottish and Irish salmon producers were changed from being out-and-out competitors to being partial allies by the 1997 Salmon Agreement. This co-opted the three salmon producers' associations into the working of the agreement and the revenue from some of the tariff on Norwegian salmon was used to finance a sales campaign for salmon generally. At least in this area there was a non-zero sum game whereby all benefited from the expenditure. In the 'pizza topping' case and in the case of salmon in 1996 Norway suffered from a lack of allies in the Commission and on the Council and, in the former case, being opposed by its Nordic neighbour and former EFTA ally, Sweden.

Identity and cultural factors have been of importance in the 'waterfalls' case, the Gas Directive, regional aid and that concerning alcopops. In the first two issues, the whole question of foreign ownership of Norwegian resources – a historically very touchy subject – has been to the fore. Regional aid has been attached to the need to keep the rural areas flourishing and thus allowing their cultures to continue. Alcopops involved an attack on a Norwegian view of the sale of alcohol espoused in particular, but certainly not exclusively, by the Christian Democrat Party. It is perhaps not surprising that the tactic used in these cases has been one of foot-dragging, either trying to prevent legislation from being adopted or challenging its implementation.

There are interests involved in all these issues but for some these are particularly strong. As indicated, Norwegian gas and fish exports are world leaders and important to the EU as a consumer of both. This places Norway in an ambiguous role: it is a provider for European needs, but it is also dependent on the European market. Both fish and gas are also key export commodities for Norway and have strong commercial interests behind them. This strength has allowed Norway to take a more promotive pace-setting approach, especially in getting its salmon accepted as a tariff-free import and in implementing the Gas Directive after it was clear that the game was up once the Commission had issued its 'Statement of Objections' to firms operating from the Norwegian offshore in summer 2001. On other occasions, as with salmon exports in 1996, the strength of Norwegian interest has been trumped by that of the Scots and the Irish.

This brings in the institutional element. To some extent it is the weight of interests and their ability to put resources into a conflict that determine its outcome, though that did not help the Norwegians in the case of the Gas Directive. The institutional element is important: it does matter whether Norway has a free trade agreement with the EU or is a member of the EEA or of the EU. An EU member has more resources than a non-EU EEA state which in turn can call upon more institutional resources than states with a free trade arrangement, but these advantages have to be paid for by greater commitments. The inequality is particularly apparent in the case of policy-making. On strictly EEA matters Norway is clearly at a disadvantage compared with even the smallest EU state, though in an area such a salmon exports, not covered by the main body of the EEA, Norwegian salmon farmers can have an input equal to that of competitors in Ireland and Scotland.

On the policy implementation side it may even be the case that Norway is at a disadvantage, as the EFTA Court and ESA cannot be seen to be lenient – otherwise they would lose the trust of the Commission – and only have to deal with cases from three small states, whereas small states within the EU may reckon on the Commission and the ECJ having a long list of important cases. However, the action of the Commission against the Swedish scheme for reduced social security contributions suggests otherwise. Governments in Norway have seen a number of issues of political importance for their supporters – alcopops (the Christian Democrats), regional policy (Labour and the centrist parties), waterfalls (most of the political parties) and veterinary and phytosanitary measures (the centrist parties at first, then the Centre Party) – decided by the ESA and the Court against their wishes, but it has always been reckoned by most parties that the overall advantage of the EEA outweighs the losses in these areas.

Another institutional element is that of the market. The disposition of a market in particular goods can be as important as the workings of the EU's institutions. This was certainly the case with salmon. In the case of the Gas Directive, the standing of the EU as a market regulator is important and this contrasts with the role that the Norwegian government had built for itself not just as a regulator of offshore gas activity but also as an organizer of and a participant in the supply end of the market. The end of much of that role indicates that the disposition of the gas market will now mean something different for the Norwegian government as well as gas producers in Norway's offshore.

A final point is salience. It might be thought that Norway would have greater success in those areas of more importance for the country, such as gas, regional aid and fisheries. This might seem to be the case if such issues were widely and well entrenched within Norwegian society. It may well be that Norway expends more political energy on these subjects, but the effectiveness is likely to depend on the importance attached to the issues by the EU and certain key member states as well as on the factors mentioned above. The EEA does not guarantee that, just because Norway considers a matter of high importance, it can have its way. However, Norwegian tactics have acted as indicators to the EU, especially the Commission, of the strength of Norwegian interest rather than effective attempts to quicken or slow down legislation and its implementation. Regardless of the outcome, a tactic of foot-dragging or, indeed, of pace-setting can demonstrate to others a lively interest. The institutions of the EEA at least allow a mechanism for such indications.

6 Norway and the CFSP

> There is only one thing in the world worse than being talked about, and that is not being talked about.
>
> (Oscar Wilde, *The Picture of Dorian Gray*, 1891)

The founding fathers of an independent Norway would no doubt be amazed to view the foreign and security policy of the country a hundred years on. To see their small state involved in places as far apart as Bosnia-Herzegovina (a name they might recognize as being a trouble spot) to Afghanistan (likewise) would make them ponder. After due consideration they might feel that some of this involvement was at least in line with one tradition, broadly that of liberal internationalism, espoused by some of their number (Leira 2002). Many, however, would wonder what had happened to the hope in 1905 of keeping Norway as a trading country with a minimal foreign and security policy.

Dilemmas about international engagement, experienced by Norway in its general foreign policy, have had a special resonance in Norwegian security policy. This has been central to the existence of Norway as a state and to the welfare of its people. Furthermore, the options for Norway in the broad area of security policy have often been varied and have represented choices between what might seem to be greater autonomy and the prospect of less autonomy but more influence within the international system. Finally, in its dealings with the EU after the 1994 referendum, the European Security and Defence Policy (ESDP) proved to be a point of some contention. For these reasons, this chapter will place more emphasis on the security aspect of external policy. Furthermore, as Norway's security position did not spring out of thin air in 1994, the background will be provided to Norwegian security until then, and to Norway's response to the Common Foreign and Security Policy (CFSP) of the European Union, including the ESDP.

A number of interwoven strands can be seen in the hundred years of Norwegian foreign and security policy, with some dominant during one period, often fading in another. The country, like many other small powers, has sought to exercise what control it could over the wider set of opportunities offered it by the international environment. It has moved between autonomy and influence in seeking this control and has become increasingly involved in a range of security institutions. There has been a growing propensity to engage with chosen partners and to exercise influence with them, especially in relation to the defence of Norway and the Nordic area more generally, but also to maintain some key 'islands' of autonomy in areas of particular concern to the wider population. However, many of the security-related policies have been a matter purely for the concern of the decision-making elites within Norway, and thus their perception of their wider environment has been crucial. Nevertheless, whatever they have thought of the international situation has to be seen against the hinterland of the wider sets of beliefs about the world, and Norwegian security in that world, by the Norwegian people. Their views have also provided a set of constraints, or an impetus to action. While the international environment has provided the framework of opportunities available to Norwegian decision-makers, the feeling of what is acceptable, and what not, to the broad spectrum of opinion within the country has affected the willingness to choose one policy rather than another.

Norwegian foreign and security policy: the background

Three strands can be seen in the Norwegian foreign policy debate, especially up to 1949, and these reflect not just the views of the decision-makers but those of the wider public. One strand placed the emphasis on Norwegian autonomy, a natural reaction after escaping the constraints felt by being in the union with Sweden. This is seen in Løvland's thoughts on foreign policy when Norway reached independence (see p. 29) and has as an operational form: the desire to have a minimal foreign policy and certainly to disengage from the struggles of the great powers and follow a policy of neutrality. It spoke to the internal needs of the country and can be seen in the resistance to the UK on fisheries matters in the inter-war period. It is thus an *intransigent* mode of adaptation to the international environment (Rosenau 1970: 5; see pp. 14–15 above). Until 1940 this strand reflected a wide spectrum of opinion throughout Norway and was dominant within the Labour Party. With its instinctive reservations about the military, it was willing to shear the defence budget from the late 1920s up to 1937 (Danielsen and Hovland 1995: 346).

The second strand placed the emphasis on influence in international affairs and was adopted by Norway's Foreign Ministry and some of the key decision-makers from 1905 to 1940. It tended to reflect Rosenau's category of *acquiescent* adaptation (1970: 5; see pp. 14–15 above) whereby decision-makers were responsive primarily to the external environment, or at least their perception of it. The hope of the politicians, not always fulfilled, was to give their external policy a preservative orientation, balancing the adaptation to international events with some response to internal pressures. The response of Norway to pressures by the UK, which turned the country into Britain's 'neutral ally' (Riste 1965), demonstrated such acquiescent adaptation.

The third strand occurred from time to time in external policy until 1940 and involved the promotion of Norway's own needs over those of others. This can be seen in the unusual events of 1930–3 when the government backed the occupation by a private group of Norwegians of East Greenland, an area claimed by Denmark (Riste 2001: 121). This was, according to Riste, 'clearly an aberration' and the dispute was soon settled, in Denmark's favour, by the Permanent Court of International Justice in its 1933 ruling. Norwegian *promotive* adaptation can be seen in a more cooperative form in the 'active peace policy' of Halvdan Koht in the late 1930s and his attempts to get the small European states – the 'Oslo states' – to press the major European powers not to resort to war (Riste 2001: 136–9).

These reactions of the new state to its foreign policy environment seemed to demonstrate a certain disdain of the world within which it found itself. The necessary deals had to be done – the great powers requested to guarantee Norway, the British assuaged in the First World War – but real engagement was limited to the moral sphere, with Norwegian representatives at the League of Nations advocating greater use of the Permanent Court of International Justice to solve disputes (Riste 2001: 131). Added to this was concern to protect Norway's commercial interests internationally and the livelihood of its fishing communities that even led the country into a running conflict over fishing limits with its assumed protector, the UK (Riste 2001: 124–6).

The wartime German invasion of Norway on 9 April 1940, and its liberation by Soviet and British forces, demonstrated the limitations of control by a small power of its international environment. It also showed that decision-makers had hoped Norway's geographical isolation would exclude it from great-power concern. This expectation was undermined by developments in both submarine and aerial warfare.

For much of the time, the three strands of adaptation in foreign policy mentioned above (pp. 133–4) – intransigence, acquiescence and promotion – were interwoven in the making of Norwegian foreign policy. In the period until 1940, there was recognition among most policy-makers that Norway could not defend itself, even if it was under threat, and that the best protector of Norway and its interests was the Royal Navy of the UK. However, even the decision-makers who accepted the need for British protection were not willing to give up their autonomy to the extent of agreeing to an alliance. Indeed, they sometimes had to face up to the British over matters such as fisheries, of seeming greater salience to sections of the Norwegian population. As a result they had little influence with the British, either in the 1916–18 period or in April to June 1940, on the matter of defending Norwegian interests. The dominance of the strand of autonomy, of intransigent adaptation, was feasible as long as those who preferred that of influence or even of promotion of internationalist ideas could persuade themselves that the British would never let Norway down or that the League (which in effect meant the UK and France) could deter reckless acts that might otherwise adversely affect small states such as Norway.

In the four years following the Second World War the weave of the strands had changed. The memory of 9 April 1940 and the liberation of 1945 – not to mention the years of occupation – had a dramatic effect on opinion in Norway. The strand of autonomy and intransigence had been weakened but was still present in the policies of caution with regard to commitment to the Marshall Plan and plans for Scandinavian economic cooperation in 1948 (Sogner 1993: 10). There were also those in the Labour Party who resisted Norway joining any form of defence alliance, though by early 1949, when Norway subscribed to the North Atlantic Treaty, these were in the minority. The events of Easter 1948 – especially the fall of the government in Prague after Communist pressure – shifted opinion to the view that some defence agreement should be made, though a Nordic defence association appeared to be the first port of call to many. However, there was acceptance that, even with this option, the link with the West should be made. The instinctive Atlantic glance given at the mention of security had to be more than a look and a hope. Easter 1948 had underlined the message of 9 April 1940 that a large section of the population seemed to accept: that autonomy in such a vital matter as the defence of the state was not going to be possible in an increasingly hostile world and that the cost of Western support was going to be acquiescent adaptation which nevertheless brought the prospect of influence. Even so, the more preservative adaptation deal that was done included some elements of autonomy, not least that of the rejection of foreign bases.

Norway in the Cold War

The basic pattern laid down in 1949 with Norway's signature of the North Atlantic Treaty, and the reservations about foreign bases, foreshadowed Norway's career as a 'cautious member of the alliance' (Grønlie 1995: 433). A serious commitment to collective defence was married to definite reservations about particular aspects of policy. Again this ambiguity reflected not just the feelings of decision-makers but a wider concern that Norway should neither be swamped by its alliance commitment nor be the cause of international tension. At the same time, the message of 'never again 9 April' was not far from the surface of Norwegian consciousness.

The history of Norway in NATO is nevertheless not one of a perfect case of preservative adaptation with external and internal factors being in balance. As shown (pp. 34 and 38), there were political battles and these were mainly fought in and around the Labour Party. From late 1950 to 1954 the Labour government increased defence expenditure four times against opposition within the party and by the centrist parties. A compromise involved a cut in the length of military service (Meyer 1989). There was also resistance to German officers being stationed at the NATO regional headquarters outside Norway. Within the Labour Party, anti-militarist and anti-German groups had some success in expressing their views in the youth groups and trade unions, leading to a no-base resolution at the 1957 Labour Party conference and a heated debate on nuclear weapons in the Easter 1958 party meeting (Eriksen 1977: 246). The resistance to nuclear weapons in Europe by Einar Gerhardsen at the December 1957 NATO summit (see p. 38) seemed to be more in accord with Labour's rank and file than the more cautious approach of the Foreign Ministry. Nevertheless, the 1960s and 1970s saw Norway even more closely integrated into the Allied defence structure, with a range of communications and intelligence stations being established.

The pressures of the New Cold War from the end of the 1970s to the end of the 1980s proved more testing, as Norway had been given greater strategic significance by the rise of the Soviet Northern Fleet and the US maritime strategy that wanted to push NATO forces into the Norwegian Sea on a more regular basis.

The response by the Labour Party on a range of issues such as port visits by US ships, plans for a Nordic nuclear-free zone and the pre-stocking in Norway of US military *matériél*, showed Labour governments trying to maintain a delicate balance between acquiescence to international pressures and intransigence based on internal needs. It was also a balance between the needs of the state, judged by the government in the light of the international situation, and the demands of social groups such as the peace movement, that often worked through the Labour Party.

Norwegian policy within NATO during the Cold War showed the weaknesses and strengths of a small state in an alliance as well as the costs and benefits of membership. The weaknesses were those arising from being dependent on the interests and goodwill of larger allies, in particular the US and, to a lesser extent, the UK. Pursuing internal demands that conflict with alliance needs can be costly in both political and economic terms.[1] Furthermore, there were costs to Norwegian society and politics. As a NATO member Norway accepted more military activity on its soil – whether listening stations or exercises – than if it had remained neutral, and defence issues tended to divide public opinion quite intensely, if occasionally. The effect on politics was more definite: the nuclear issue was a major factor that led to expulsions from the Labour Party and the formation of the Socialist People's Party and it was an issue that added extra tension within the Labour Party of the late 1970s and possibly contributed to that party's fall from power in 1981 (Riste 2001: 231).

The strength of Norway within NATO was its strategic position close to the Soviet Union and, from the 1970s, the Soviet Northern Fleet. On the whole Norwegian governments used the 'loyalty' card rather than threatening exit from the alliance, although sometimes it did voice its concerns, as in December 1957.[2] Being the 'good boy' allowed Norway some influence in the alliance which, however, it could use only sparingly, for example by making sure that there was an arms control 'track' in the December 1979 'Dual Track' decision by NATO (Tamnes 1991: 290). The benefits of membership can be seen in terms of security for Norway. This is hard to calculate, as there is no way to estimate how secure Norway would have been outside NATO. The assumption – made by a majority of its population and all its governments – is that it certainly would have *felt* less secure. Furthermore, there were particular gains in terms of US military assistance, especially in the 1950s, and benefits to Norwegian defence-related industries (Devold 2003: 4). Finally, membership of NATO gave Norway the experience of integration in a policy area of key importance for the existence of the state. Though Norway's reservations kept at bay some of the more intrusive aspects of alliance membership, the Norwegian people, politicians and officials had constantly and almost on a daily basis to adjust their own feelings and needs to the requirements of other states, and had to articulate their own wants in such a way as to persuade their allies. This experience was, however, within an inter-governmental and Atlantic framework.

Given the centrality of defence issues to the existence of a state and a nation – a lesson well learned by Norway during the Second World War – why did not NATO membership, and the subsequent issues arising from it, have a greater effect on the political system? Why was it not this issue, instead of EC membership, that divided the country and led to such an internecine political battle?

Part of the answer is that defence did leave scars on the body politic: the expulsions from the Labour Party in 1958, the collection of 100,000 members for the 'No to nuclear weapons' campaign in 1979 and the possible effect on the 1981 election. Nevertheless, from the beginning in 1949, NATO and Norwegian membership always had the support of an overwhelming section of the Norwegian public. This was reflected within the Labour Party, where the opponents of the official defence policy were in a minority. Perhaps the reason why NATO membership in 1949 did not create more of a stir was that it was seen not as Norway giving up autonomy, but as losing less autonomy than might be the case had Norway followed Czechoslovakia into the Soviet bloc in 1948. With the signing of the North Atlantic Treaty the fear of Soviet action against Norway had subsided, but in early 1948 that real fear led Norway to discuss an alliance, albeit a Scandinavian one. By the time it was clear that this would not suit Norway's requirements, potential critics had lost the argument about the country's autonomy. Unlike the signature of the Treaty of Rome, the

Washington Treaty did not automatically lead to policy changes that could even be imposed by majority voting in a council of ministers. Further policy steps had to be accepted by *all* alliance members. It also provided small states with a forum for influence in an area – international security – in which they would otherwise be objects of great-power policy (Honkanen 2002: 22–38). The Labour Party was able to demonstrate in 1949 – with its statement on bases – that membership of an alliance was not a blank cheque, one of the most telling criticisms made of EC and EU membership. Even when demands that touched public opinion were made later in NATO's life – about nuclear weapons and the stationing of German officers – the Norwegian government could show a degree of intransigence.

Post-Cold War: Norway and the new NATO

The end of the Cold War swept away the *raison d'être* of NATO, which nevertheless remained as a going concern. What consequences have the end of the Cold War and the continuation of NATO had for Norway in its relations with the EU and, especially, its European Security and Defence Policy? Has the issue been one of how best to adjust to new institutions and policies or have deeper questions of identity been involved?

It seemed that at the end of the 1980s and the start of the 1990s, though welcoming the developments in Eastern Europe and the Soviet Union, the leadership of Norway, especially the military, was cautious about the consequences for its country (Archer 1994b). Unlike any other NATO country in Europe, Norway had a small land frontier and a massive sea border with the Soviet Union. The feeling was that what could be changed favourably might be changed back. The initial cautious response to the end of the Cold War can be seen in the report, in March 1992, of the Norwegian Defence Commission of 1990 (Forsvarskommisjonen av 1990 1992). The historian Olav Riste expressed this succinctly:

> Russian democracy is unstable, and Russia remains a power with an enormous arsenal of nuclear weapons. Norway also has an unresolved territorial dispute with Russia concerning jurisdiction in the Barents Sea and Arctic ocean. In Norwegian eyes, while the threat might have disappeared, there remained a long-term uncertainty.
>
> (Riste 2001: 278)

By the mid-1990s it was still not clear how the post-Cold War scene would look. After the Maastricht Treaty, the EU was starting to develop its own Common Foreign and Security Policy and the Yugoslav conflict demonstrated that the end of the Cold War would not necessarily bring peace to Europe. In this security turmoil at the start of the 1990s, Norway found that its security 'menu' had lengthened considerably. However, it remained firm on its first choice: a close security link with the US through NATO.

The main question for Oslo was the form of any future US commitment to the defence of Europe in the changed conditions, and how this might affect Norway. Tied to this was a general Norwegian approach to the new security situation, that represented a recasting of the view of the world in a way that allowed Norway to respond without too sudden a change in its defence posture. However, by the end of the 1990s this gradual approach was beginning to wear thin and more drastic change had to be considered. A review of Norway's relations with the burgeoning ESDP was part of that development.

The question of the US commitment has led to a discourse among Norwegian defence experts and politicians: that of *marginalization*, and it is one that has consequences for Norway's relations with the EU.

Marginalization draws on a number of fears. The first is that Norway has not benefited from the end of the Cold War as have, say, Denmark or the Central European states (Forsvarskommisjonen av 1990 1992: 34). The second is that, as the urgency of the Cold War threat declined, US and other allied forces would lessen their involvement in the defence of Norway. Third, there was concern that Norway would disappear off the conceptual map of those making new security arrangements in Europe. It is a relief not to be talked about as much as Serbia, Cyprus or Georgia, but there is a certain feeling of rejection on being ignored altogether. In the post-Cold War security foursome in the north, Norway might still find itself faced by a surly Russia, so it had to make sure that it had at least the US or the EU by its side. The worst case would be to be neglected by both (Neumann 2002b: 20–1).

The supposed danger of marginalization gained the attention in October 1991 of the Minister of Defence, Johan Jørgen Holst (1991: 26). This danger of 'marginalization and isolation' would be worsened by Norway's 'self-imposed isolation in Europe' but he saw a possible way out: an application for EC membership. Nevertheless, he recognized that the foreign and security considerations might be counterbalanced by 'other policy interests' (ibid.: 27). Holst was prepared to bolster one waning restraint on Norwegian autonomy – NATO – with another – the EC/EU – as a means of ensuring Norwegian influence in the redrawing of the post-Cold War security map of Europe.

This point was taken up by Gro Harlem Brundtland, the Labour Prime Minister, during her 1994 EU referendum campaign, when she claimed that Norway should not be 'a second-rank security policy nation in Europe', therefore providing strong foreign and security reasons for full Norwegian membership of the EU (Brundtland 1994b: 9).

Norwegian decision-makers developed another strand in their post-Cold War security policy, and this also pointed to a closer link with Europe. The wider security concerns of the decision-makers attempted to address the increase in security risks identified by the 1990 Defence Commission (Forsvarskommisjonen av 1990 1992: 34) and create more stability, especially in Europe. The Commission considered that 'organizing a comprehensive pattern of cooperation seeks to counter the tendency to international anarchy' and the level of norms and rules followed by most countries would be a desirable aim (Forsvarskommisjonen av 1990 1992: 37, author's translation). This followed in the footsteps of Koht's promotive policy, noted above (see p. 134).

The government sought to encourage such cooperation, based on norms and rules, in its own vicinity. In 1992 it inaugurated the Council for the Barents Euro-Arctic Region, with the aim 'to replace the previous hostility in the North with an active form of cooperation' (Stoltenberg 1994: ix.) Similarly, Norway became involved in the Council of Baltic Sea States which brought together the Nordic countries, Russia, the Baltic states, Germany and Poland.

It was correct of the Ministry of Defence (1993: 2) to recall that '[t]raditionally Norway has applied a broad approach as the basis of its security policy', that the country 'quite early tried to integrate more political instruments as part of a more *comprehensive* security policy'. NATO's new strategic doctrine stressed dialogue and cooperation in achieving security and, in re-evaluating its policy instruments, Norway found that the political aspects had gained in weight 'at the expense of the military ones' (ibid.: 5). In seeking the economic and political aspects of security, 'the process of European integration, or EC, is at the core' (ibid.: 14).

Likewise, when considering common security throughout Europe, Norway had to be 'willing to contribute to security, stability and possible collective military defence in other parts of Europe' (ibid.: 9), if only as a *quid pro quo* for a similar commitment to northern Europe by allies.

This trend in security policy in the lead-up to the negotiations for EU membership and the referendum can be seen in two perspectives. One would view Norway's position in post-Cold War Europe and would see strengthening the Western European Union (WEU, the defence operational arm of the EU) in the Treaty of Maastricht as a good way to keep the US engaged and offering an alternative if the Atlantic powers cut loose. This was the view expressed by Holst. A second opinion had more to do with the 1994 referendum. One way to get obstinate Norwegian voters to support EU membership might be to persuade them that Norway's security and stability would anyhow be increasingly tied to the rise of the EU. The first approach feared an Atlantic estrangement; the second almost predicted it.

In the end, the electorate did not see security as a salient issue in the EU referendum of November 1994 and made their minds up on other issues (Archer and Sogner 1998: 134–5). While the US did draw down its military presence in Europe, it did not pull out altogether and indeed was closely involved in former Yugoslavia in the mid and late 1990s. Though

Norway did not join the EU, it still sought to be closely involved both with the WEU and the EU's ESDP. The rise of that policy and the Norwegian response will be briefly examined.

Norway and the CFSP

Cooperation in foreign and security matters, developed in the Maastricht treaty, basically remained an intergovernmental arrangement with the *communautaire* institutions – the Commission, the European Parliament and the European Court of Justice – held at arm's length. This process has been refined in the Amsterdam and Nice treaties.

Norway had already engaged in a dialogue with European Political Cooperation (EPC), the CFSP's predecessor, and was anxious to be associated with the CFSP (*Stortingsmelding* 12 2000: 21–2).

The CFSP provided a set of policy positions, together with occasional action, with which Norway could associate itself. Indeed, Norway has aligned itself with practically all the EU's declarations on foreign policy issues, from Burundi to Myamar. However, in the foreign relations that were of greatest import for Norway – those with the US, Russia and Central and Eastern Europe, especially the Baltic states – Norway was able to conduct its own policies and to work through other institutions, quite often with EU countries, such as the Barents Euro-Arctic Council, the Council of Baltic Sea States and the various NATO institutions. Furthermore, after the 1994 referendum, Norwegian governments spread their wings internationally and remained active across four continents – in Guatemala, Sudan, southern Africa, the Middle East, Sri Lanka, the Philippines and former Yugoslavia. These activities can be seen as buying influence internationally, 'diplomats for influence' to paraphrase Nina Græger (2002). They can also be interpreted as helping to ensure the sort of world that Norway wanted and which it felt best served the needs of a small, rich, democratic state. In that sense Norway was acting as a 'norm entrepreneur' (Ingebritsen 2002) and one that was prepared to put resources where its preferences lay. It was a pace-setter in certain sorts of peace operations.

Perhaps the greatest test for Norway's external policy after the end of the Second World War has come in the area of defence and security. This is not because of any direct threat – far from it. The end of the Cold War meant a reduction in military threats to Norwegian soil or offshore areas. It was more the challenge of finding an appropriate form of defence structure and framework for security policy. Of course, the traditional structure for Norwegian defence and security had been NATO, but the Atlantic alliance was changing after the Cold War and the creation of the EU provided an emerging supplement, or even alternative, to NATO.

Norway's dilemma

The defence and security dilemma facing Norway since the end of the Cold War has been one of adjustment to a new environment that never remains still. The internal pressures have been to spend less on defence[3] but to keep a defence presence in the north of the country, not least to help the economic infrastructure there. Norway has also had to move its defence posture away from that of the Cold War that was based on territorial defence, postulated on Allied support, to a profile that addresses the security needs of a small state in the post-Cold War world. It has tried to reform its armed forces and the internal balance of its defence expenditure. As many of the insecurities are Europe-wide, not to say global, Norwegian defence and security policy has increasingly had to look outwards. A number of partners have been available for Norwegian activity – the UN, the OSCE, *ad hoc* coalitions, NATO and the EU. The creation of the ESDP presented Norway with the two emerging and related problems. The first was that, over the long run, such a system might detract from the primacy of NATO in the defence of the North Atlantic area and thus undermine the very Atlanticist basis of Norwegian security. The second was that, in the meantime, Norway would have to fashion a relationship with the new system. Given that the WEU, of which Norway was an associate, was the operative arm of the ESDP at the start of the EU's existence, that did not create an immediate problem, but the question became of interest perhaps sooner than most Norwegian decision-makers thought would be the case.

The first problem was one of priorities. How much attention should be given to Norway's first choice – NATO – and how much could be spared for ESDP? Should Norway encourage what could become the cuckoo in the North Atlantic nest or would it not grow anyhow, despite anything Norway did? By agreeing to the ESDP the members of the EU had signalled that they were not content to allow the WEU to continue as before as the institutionalization of European defence within the Atlantic Alliance. Something had to change. There was some disagreement among EU members on how it should progress. After the 1994 referendum, Norwegian Ministers were anxious to demonstrate that the country was loyal to NATO and the Atlantic link. The cover given by Europe and the US to Norway in its dealings with Russia was seen as critical (Kosmo 1995: 3). It was crucial to Norway for the US to continue its defence commitment to Europe and to recognize that Norway's defence-related problems – with its need to defend against invasion – were different from those on the European continent, according to the then Labour Defence Minister (Kosmo 1995: 6). The emphasis was thus placed on allied, especially US, commitment to the NATO Composite Force (NCF), the sole NATO force then, with Norway as the only potential area of operation.

The good news for Norway was that, by 1995, the scope of US security involvement in Europe had been enlarged, with President Clinton's engagement in issues such as Bosnia, Northern Ireland and the Greek–Turkish dispute (Godal 1995: 16). As well as this strong stress on the Atlantic link, Norwegian Ministers were prepared to see the WEU – which they regarded as the European pillar of NATO – become more involved in the Petersburg tasks.[4] While 'Norway should be given an opportunity to become linked or associated with this part of the European cooperation', there was also a warning against 'exaggerated "Europeanization", which could in reality call into question the entire notion of the transatlantic community' (Godal 1995: 25). Norway stood shoulder-to-shoulder with its Atlanticist ally, the UK, on the future of the WEU.

From mid-1997, when it became clear that the Treaty of Amsterdam would lead to the virtual inclusion of the WEU and its Petersburg tasks by the EU, it should have been apparent to Norway that its position in European security would change. Thus the second problem arose. ESDP was here to stay; how should Norway interact with it? Official defence statements from then until 2004 show something of an initial reluctance to be fully engaged in this development followed by grudging acceptance of involvement.

In the chapter on security and defence in the 1997 Norwegian Defence Budget, issued in September 1996, the WEU's future role was seen to be more certain after the June 1996 NATO meeting in Berlin:

> but there is nevertheless still considerable doubt as to the WEU's institutional links. From a Norwegian viewpoint it is desirable that the WEU should remain as an independent organization. This means that the WEU would in the future continue to have more or less equal links with the EU and NATO ... Norway would wish to see clarification of the status of associate members.
>
> (Ministry of Defence 1996: 3)

Both the defence minister in the Labour government in power until 1997 and his successor in the centrist government saw greater European security cooperation within NATO, the WEU and the EU. The latter considered that this would:

> bring particular challenges to Norway because of our associate membership in the WEU and our position outside the EU. These facts should be considered in framing Norwegian attitudes towards the development of a European security and defence identity.
>
> (Fjærevoll 1998)

Here Fjærevoll referred to the NATO plans for a European security and defence identity but not to the EU's European Security and Defence Policy. Indeed, he was insistent:

> Norway has considered the idea of increased European responsibility for security and defence policy favourably. In particular, we have advocated that ESDI evolves within the alliance. Nevertheless, it is instrumental that the development of ESDI proceeds with American blessing.
>
> (Fjærevoll 1998)

The centrist coalition's Foreign Minister, Knut Vollebæk (1998: 2), was able to make his major statement to the Storting on foreign policy in January 1998 without mentioning the EU's ESDP at all, despite his overview of the government's 'active policy towards Europe'. The activity clearly did not include defence and security. However, the Anglo-French meeting at Saint-Malo in the autumn of 1998, and Tony Blair's seeming conversion on the road to Damascus in relation to European defence, showed that this tactic of denial could not last long. The Defence Minister devoted two paragraphs to what was still headed with the NATO phrase 'European Security and Defence Identity' (ESDI) in which the preference for NATO in realizing the primary military capabilities was expressed. If the growth of the EU's CFSP 'and the development of a common defence *within the EU*' became apparent, then 'Norway will face considerable challenges'. Norway wanted the ESDI to evolve in a way giving 'equal rights' to all European NATO members (Fjærevoll 1999: 3, original emphasis).

The first real impact of the NATO April 1999 Washington Summit, at which the alliance's new Strategic Concept was promulgated and three new Central European states were welcomed as members, and of the development of the ESDP can be seen in the Defence White Paper of 1999. Importantly, it also bore the imprint of Norway's Kosovo experience but in a different way from that seen in the UK's embrace of ESDP.

Much of the thinking behind the White Paper was explained in a speech by Fjærevoll's successor as Defence Minister in the centrist government, Eldbjørg Løwer, to the Oslo Military Society in January 2000. She stressed that the international dynamic was dramatically different from that seen in the Cold War, but that the security situation was still one of considerable uncertainty. 'Society at large has also become more vulnerable', with greater dependence on information technology leading to 'increased vulnerability to sabotage', an important factor for an oil- and gas-producing country such as Norway (Løwer 2000: 2). She also saw a new opportunity. Norway's interests could be served by 'associating itself as close as possible with European cooperation in the field of security and defence policy and by offering our own resources for the furtherance of joint European endeavours'. The intention was cooperation 'in a spirit of mutual commitment with our Nordic, European and North American partners' (Løwer 2000: 4–5). This reflected a policy that has been described as 'troops for influence' (Græger 2002: 35). In the context of NATO, it was seen as a reciprocal process whereby 'the ability to operate jointly with the forces of other NATO countries ... applies not only when Norwegian forces are deployed abroad but also in the cases where we might need reinforcement of our own national defences' (Løwer 2000: 7). NATO was the organization that was seen as the prime forum for Western defence and security cooperation and it was one where Norway was part of transatlantic security consultation (ibid.: 3–4).

In the case of the EU, there was no indication from other states that such a mutual bargain as 'troops for influence' was on offer. In that context it was more a matter of *expectant acquiescence* (see p. 15), whereby Norway contributed to a process that it clearly did not wish, in order to influence the future development of that process. This called into question the form of the bargain.

Referring to the Defence White Paper (*Stortingsmelding* 38 1999), Løwer saw the recommendations there as pointing towards an improved ability 'to operate jointly with allies and partners', with the future trend envisaged as 'closer integration of our force elements with the multinational forces of which they form part'. This would mean a 'greater degree of joint procurement, operations and training for the various forces concerned'. The search was on for 'partners with whom we can enter into long-term strategic cooperative arrangements in a range of different areas'. All this was placed in the context of adapting the defence establishment 'towards a more Alliance-oriented structure' (Løwer 2000: 7). However, when turning to the development of the ESDP, the Minister admitted, it would 'have very definite consequences for Norwegian defence', a matter that had 'occupied [her] mind greatly during the past year' (ibid.). She then outlined what she thought might be the deal between Norway and the developing EU.

Norway would contribute components to larger international units, and the EU countries were 'our natural partners here', but Norwegian participation would require a 'satisfactory framework' (ibid.: 8). There was the constitutional question of 'to what extent can Norway contribute forces towards an EU led operation without any assurance of full participation in the planning of the operation' (ibid.). As the lives of Norwegian troops could be at stake, 'consultation after decisions have been taken will not be acceptable to Norway in this respect. It cannot be assumed, therefore, that Norwegian forces declared to the WEU's force register will automatically be transferred across to the EU's force register.' Norway wanted a say in the planning of EU-led operations in which its troops could be used. However, the record of the EU was not to allow non-members the same rights as members in its policy-making process.

Towards a solution

The nature of the basis for cooperation with the EU had been set out from the Norwegian side in the note (pro memorandum or 'PM') sent to EU and NATO countries by Knut Vollebæk in preparation for the EU's

European Council in Helsinki in December 1999. In this he stressed that any new structures for European security should 'build on the arrangements and practices developed in the WEU, encompassing all EU members and non-European allies' (DNAK 2002: 1). As Norway had 'a fundamental interest in the security and crisis management arrangements now being developed in the European Union' the country wished 'to be fully involved in these endeavours'. It was stressed that Norway's alliance membership was 'also of fundamental importance in the context of EU-led crisis response operations'.

Close relations between the EU and NATO were emphasized, as was the need to 'ensure the fullest possible involvement of non-EU European allies in EU-led crisis response operations'. It was recognized that Norway had a close relationship with the EU and had been a substantial contributor to conflict prevention and conflict management. In intending to strengthen its contribution 'to European and future EU-led crisis management' Norway wanted these to be based 'on full participation in the decision-shaping process' (ibid.: 2). It should be noted that the term 'decision-taking' was not used, suggesting that the emphasis was to be on having an input to content rather than just on the formality of any voting or consensus arrangement. Indeed, the following EU activities were important to Norway:

- Day-to-day consultations and non-operational activities relating to defence and security issues.
- Consultations and the shaping of policy related to crises 'in all phases, including the stage before an EU decision in principle on planning for or initiating an operation'.
- EU-led crisis management operations (DNAK 2002: 2).

The Minister advanced Norway's own ideas about how non-EU European allies might be included in the new EU defence and security arrangements:

- Consultations in the proposed Political and Security Committee and its working groups with non-EU European allies having the rights to speak, make proposals and to have access to all relevant information and documents. This would also be the basis of consultation in the Military Committee.
- Non-EU European allies would be invited early on to participate in EU operations not drawing on NATO assets and capabilities. Once participation was confirmed, these states would have the same rights in the operation as EU member states, including full participation in planning and preparation.
- The non-EU European allies would meet the EU states at political level to discuss security and 'confirm participation in EU-led operations' (DNAK 2002: 2).

This PM indicated Norwegian awareness of the EU's sensitivity to allowing non-members the same decision-making rights as EU states and satisfied itself with a high level of consultation and participation on the basis of being part of the planning process. Or, put the other way round, Norway would not expect to contribute to an operation when it had not been invited to its preparation.

The outline of a solution to the participation of NATO non-EU states in ESDP-led activities started to emerge at the end of 2002.

If, as claimed by Nina Græger (2002: 35), the basis of this policy was 'troops for influence', there were two elements to the emerging deal – both of which were problematic – Norwegian troops, and influence with allies. The first element refers to what Norway had on offer. As long as Norwegian defence was basically aimed at territorial defence (as it had been throughout the Cold War), then Norway's broader international contribution was willingness to provide personnel for international peacekeeping operations. Welcome as this was, it was scarcely substantial. As the 1990s unfolded, more organizations – the OSCE, WEU, EU and NATO as well as the UN – crowded into the peacekeeping business and operations were extended to include humanitarian and rescue operations, as well as peacemaking (basically, with peacekeeping, the Petersburg tasks). Furthermore, the realization was dawning, even in Norway, that the continued devotion of most defence resources to the territorial defence of the country in the absence of a likely threat was a waste of money. The taxpaying public and their representatives in parliament were not prepared to finance a structure aimed at a phantom. Unsurprisingly, defence budgets shrank and looked like continuing to do so unless some other worthy activity was found for the defence forces. It seemed that it was either 'out of Norway or out of business' for Norwegian defence.

The 1997 Long-term Defence Plan for 1998–2001 tried to struggle with this dilemma but the outcome of its considerations was still half-hearted, for a number of reasons. First, what Norwegian defence had done – and had done well – for the previous fifty years was territorial defence within the context of NATO. To expect it to alter its tasks within a couple of years was perhaps unreasonable. A supertanker needs space and time to change direction. Second, there was still the belief in a residual threat to Norway's homeland (Neumann 2002b) and so a wish to keep some capability to deal with that eventuality. Third, defence activity was an important economic factor in the life of north Norway in particular and there was the fear that, should emphasis be placed elsewhere, this contribution to the infrastructure of the north could be lost. Finally, there was the national construct of Norwegian defence. The armed forces were based on conscription and their existence was tied to the defence of the country and the nation. Troops that had been spared for peacekeeping had been volunteers. Nevertheless, it was clear by the end of the 1990s and the start of the new century that, if Norwegian defence was to mean anything, it had to be part of the international operations that were occurring not just in the Balkans but farther afield, in Afghanistan, the Middle East and Africa. These were far from traditional peacekeeping operations

The Long-term Defence Plan for 2002–5 (Forsvarsdepartementet 2001) confronted this dilemma. It started with the admission by the then Defence Minister, Labour's Bjørn Tore Godal, that Norway had 'not managed to create a flexible and credible Defence that is properly attuned to the tasks and challenges to be met'. The defence structures 'would not be capable of meeting the challenges that we must be prepared to face in the future'. What were needed were 'high-quality mobile and flexible forces capable of rapid reaction' but these had to 'measure up to the quality requirements set by NATO' (Forsvarsdepartementet 2001: 1).

The aim was that the forces should make a 'greater contribution to the defence of the NATO area as a whole, and ... capable of contributing to other international initiatives under the auspices of the UN, NATO or the EU' (Forsvarsdepartementet 2001a: 3). Conscription was to be kept, though radically revised, and civil–military cooperation was to be enhanced. The armed forces would continue to be strongly represented in the north of the country and some communities hard hit by the structural changes would receive support to aid local redevelopment (Forsvarsdepartementet 2001: 5). Critics have pointed out that both elements in the armed forces and politicians have clung to traditional beliefs about conscription and the defence of north Norway (Ulriksen 2002: 238).

In introducing the defence budget for 2003, Kristin Krohn Devold, the Conservative Defence Minister, stressed that the terrorist attacks of 11 September 2001 in the US underlined the necessity 'to enhance flexibility, readiness and the ability to work together both nationally and internationally' (Forsvarsdepartementet 2002: 1). By early 2004 she was able to report that personnel from the Telemark battalion had been active in Afghanistan in the NATO-led stabilization force, ISAF, and had contributed to the NATO standing force in the Mediterranean and its operation, Active Endeavour, and to the NATO force in Kosovo. After the adoption of UN Security Council resolution 1511, Norway had sent elements of an engineering company to the British-controlled sector in Iraq. Staff officers and observers were active in a range of UN operations in the Middle East, the Balkans, the Horn of Africa, the Congo, Liberia and Sudan. To quote the Defence Minister, 'Norway's sphere of interest thus today stretches from the border [with Russia] at Jacobselv to the streets of Kabul' (Devold 2004b: 6).

Norwegian forces are undergoing a transformation that will increase in pace during the period of the 2005–8 defence plan (Forsvarsdepartementet 2004). The key words for the forces are flexibility and usability, with 'the "plugging in" of relatively small Norwegian units into larger multinational forces' (Devold 2004a: 2) and justification having to be made for any capability that cannot be used internationally.

To what extent do these changes make Norway more prepared to be part of ESDP? Without them – with Norway sticking to territorial defence and some peacekeeping operations – Norwegian defence would have been of little use. There would have been few troops to exchange for influence. The reforms not only made Norway ready for NATO's new tasks, they offered the possibility of involvement in EU-led operations. The questions remaining were those of the quantity of forces to cover more than one substantial operation and their readiness to participate. The latter element was recognized by the former Defence Minister in her 2000 speech (Løwer 2000: 6–7), though by 2004 improvements had clearly been made, with more promised.

The above section shows that the 'troops' in the 'troops for influence' equation were a long time coming. Nevertheless, they were there in important operations in Bosnia, Kosovo, Afghanistan and even post-war Iraq (International Institute of Strategic Studies 2003: 52) and have useful capabilities for most international operations. What of the influence element? Where could that be exercised in the ESDP?

The PM mentioned above indicated the Norwegian hopes.[5] Norway had been an associate of the WEU. According to the Petersburg Declaration of the WEU, this meant it could participate fully in Council meetings and subsidiary bodies, but could not block decisions by full members (Archer 1994a: 249). Norway was involved in WEU military planning cells and contributed significantly to the EU-run operation in Mostar. With plans to integrate the WEU into the EU in the air, Norway wanted its rights as an associate transferred to any new arrangement, but this was opposed by Greece, which was concerned less with Norway than with Turkey, another non-EU European NATO member. After the Amsterdam treaty came into force, the EU members, meeting in Helsinki in 1999, agreed on the transfer of WEU tasks to the EU, but not its structures, except when it suited them in the satellite centre and the WEU institute. At the Nice European Council meeting, the idea of non-EU states participating in contributors' groups for particular EU operations was accepted, but there was still no acceptance of their right to participate in the decision-making leading to such operations. However, there followed a long wrangle between the EU, especially Greece, and Turkey, about the arrangements to be made between NATO and the EU with regard to access to NATO assets for any EU-led operation. Turkey held out against the EU using NATO facilities on this basis. Though Norway was less prominent in the debate, it agreed with the principle of the Turkish argument.

This disagreement was only settled at the end of 2002 after the NATO Summit in Prague and the Copenhagen European Council. The deal between the EU and NATO was in fact better than that at the time of the 2000 Nice European Council and it seemed to satisfy the requirements of the Norwegian 1999 PM. Norway would continue to discuss ESDP matters with the EU at all levels. Nevertheless, the numbers game of the

EU consulting with the accession states who were to join in May 2004, as well as non-EU NATO countries, meant the attention Norway could expect was minimal.

At the same time, reforms of NATO's headquarters and the renewed NATO activity in Afghanistan has been met with active Norwegian participation. A Joint Warfare Centre has been established in Stavanger under NATO's Allied Command Transformation and an Allied Centre of Excellence for Winter Operations is being set up in Jåttå (Devold 2004b: 3). Norway has tied its military reforms to NATO's Prague Capabilities Commitment (PCC) and has also focused attention on cooperation with other North Sea NATO members, the UK, Denmark, Germany and the Netherlands (Devold 2004a: 2). Meanwhile, by 2004 Norway had received no reply from the EU concerning the contributions it had declared in 2003 to the ESDP's Headline Goals. Its interaction with the EU has been a matter of exchanging information rather than of consultation. The Defence Minister, reporting on Norway's willingness to support a division of roles and cooperation between NATO and the EU, said in January 2004, 'I wish I could say that we had succeeded here . . . our position as EU "outsiders" has meant that the results are decided by others than ourselves' (Devold 2004b: 4). The signs are that while the Norwegian answer to a choice between NATO and the EU would be 'Both, please', the EU's preoccupation with the politics of the NATO–ESDP relationship and with integrating its new members has meant that the useful resources that Norway could offer have been overlooked. In an area where Norway has been promotive, the EU has not rushed to respond.

Conclusions

Norway's relationship to the EU's CFSP is complex. It follows in the trail of the CFSP's policy declarations. However, it also conducts a very activist foreign policy of its own that has a global reach. By its active diplomatic role and its involvement in military operations, Norway has shed many of its fears about marginalization. There are still residual concerns about Russia, but concerted bilateral, trilateral (with the US) and multilateral initiatives have brought some calm in that relationship.

Norwegian defence and security policy faces the question 'Where is it going?' This is not a dilemma exclusive to Norway. Indeed, most European states have been asking it about their security policy since the end of the Cold War, but for Norway there was increased uneasiness after a period, the Cold War, of relative certainty. Despite a slow start, Norway seems to have decided that, increasingly, its defence forces must be able to be part of wider operations, not just within Norway (as was the case with NATO) but outside the country, indeed almost anywhere in the world. It has become much more promotive of its own view of security.

While Norway has shown itself willing to participate in EU operations in 2003 (such as Concordia and the EU Police Mission in Macedonia), it is clear that involvement in too many activities stretches the resources of Norway's defence. This indicates more hard choices being made – with Norway more likely involving itself in NATO operations and retrenching its maritime tradition with North Sea neighbours – and the continued radical transformation of Norwegian defence. 'Holy cows' such as conscription, the remaining emphasis on north Norway and procurement of new frigates are politically sensitive issues that are still on the political agenda (Forsvarsdepartementet 2004).

Clearly Norwegian defence will not return to territorial defence. The changes started at the turn of the twenty-first century placed an emphasis on the protection of Norway's resources and also on creating more mobile and interoperable forces. But into which generator should they be plugged? The government has to decide on the sort of preferred operation, and this returns to the question of influence. So far, Norway has chosen to exercise what influence it can through NATO, its links with the US and the UN. This leaves only limited resources for other operations, such as those run by the EU, where it is excluded from decision-making. To change that, it will have to become a member of the EU.

7 Norway and Justice and Home Affairs

> The social progress, order, security and peace of each country are necessarily connected with the social progress, order, security and peace of all other countries.
>
> (Pope John XXIII, *Pacem in Terris*, p. 150)

The Treaty of Maastricht's 'third pillar' covered the area of Justice and Home Affairs (JHA). The members of the European Communities – in some cases not all of them – had been cooperating in these and associated policy areas before Maastricht and a network of cooperation has developed since then. This chapter examines Norway's relations with the European Union in the general area of justice, border controls and control of criminal activities, especially that undertaken through the Schengen agreements.

These elements of policy relating to the internal order, security and peace of the country have a particular importance not just for Norway but for most modern states, as they are important elements in their survival as states. In the context of Norway's cooperation with the EU, there are deep issues to consider. The nature of the law in Norway reflects the cultural and institutional elements of the country's history (see Figure 1.1). It is based on a Nordic tradition rather than the Roman law basis of much Continental law. Any cooperation internationally had been mainly with other Nordic states. Norway has traditionally been a country within which law is built on consensus and has a certain social acceptance backed by solidarity, as mentioned in Chapter 2. It is not a country with any substantial minority or alienated group that has threatened the integrity of the state. It has not suffered terrorist attacks. It is thus lightly policed. The government of Norway has championed human rights internationally and has accepted obligations under international agreements. Until the 1990s the only requirement for international treatment of legal and justice matters was through Nordic cooperation or through the various agreements associated with the Council of Europe and the United Nations.

The rise of increased cooperation on legal matters within the EU and the inclusion of some Nordic states within that system posed problems for Norway. It could either end the arrangements it had with the other Nordic states and return to almost complete autonomy in legal affairs or it could seek an agreement with the EU system as a way of exercising some influence. Before analysing how Norway dealt with this dilemma, a brief account will be given of the EU's treatment of Justice, Home Affairs and other related matters.

Developments in the EU

The background

The European Communities were based on the notion of creating a 'common market' whereby economic barriers would be removed between member states. As this was achieved, the notion of free movement of labour in the area became more than just an aspiration. As such free movement became easier between EC member states, the opportunity grew for drugs, criminals and terrorists also to move more freely within the EC. Migrants coming to one member state could cross over to another EC country. By the time the Maastricht treaty was signed in 1992, two strands of cooperation had developed between the EC states, one dealing with the freer movement of individuals and the other concerned with some of the negative aspects of that freedom.

With the rise of terrorism in the 1970s, the heads of state and government of the EC, meeting in the form of European Political Cooperation (EPC), often discussed common action against the phenomenon. From 1975 Interior and Justice Ministers of the EC met regularly on an intergovernmental basis to discuss reactions to terrorism and serious crimes.

The 1984 decision of the Fontainbleau European Council to abolish, at least in principle, customs barriers between EC members was followed by a Franco-German initiative to end border checks. This notion of allowing free access between member states was taken up by France, Germany and the three Benelux countries in the 1985 Schengen agreement and the 1990 Convention of Application, which was later joined by Italy, Spain, Portugal and Greece, though the signatories had difficulty in implementing the open borders idea (Kostakopoulou 1998). The Schengen Information System (SIS) allowed the authorities to exchange passport information. The Schengen system was aimed not just at opening the borders but also included the harmonization of visa policies and laws on the regulation of drugs and arms, and cooperation in the fight against international crime.

Maastricht

The third pillar of the Maastricht treaty was headed 'Provisions on cooperation in the fields of justice and home affairs' and Article K1 set out the issues that were of concern: asylum policy, rules controlling people crossing the external borders of the member states, immigration policy for nationals of third countries, combating fraud and drug addiction, cooperation in both civil and criminal judicial matters and over customs and specific police action to combat terrorism, drug trafficking and serious international crime. A Coordination Committee of senior officials (the 'K4' committee) took over from the existing Group of National Coordinators, three steering groups were established, as was a European Police Office (Europol) and a European Drugs Unit (EDU). The structure was intergovernmental with the role of the EC institutions being limited. Schengen continued its separate existence with the UK, Ireland and Denmark not being members. Meanwhile, EC members had agreed a separate Asylum Convention, signed in Dublin in 1990 but ratified only in 1996. The question of visas was to be dealt with under the Community-based Pillar One of the Maastricht treaty.

When Norway applied for EU membership in 1992, the subsequent government report spent seven out of 477 pages on 'justice cooperation', which covered the Third Pillar of Maastricht and Schengen. The stress here was on better protection against increased internationally organized crime and on the intergovernmental nature of cooperation. One section, that on inter-state cooperation on asylum and immigration policy, suggested an area where the Norwegian Labour government might be promotive. EU membership would give Norway 'increased opportunity to influence the developments in Europe as promised by our humanitarian tradition' (*Stortingsmelding* 40 1994: 349). Norwegian cooperation in Schengen cooperation was to be considered 'in a Nordic perspective' (ibid.: 350). The Norwegian 'no' to joining the EU and the continued EEA membership meant that Norway was excluded from Pillar Three cooperation and, it seemed, from Schengen.

Amsterdam

The 1997 Treaty of Amsterdam shifted the borderline between those elements that were treated under Pillars One and Three. Essentially matters concerning immigration and asylum were moved to Pillar One, and Pillar Three was renamed 'Police and judicial cooperation in criminal matters'. Combating racism and xenophobia was added to this group. The Schengen agreement was incorporated into the Amsterdam treaty but spread across the First and Third Pillars. However, the UK, Ireland and Denmark reserved the right to stay out of the arrangements in Pillar One, though they could decide to apply particular elements. The changes represented 'reform at the price of fragmentation' (Monar 1998), but with the implementation of the Amsterdam treaty in 1999 cooperation expanded in the areas covered by Schengen and police and judicial matters. The attack on the US on 11 September 2001 led to a further expansion of the European effort in the 'war against terrorism', reflected in the activities of the EU (European Union 2002).

Norway and Schengen

The Nordic countries created a common Nordic labour market in 1954 and a passport union in 1958. With the original absence of Denmark from the Schengen arrangement, this northern arrangement went unchallenged. However, with the entry of Finland and Sweden into the EU on 1 January 1995 the situation changed. The three EU Nordic states became members of Schengen and Norway, plus Iceland, signed agreements with the Schengen countries on 19 December 1996 (Schengen I), ratified by the Storting on 9 June 1997. With the rolling up of the Schengen agreement into the Amsterdam treaty in June 1997, Norway and Iceland had to renegotiate their relationship with the EU states on Schengen issues. An agreement – Schengen II – was signed between Norway and Iceland and the EU on 18 May 1999 and came into force on 26 June 2000 (*Stortingsmelding* 12 2000: 11).[1] Both occasions provided an opportunity for the political forces within Norway to fight battles about Norway's sovereignty and its relations with the process of European integration.

Schengen I

With Finnish and Swedish membership of the EU, and in the wake of the lead-up to the Treaty of Amsterdam, it became apparent in 1995 that, if Sweden and Finland wished to join Schengen, then not only would Denmark be swept along, but also Norway would have to respond. Danish involvement in Schengen was encouraged by the prospect of increased border controls between Denmark and Germany if Denmark remained outside (Bull 1999: 66–7). All the five Nordic states wanted this to be done in such a way as not to interfere with the free movement of people in the Nordic region by drawing a line between the Nordic members and non-members of Schengen. If Sweden and Finland had joined Schengen, then passport controls would have to be instituted along the long Norwegian land border with Sweden and the northern border with Finland. If Denmark had been brought into the Schengen system, then ferries and air traffic from Norway would be treated as coming from 'the outside world' rather than the Nordic region, turning the clock back on one of the major achievements of Nordic cooperation.

However, this faced the Nordic states with an institutional dilemma – one of them was an EU member with an opt-out from justice issues (Denmark), two were new members with no such opt-out (Finland and Sweden) and two were non-EU members but part of the EEA (Iceland and Norway). An obvious solution was for all five Nordic states to join the Schengen system, thereby keeping EU Nordic doors open to Norwegians and Icelanders. The problem was that Schengen, even before it was cut-and-pasted into the Amsterdam treaty, was open for full membership only by EU states, which excluded Norway and Iceland. Nevertheless, pre-Amsterdam, the separation of Schengen from the EU gave some latitude in its development and it was certainly worth the Nordic states' while to make a joint approach, which they did. Denmark, Sweden and Finland, having joined the Schengen system (the 1985 agreement and 1990 convention), Norway and Iceland signed an agreement with the Schengen countries on 19 December 1996.

The proposition to the Storting on the issue placed the question in the context of Nordic cooperation, the Schengen agreements and the free movement of persons promised by the EEA agreement (*Stortingsproposisjon* 42 1996). It set out the Schengen *acquis* that Norway and Iceland would accept and also their place in the formulation of decisions. The two countries would be able to take part in the Executive Committee, other organs and all other working groups that prepare decisions. Norway and Iceland could make their own views and particular interests known and could make their own proposals, but could not take part in votes (Article 2). However, both states had the right to subscribe to Schengen decisions on an individual basis and, in the cases where either Iceland or Norway had made it clear beforehand that they could not support a proposal, the Schengen Executive Committee would not adopt that proposal until they had especially appraised that viewpoint (Article 3). The provisions of the agreement were not to prejudice cooperation in the framework of the Nordic passport union 'to the extent that such cooperation is not in variance with or hinders the implementation of the agreement' (Article 4, author's translation).

The report on the proposal from the Foreign Affairs Committee to the Storting showed a split down party lines. On this occasion it was the Conservatives, Labour and the Progress Party forming the majority in favour of the Schengen agreement and the Centre Party, the Socialist Left and the Christian People's Party against.[2]

The first battle concerned whether the agreement could be accepted by a straightforward majority vote or whether it had to be accepted by a three-quarters majority of the Storting, according to paragraph 93 of the constitution. The majority of the committee considered that the agreement was a traditional inter-state agreement without supranational features. They rejected the argument of Professor Ståle Eskeland of Oslo University, who had considered that power would be handed over to the Schengen Executive Committee and had pointed out that though, according to Article 103 of the EEA agreement, Norway had not been legally bound by EEA Committee decisions, still the Storting had used paragraph 93 of the constitution for the EEA (Innst.S. nr 229 1997: vedlegg (appendix) 3, 27–35). The majority considered that the reason for this process had been the delegation of authority to the ESA and the EFTA Court, which could make decisions of direct effect on Norwegian citizens. This was not the case for Article 103 of the EEA or for the Schengen agreement, where the Norwegian government was given the choice whether to accept the decisions of the Executive Committee. The majority group considered that it would be 'unthinkable' for any government to accept any Schengen decision without previously having obtained the necessary legal decision in the Storting, and indeed the government set out how it would consult the Storting's organs before a meeting of the Executive Committee. The majority parties pointed out that Norway would be able to participate in the Executive Committee on an equal basis with member states, though it would not be able to vote. However, there would be three other Nordic states on the committee with votes and all decisions had to be unanimous. If a decision was taken that was unacceptable to Norway and was of such a nature that Norway had to leave Schengen cooperation, then a border control would have to be established between Norway and its Nordic neighbours, just the situation that those countries had struggled to prevent. The implication was that Denmark, Finland and Sweden would never allow a substantial decision to pass in the Executive Committee that Norway opposed (Innst.S. nr 229 1997: 1–4).

The minority on the Foreign Affairs Committee, consisting of the Centre Party, the Socialist Left Party and the Christian People's Party, considered that many constitutional questions were brought up by the agreement and wanted them dealt with by independent judicial sources and even a revision of the constitution. These members placed emphasis on Norway having an international law obligation to carry out decisions taken in the Schengen organs when no explicit reservation had been made as to the Storting's consent. Second, they considered that there would be a real relinquishing of sovereignty. The agreement covered so many important areas of cooperation and would leave Norway without a vote or veto – all it could do would be to threaten to leave, pulling down the pillars of the Nordic passport union in the process. The third reason given by the opponents of ratification was that the agreement would allow foreign police authorities to have dealings with direct effect on Norwegian citizens, a reason that had led the Finnish and Swedish governments to ratify Schengen with qualified majorities (Innst.S. nr 229 1997: 4–6).

These were basic arguments about constitutional questions, and they had political implications. Had paragraph 93 been used, then the parties opposing the Schengen agreement would have been able to defeat it, and for most of the Storting members from those parties the agreement really did represent a challenge to Norwegian autonomy and bit into the core element of sovereignty, the control of external borders and police powers.

The conflict between the two sides continued with the debate on substance. The parties in favour of ratification had three basic elements underlying their arguments. The agreement secured the continuation of the Nordic passport union, it extended such a union to the other countries in the Schengen cooperation, and it strengthened police cooperation to fight the misuse of narcotics and international criminality in a more effective way. Those opposing ratification pointed out that the Schengen agreement would be partly or fully integrated into the EU in June 1997, thus making Norwegian association counter to the people's wish to stay outside the Union. Norway would have to leave such integrated cooperation, anyhow, destroying the Nordic passport union. The minority also stressed the need to fight international criminality, but through Interpol, and stressed that they considered that an ending of passport control at Norwegian borders to Schengen would make this struggle more difficult (Innst.S. nr 229 1997: 1).

On each issue of detail covered by the committee there was a split between the majority consisting of the Conservatives, Labour and the Progress Party and the minority from the Centre Party, the Christian Democrats and the Socialist Left. On visas, the majority considered that the introduction of visas by Norway for people coming from states that were until then visa-free was a drawback, made bearable by those having a visa being able to use it for the Schengen area and not just Norway. The minority disagreed with this balance and introduced the criticisms of the Schengen visa system made by the UN High Commission for Refugees (Innst.S. nr 229 1997: 9–12). Fridtjof Frank Gundersen of the Progress Party praised Schengen as a step towards hindering illegal immigration into Europe from the 'overpopulated' Third World and specifically saw this as important in defending 'Norwegian culture and our traditional national values' (ibid.: 12–13, see also his questioning of Professor Thomas Mathiesen in ibid.: vedlegg 3, p. 10), an end to which those in the minority may have aspired but not by means of Schengen. Neither would they have seen the threat coming from the same source as Gundersen, but more directly from the EU itself. Gundersen perceived members of the EU as in the same boat and coming under attack from a threatening and growing non-European world. The minority parties identified the threat as being less ethnic-based and closer to home – the EU itself – which threatened Norwegian autonomy and their version of the culture, rather than bolstered it.

The majority group saw police cooperation as the most important section in the agreement, as Norway had suffered from the general increase in organized international crime during the 1990s. Schengen police services would be able to make a 'hot pursuit' of suspected criminals over the Norwegian border and would be able to hold a 'discreet surveillance' in Norway, but under strict conditions (Innst.S. nr 229 1997: 13). The minority group, which supported police cooperation with other Nordic states and Interpol, saw the dangers of an increased use of border-crossing police operations, especially when the foreign police were armed (ibid.: 13–14).

There was also disagreement about the Schengen Information System

(SIS), the electronic data system attached to Schengen. The majority saw it as very restrictive and the Norwegian entries being controlled by Norwegian law. The minority did not consider that SIS would be a suitable 'compensatory measure' to balance against the increased danger of transnational criminality. They had grave doubts about who would be registered by SIS, thought that 90 per cent would be people unwanted in Schengen and that the system would be used to keep foreigners out of the Schengen area rather than to fight crime. They cited criticism of the Joint Supervisory Authority, the control organ of SIS, by the director of the Norwegian representation on the JSA, the Data Supervisory Authority (Innst.S. nr 229 1997: 17, see also the questioning of Apenes, ibid.: vedlegg 3, pp. 10–18).

The main differences cited above were between those who considered that a European basis was the most appropriate form of cooperation in the fight against criminality, and were prepared to give up the remaining Norwegian border controls to a common system, and those who wanted to keep national or, at most, Nordic controls. The Progress Party saw the issue in 'us against them' terms, with 'them' being immigrants from the Third World. Both Labour and the Conservatives saw 'them' as being international criminals, and the way to tackle them was that which would function best internationally, which meant the Schengen system. They also recognized it as the way to maintain the passport union with the other Nordic countries – in effect by dissolving it into the wider Schengen system. On the whole the majority group seemed in favour of fairly acquiescent tactics, making substantial changes to the Norwegian system to blend in with the Schengen system, even if it meant loss of national control in important areas of state activity.

The minority group rejected the Schengen system. For the minority parties, the threat came from international criminals but also from 'them' in Brussels who would take away Norwegian sovereignty. They gave preference to both the Nordic and the wider international solutions over those based in Western Europe. If Norway was to be part of Schengen, they wanted a show of intransigence, with feet being dragged on a number of issues and the reintroduction of national controls kept as an option, though that would have meant an end to the Nordic passport union. They called upon a defence of Norwegian *interests* in their support – the Schengen system would not be effective in keeping criminals out of Norway, would be expensive and would threaten individual rights – but they also used elements of *identity* to support their cause, rejecting foreign methods and impositions.

When the report reached the Storting, the majority vote was backed by seventy-five votes, with supporters coming from Labour, the Conservatives and the Progress Party, while the Centre Party, the Socialist Left and the Christian People's Party, together with three Labour rebels, two independents (former Progress Party members), the sole Liberal and only member from the Red Electoral Alliance garnered forty-nine votes for the rejection of Schengen. As the resolution needed only a simple majority, the government's proposal passed (*Stortingstidende* 1997).

The institutional arrangement that Norway had gained in Schengen allowed a greater possibility of foot-dragging than in the EEA. Apart from the formal arrangements, the position of the Nordic states as a bloc until their Schengen membership made it more likely that Norway would receive support from at least three voting members on issues of national importance, and only one vote was needed to block. The whole question of borders and the police was central to all the member states, so the system was run on an intergovernmental basis. Furthermore, the area of cooperation covered policy areas where there had been a long tradition of Nordic cooperation based on the cultures and traditions of the states involved. All this placed Norway in a stronger institutional position in Schengen I than in the EEA.

Schengen II

As had been foreseen in the 'Schengen I' debate, a reprise was in the offing. The moving of the Schengen treaty into the Treaty of Amsterdam and the placing of certain elements into the Community-based Pillar One meant that Norway's relationship with the system had changed.

By the time the issue came before the 1998–9 session of the Storting, the political situation in Norway had changed. The September 1997 general election had resulted in a minority government consisting of the three anti-Schengen parties – the Centre Party, the Christian Democrats and the Liberals. However, the parties that had supported the agreement with Schengen in 1997 – the Conservatives, Labour and the Progress Party – had a clear majority in the Storting.[3] Norway was in the position, not for the first time, of having a government that was opposed to a policy which was favoured by a majority of the parliament. In the platform that formed the basis of the centrist government – the Voksenås declaration – the three parties had agreed to remain opposed to Norwegian involvement in Schengen in principle. However, the government had to face the reality that once Denmark, Finland and Sweden had ratified the Amsterdam treaty and it came into force, then the Schengen institutions and cooperation would be within the EU institutions, not parallel to it as before. Without a new agreement between the EU and Norway and Iceland, a border would be created between the three Nordic states within the EU and the two outside.

The government took as its starting point the reality that a majority of the Storting wanted negotiations with the EU over Schengen and it decided to work to protect Norwegian interests, especially the Nordic passport union. However, they warned that they would 'carry out an evaluation of the constitutional questions tied to a new Schengen treaty' and to this end they had proposed a 'reference group' of five independent judicial experts to evaluate and advise on these questions (*Stortingsproposisjon* 50 1999: sammendrag 1.2). The government decided to continue with the negotiations with the EU already opened by the Labour government before it lost power in October 1997, but said that it would not agree to any institutional development beyond those accepted in the Schengen agreement of 19 December 1996. The judicial reference group had accepted that a new agreement could be accepted by a majority of the Storting, though they disagreed on the basis for such a decision.[4] Nevertheless, the three governing parties divided on the issue. The Christian Democrats and the Liberals joined the Labour, Conservative and Progress parties in support of the changes, while the Centre Party joined the Socialist Left as opponents. Why had the opponents of EU membership fallen apart on this issue – as they had done on the EEA – yet been so united in their opposition to 'Schengen I'? After all, from a number of perspectives, 'Schengen II' presented greater constraints on Norwegian autonomy.[5]

The government started from the basis that, dislike it as they did, Norway was part of Schengen and these relations had to be renegotiated. Given that a majority of the Storting wanted this, a refusal by the government to undertake such negotiations would have led to its demise. Though the Schengen structure reached into the heart of sovereignty, it did not cover so many aspects of socio-economic activity as the EEA. The agreement reached did not provide for any supranational authority over Norway and also meant that Norway could be bound only by laws which it had accepted, key points for the Christian Democrats and Liberals (*Stortingstidende* 1999a: 29–30).

The deal that was reached, after somewhat difficult negotiations between Norway and Iceland and the EU (*Stortingsproposisjon* 50 1999: section 2.6.1), was based on 'Schengen I' with changes arising from the inclusion of Schengen in the Amsterdam treaty. Some EU member states were unhappy about giving non-member states what they regarded as a privileged position with regard to Schengen and there were heated negotiations within the EU before a common negotiating line was agreed. At that stage it was important that the Nordic EU members had a common interest with Iceland and Norway – the continuation of the common Nordic passport union, albeit through Schengen.

In Article 6 of the Treaty of Amsterdam's protocol integrating the Schengen *acquis* into the framework of the European Union, reference was made to associating Norway with the implementation of the Schengen *acquis* and its further development 'on the basis of the Agreement signed in Luxembourg on 19 December 1996', asking that 'appropriate procedures' be agreed with Norway (and Iceland) by the Council (Duff 1997: 282–3).

With the inclusion of Schengen in the structure of the EU, the work of the Executive Committee was taken over by the EU Council. While this seemed to guarantee Norway no worse a deal than that agreed in December 1996, it was also clear that the exact nature of Norwegian involvement in decision-making, taking and implementation would also be determined by the wish of the EU members to keep their own autonomous decision-making and treaty-based cooperation (*Stortingsproposisjon* 50 1999: section 2.6.1).

The agreed answer was for Norway and Iceland, the EU members and the European Commission to participate in a Mixed Committee that would handle all Schengen matters. It would cover the implementation of Schengen rules, as well as their development, and would be an organ for the settlement of disputes between either Norway or Iceland and the EU or a member state. It could also take up matters raised by Norway or Iceland. It could meet at expert, official or ministerial level. As with the EEA, Norway would have the right to participate in the formulation of Schengen decisions on the same basis as experts from EU member states but, of course, could not participate in the decision-taking in the Council. In the Mixed Committee, Norway and Iceland would each decide whether to adopt these decisions. If Norway (or Iceland) decided not to implement a decision, then the Mixed Committee would have ninety days to negotiate a solution and, if that failed, the whole agreement would cease after a further three months. Likewise, if the Mixed Committee failed to resolve a dispute about the interpretation or practice of Schengen regulations, then cooperation would be discontinued after six months. Any of the parties could end the cooperation without notice (*Stortingsproposisjon* 50 1999: section 2.6.1). This could be seen as a major institutional change from Schengen I, though in reality the system worked much the same (Bull 1999: 70).

In his positive evaluation of the agreement to the Storting, the Minister of Foreign Affairs, Knut Vollebæk of the Christian Democrats, stated that an important element in the agreement was that it gave neither the European Court of Justice nor the Commission authority in Norway, and it would be based on international (not Community) law. He pointed out that the arrangement would allow Norway to remain informed of other EU Justice and Home Affairs matters that were not under the Schengen label but which had relevance to Schengen cooperation. Furthermore, as the European Parliament (EP) had a standing in the legislation that was agreed under Pillar One, the EU had agreed with Norway and Iceland that there should also be parliamentary cooperation between the EP and the Storting and the Icelandic Althing (*Stortingstidende* 1999a: 29–30).

One puzzle about Schengen II is not so much why the Norwegian government accepted it as why the EU was prepared to put up with what looked like a strengthened version of the EEA. The need of the Nordic EU members to reach a solution that kept their Nordic passport union intact was a strong factor, but the perceived weakness of the Norwegian government may offer an extra explanation. The very weakness of the government and its division over EU issues meant that a poor solution in Brussels could lead to the fall of the government. There had to be enough for at least the Christian Democrats and the Liberals to support. Another element in Norway gaining what was seen as a satisfactory result was the advice given the government by the judicial expert group during the negotiations with the EU which permitted the government to be more 'offensive' in its negotiations. The experts, who were divided on their views of the EU, had over fifteen meetings with Norway's negotiating team and had access to all the documents. The Commission was certainly aware of the monitoring role of the negotiations by these experts. These factors allowed the government, compared with the lead-up to the 1996 agreement, modestly to drag its feet in the 1998 to 1999 negotiations with the EU.

In effect, the government was playing a two-level game. Such an analysis of the negotiations examines both the international level (Level One between Norway and the EU) where 'national governments seek to maximize their own ability to satisfy domestic pressures, while minimizing the adverse consequences of foreign developments' and the national level (Level Two) where 'domestic groups pursue their interest by pressuring the government to adopt favorable policies...' (Putnam 1988: 434). Putnam's conditions for when conflict in a two-level game can be solved are 'win-sets' where international agreements have the support of the domestic constituencies necessary to obtain ratification. The size of these 'win-sets' are affected by three elements. The first is the 'distribution of power, preferences and possible coalitions' among the domestic constituents, with 'the lower the cost of "no-agreement" to constituents, the smaller the win-set' (Putnam 1988: 442). Second, the breadth of the 'win-set' will also depend on domestic arrangements about the autonomy of decision-makers and ratification processes (ibid.: 448). His view is that 'the stronger a state is in terms of autonomy from domestic pressures, the weaker its relative bargaining position internationally' (ibid.: 449). The 'win-set' also relates to the negotiators' strategies. A small 'win-set' means that while negotiators may know what to try for, their limited room for manoeuvre resulting from domestic constraints could lead to a breakdown in negotiations (ibid.: 450). However, Level One negotiators are 'often in collusion', helping each other to get an agreement ratified (ibid.: 451).

Thus the seemingly weak position of the government could be seen as a strength at the negotiating table in Brussels, especially as both the Commission and at least the Nordic EU states could see their way to 'collude' with the Norwegian negotiators. Although there was still a majority that could be relied upon to ratify any Schengen agreement, it had become more precarious after the 1997 election and an adverse evaluation by the judicial experts and/or by the Foreign Minister of any deal could have led to its rejection by the Storting.[6] The Foreign Minister, while more 'pro-European' than most of his Christian Democrat colleagues, could not be seen to support an agreement that was perceived as 'worse' than Schengen I. Given that what could be offered was dependent mainly on Schengen I, there was only modest room for manoeuvre but this was nevertheless exploited by the minority government. Furthermore, the presence of the three Nordic EU states increased the interest of the EU side in 'colluding' with Norway to gain a suitable settlement.

The arrangement with the Mixed Committee thus allowed Norway the possibility to accept or reject Schengen legislation and, if accepted, then to introduce it internally in Norway (*Stortingstidende* 1999a: 30, Vollebæk). Also Norway was able to make its input into the formulation of such policy and had contact with the wider justice and police cooperation in the EU.

The opponents of the new agreement compared it with the existing one and found no improvement. While the Foreign Minister talked about Norway having influence in the new system, for Centre Party opponents it was a matter of whether Norway could be 'governed and managed according to our own regulations and basic law' and whether Norwegian citizens' interests and integrity could be looked after according to the democratic and human rights principles and traditions 'on which we have built until now' (*Stortingstidende* 1999a: 39, Gløtvold, Centre Party, author's translation). The Socialist Party agreed with the Centre Party that the vote should have been under paragraph 93 of the constitution and saw the agreement bringing Norway further into unwelcome police cooperation with the EU states (*Stortingstidende* 1999a: 38, Valle). The move to have the vote under paragraph 93 was lost by eighty-one votes to twenty-three, while the agreement was accepted by eighty-five votes to nineteen (*Stortingstidende* 1999b).

Implementing Schengen

The programme and institutions

The decision-making process in Schengen and other EU judicial and police matters settled down after the Amsterdam treaty was ratified (which was only in 1999) and after the agreement between Norway, Iceland and the EU became operative on 25 March 2001. The October 1999 meeting of EU justice and interior ministers in Tampere set out an ambitious programme of work between EU states that built on agreements in an earlier Council meeting in Vienna and gave substance to the notion in the Amsterdam treaty of the 'Progressive establishment of an area of freedom, security and justice' (Finnish presidency of the EU 2000). It demonstrated that further cooperation in this area would be pursued within the EU. The expansion of EU involvement in justice, police cooperation and frontiers and the inclusion of Schengen in two pillars of the EU muddied the borders between that agreement and EU cooperation.

The EU Council and Group of Experts meet to discuss such matters in two formats. One is for non-Schengen matters and includes all EU members. The other is the Mixed Committee, which normally excludes the UK and Ireland from voting, but which includes Norway and Iceland. The Commission and the Council have to agree what matters should be taken under which of the two headings, Schengen or non-Schengen, and they do not always see eye to eye. If matters come under the Schengen heading, then Norway and Iceland attend what is a Mixed Committee and sometimes Norway and Iceland are invited to attend discussion of non-Schengen matters, but that is at the EU members' discretion.

An example is that of the European arrest warrants. The Commission considered that it should be a Schengen matter, but the UK opposed this ruling and was supported by the Council legal service. This meant that Iceland and Norway were excluded from the discussions on a European arrest warrant. Nevertheless, the Council presidency invited Iceland and Norway to be associated with the agreement.

The Labour and 'cooperation' governments

Mr Stoltenberg's minority Labour government, in its White Paper on Europe in May 2001, presented cooperation over judicial matters in a positive light. It mentioned Norwegian cooperation on justice matters within other forums such as the Council of Europe, Interpol, Nordic cooperation and the Baltic Sea region, but considered cooperation within the EU to be 'broader and more integrated than other cooperation'. The government wanted the 'tightest possible cooperative connection with the EU members' justice cooperation' (*Stortingsmelding* 12 2000). Norway was negotiating with the EU in a number of areas, including Europol and Eurodac, the registry of fingerprints. It was pointed out that Norway's Nordic EU neighbours were also cooperating within the EU over asylum and migration matters, issues not covered by Schengen. However, the implication – made quite clear – was that Norway would have to get more closely involved in these matters as they affected Schengen issues.

In the parliamentary debate the Minister of Justice, Hanne Harlem, portrayed the development of criminality that faced Norway as part of a wider international scene that needed a more coordinated response between the authorities of various countries. Norway was to be associated with the EU's Tampere programme, 'to a greater or lesser extent', and this included cooperation over Europol, Schengen, Eurojust, the European police academy and a convention on criminal law. In the case of Europol, Norway was the first non-EU state to sign an agreement with the EU version of Interpol in May 2001, and this allowed practical participation, with a Norwegian liaison officer based in the organization's headquarters in the Hague. The Minister was able to report that Norway had been recognized as 'a good cooperation partner' and that police cooperation through SIS had already provided results for Norway. Also, the justice department had accepted an offer from the Swedish EU presidency to take part as an observer in Eurojust meetings.[7] The Norwegian Police Academy had met with the European Police Academy in discussions about improved police training in the EU. The Justice Ministry had responded positively to attend meetings working on an EU convention on criminal law cooperation when such matters were 'Schengen-relevant' (*Stortingstidende* 2001b: 3159).

The other parties reflected their earlier feelings about 'Schengen II' in their comments. The Christian Democrat spokesman (Steensnæs) pointed to all this cooperation as what could be achieved without full EU membership but was concerned about the consequences for Norway's refugee and asylum policy, while the Conservative spokesman (Hernæs) preferred cooperation with the EU as a member and stressed fighting criminality rather than being concerned with refugees and asylum-seekers. Johan Jakobsen from the Centre Party rehearsed the criticisms of many of the EU member states' asylum and refugee policies by the UN High Commissioner for Refugees (*Stortingstidende* 2001b: 3159–61). Carl I. Hagen of the Progress Party stressed the importance of Schengen cooperation in moving towards stronger control of access to Europe to decrease the numbers of illegal immigrants and smugglers of people (*Stortingstidende* 2001b: 3154), quite a different emphasis from that of the Christian Democrats and the Labour Minister.

The Labour government was basking in the warm spillover from Schengen cooperation into other areas, while the Centre Party and the Socialist Left could say 'We told you so.' Even before 11 September 2001 international events – an increased flow of people across frontiers and more cross-border crime – seemed to point towards increased cooperation on justice and police matters for a small country such as Norway. This was accepted by all Norwegian politicians, the points of dispute were about the most appropriate forums and extent to which Norway might have to change its own ways – in other words, adapt.

The European platform of the 'cooperation government' that came to power in October 2001 mentioned Schengen as one of the 'suitable cooperative arrangements with the EU'. Building further on formal and informal cooperation with the EU on justice policy is included in its goals concerning the EU and EEA. In relation to Europe's global responsibility, there is specific mention of working to ensure that refugees and asylum-seekers who come to Europe are treated in accordance with the UN refugee convention. Active use of European cooperative organs in the work for human rights and to give the UN an active role in the international cooperation against terrorism are also listed. The government stated its wish to develop common Nordic standpoints on, *inter alia*, cooperation over justice policy and the fight against crime (*Stortingsmelding* 27 2002: vedlegg 1, pp. 3–5).

Refugee and immigration policy is one area where there was some political disagreement. It is an area where Norway has, in theory, retained its independence of action. While it is not part of the Schengen agreement with the EU states, this agreement, according to the Minister of Local Government and Regional Development in the 'cooperation government', 'has had a significant impact on our immigration policy' (Solberg 2002: 2). The increased interconnectedness of issues such as immigration, asylum, visas, international crime and terrorism has made it difficult to deal with them in a compartmentalized fashion, making the distinction between Schengen and non-Schengen or between Pillar One and Pillar Three justice policies harder to discern. The factors affecting these issues are external to Norway (and the EU) and the response by the EU tends to set the pace for the rest of Europe. Should Norway get too out of step with the EU, for example by being more liberal in its asylum policy, it will not only have to answer questions internationally about being a safe haven,[8] it will find that genuine asylum-seekers and those abusing the system will both target its shores rather than more difficult points of entry into Europe. Likewise a more restrictive policy may bring a reaction from neighbours who have to deal with the surplus cases.[9] The flow of people from the outside to Europe comes to resemble a market with restrictions in one area rarely staunching demand, more deflecting it elsewhere. This leaves Norway less and less leeway in its immigration and asylum policies. Indeed, the 'cooperation government', though consisting of parties that have traditionally favoured a more liberal approach on these subjects, has tightened up the law on, for example, refugee status (Johnsen 2002). In other words, on both Schengen and non-Schengen matters, Norway will increasingly have to follow the 'market leader', the EU. This will also fit in with some of the internal political pressures – for example, from the Progress Party – to fall in line with what is perceived as a tougher EU policy towards immigration and refugees (*Stortingstidende* 2001b: 3154). Norway will also have to reflect the increasing overlap between Justice and Home Affairs matters and ESDP issues as the 'war on terrorism' affects the EU more. In the EU's 'European Security Strategy', adopted in December 2003, three of the five 'key threats' – terrorism, state failure and organized crime – directly affect the internal affairs of member states, a matter reflected in the call for 'better coordination between external action and Justice and Home Affairs policies' in the EU (cited in Missiroli 2003: 324–33). This development can only add to the already complicated links between Norway and the EU.

Conclusions

The policy areas covered by the Third Pillar of the Maastricht treaty, changed by the Amsterdam treaty and partially implemented through the Schengen process are those which reflect two important tasks of the modern state, to provide both security and justice for those living within the state. In doing this, the state must protect the nation and society and also maintain the rule of law. As yet, the EU has taken over few of these tasks, though it has provided a common approach in the external aspect of the tasks and has encouraged the establishment progressively of 'an area of freedom, security and justice' (Treaty of Amsterdam, Article 73 I) consequent to the abolition of most barriers to the free movement of persons internally.

Norway has had to respond to the growing level of EU cooperation over 'justice' matters from the early 1990s onwards. A response was required first because of potential Norwegian membership of the EU and then because of actual Danish, Finnish and Swedish membership. This provided a break with Norway's previous external reference point on such matters, the Nordic states. Adaptation to agreed Nordic standards was fairly painless,[10] but that to the EU would be more costly. Being on the outside of the decision-making and decision-taking in the Schengen system would have meant either getting out of step with the Nordic neighbours – and eventually building barriers with them – or signing a blank cheque by accepting Schengen rules in an important section of justice policy. In two steps, Norway again chose a form of association that allowed a distinct input into the decision-making, one that was strengthened by the presence of three like-minded Nordic EU members. However, Norway had to rely on those Nordic states, and other friendly member states, at the decision-taking stage. There was still the possibility of Norwegian rejection of Schengen rules but that would have been a Samson-like response that would have demolished Norway's association with Schengen. This has pointed to a fairly acquiescent Norwegian policy on Schengen matters, though a streak of intransigence was shown by the centrist government that negotiated Schengen II. This allowed an institutional structure more to its liking than that of the EEA, though the net effect will be little different.

Justice, police, immigration and asylum policies have traditionally reflected the culture and institutions of Norway. After the Second World War the country had an open-door policy for immigrants and asylum-seekers but found few takers from outside the Nordic region. The country was lightly policed, as the crime rate was low. Modest adaptation was needed to fit policies into a Nordic framework, with its achievement of a Nordic passport union. Norway pursued a liberal immigration policy, with restrictions on labour immigration being introduced in 1975 'at the same time as several European countries introduced similar restrictions'. Since then immigration has been allowed for EEA citizens and for other foreign 'highly skilled labour' (Ministry of Local Government and Regional Development 2002: 2). Internally, the trade unions and the anti-immigration Progress Party have pushed to shut the door more tightly, a process helped by the restrictions introduced by the EU members. These have not only fed into Norway through the Schengen agreement but have also provided a lead for Norway. Likewise, policing has reacted to internal demands for a response to the perception of increased crime and to external requests for Norway to keep up in its anti-terror and anti-international crime responses. As Norwegian society has come to resemble more closely that in the rest of Western Europe, so have the 'stumbling blocks' on the path to 'an open global society' – violence, terror, crime and the change in the nature of migration – become more apparent (Solberg 2002: 1). The efforts to overcome, or at least respond to, what are global phenomena is unlikely to be undertaken purely at a national level. The most likely framework for collective action by all the Nordic states is that of the EU. The 1995 enlargement made sure that Norway, even if it did not become an EU member, would be dragged along by its Nordic EU neighbours. The only question was the extent to which it would pick up its feet and walk instead of being pulled along.

8 Change, choice and conclusions

> You pays your money and you takes your choice.
>
> (*Punch*, vol. 10, 1846, p. 17)

Norway and the EU in changing times

This book has examined Norway's relations with European integration, especially in the form of the European Union since the country decided against EU membership in November 1994. In the decade after that decision, Norway has changed the political colours of its government and, despite its burgeoning petroleum economy, has come to resemble other West European countries in some of its culture and in its openness to the forces of globalization (Udgaard 2004). It has also been tied to the EU by the EEA for over a decade and has built up a relationship with EU member states in the fields of defence and security and justice and police matters.

During this time the other partner in the relationship – the EU – has also changed. This has included the Lisbon Strategy aimed at making the EU more competitive in the world market. A majority of members are part of the Economic and Monetary Union and now share one currency, the euro. Institutionally, it has been reformed by the treaties of Amsterdam and Nice and by a number of European Council decisions that have developed the way that the EU does business. The EU has also undergone an introspective discussion concerning its future in the form of the European Convention and the planned treaty on the constitution. These institutional changes have been associated with the main development in the EU, that of the May 2004 enlargement with its inclusion of ten new members. These developments will be briefly examined to see how they have affected Norway and how it has reacted.

Internal EU developments

The Lisbon Strategy

The EEA provides a continuous process for the extension of market legislation to the EEA EFTA states. Certain other areas associated with the creation of the single market were included. However, it is restricted to the areas covered by the 1992 agreement and conspicuously cannot include innovations within the EU framework since then. In the European Policy Platform of the 'cooperation government' there was a recognition that there would be developments within the EU in areas not covered by the EEA and that one of these would be the Union's strategy for making its economy 'more competitive, socially cohesive and sustainable in the period 2000–10, among other things by further developing the internal market (the Lisbon Strategy)'.[1] It was noted that the EEA agreement did not allow Norway 'to participate directly in new cross-sectoral cooperation areas and forms of cooperation in the EU such as the Lisbon Strategy' (UD 2002: sections 2.2.2 and 2.3).

Later in the Platform the government listed ten bullet-points in relation to the Lisbon Strategy that aimed at closer Norwegian links with the strategy, policy action within Norway to keep pace with aspects of the strategy (for example, promoting lifelong learning) and contact with the social partners (such as business and the unions) and EFTA over the strategy (UD 2002: section 4.2.1). The Lisbon Strategy represents a move away from a more rule-based EU towards the 'open method of coordination' which uses more voluntary and intergovernmental forms of cooperation such as benchmarking and best practice – methods with which Norway is familiar within the OECD – but, by doing so, excludes Norwegian participation on the basis of the EEA agreement (Traavik 2002). The Lisbon Strategy is a dual-edged sword for Norway. On the one hand, it can mean a move away from the formal Community-based decision-making in which Norway is involved through the EEA. This could negatively affect Norway's ability to influence the likes of EU social policy, an area that has developed significantly (*Stortingsmelding* 27 2002: section 5.4). On the other hand, it allows states to choose the method of achieving various goals and uses means less rigid than legislation, thereby allowing EEA EFTA states to shadow such activities and also to cooperate on such matters with the EU through EFTA.

EMU

Another area where Norway has been on the outside has been that of Economic and Monetary Union (EMU). As a non-EU country, it has not had the opportunity to become a member of the EMU. However, any divisive impact has been softened by the non-membership of the EMU of the three

EU states perhaps closest to Norway, the UK, Denmark and Sweden. Furthermore, as a major oil-producing state, Norway's economy is often out of synchronization with that of the EU (*Stortingsmelding* 27 2002: section 5.5) and in monetary matters can be more affected by the value of the dollar more than by that of the euro, as its oil sales are designated in dollars.

Nevertheless, the existence of the EMU and the policies it pursues clearly affect the Norwegian economy, especially the macro-economic stability of the country (*Stortingsmelding* 27 2002: section 5.5). This has led the government and the Bank of Norway to maintain close contact with the EU Council of Economic and Finance Ministers, the European Commission and the European Central Bank on EMU affairs. The poor performance of the economies of the euro-zone during 2003 compared with the UK and US economies and the slackness in the treatment of French and German breaking of the Stability Pact have made the EMU less attractive in the short term. Should the UK, Denmark and Sweden, as well as the new members of the EU, become full members of EMU, and should the EU deal with some of its structural weaknesses, it will offer a powerful economic magnet to a country such as Norway, an overwhelmingly part of whose trade would be with the area.

Institutional and policy changes

The Amsterdam and Nice treaties made a number of changes to the Maastricht treaty, though they did not alter the fundamental shape of the EU's internal market, the basis of the EEA. However, with each change, especially in the decision-making process, the EEA agreement became more outdated.[2]

Plans by the EU to hold a convention leading up to a treaty on a constitution threatened a further ageing of the EEA agreement, though the failure to reach agreement on such a treaty at the end of 2003 gave some respite. In the general debate surrounding the convention there was a near silence from the Norwegian government, which no doubt felt it was not appropriate to have views about changes in an organization of which it was not a member. Furthermore, any statement beyond the most bland would have split the government. Jan Petersen, the foreign minister, speaking before the European Council had considered the treaty on the constitution, described the convention as confirming that the EU would continue as intergovernmental cooperation with supranational element in some areas. However, he admitted that the transfer of authority from the member states to the EU was greater than in previous treaty changes and foresaw further treaty revisions (Petersen 2003). A similar prognostication could be made by anti-membership politicians, only with a greater sense of foreboding. For the time being the EU, for all its changes in the 1990s, has not evolved into anything too different from the creation that emerged with Maastricht.

EEA and enlargement

The details of the enlargement process were soon finalized with the Copenhagen Summit in December 2002 providing the showpiece ceremony whereby ten states were welcomed as members as from 1 May 2004, two others (Romania and Bulgaria) handed rain-checks and Turkey given another, but more definite, ambiguous promise. Article 128 of the EEA agreement stipulated that a country joining the EU should also apply to join the EEA. As pointed out by Kim Traavik, the State Secretary dealing with the negotiations, 'the EU enlargement negotiations have in effect also been conducted on behalf of the EEA EFTA countries, since the adaptations and transitional periods agreed upon will by and large also have to apply in the EEA' (Traavik 2003b). External events (the EU enlargement) were to the fore and there was little opportunity for states such as Norway to alter this process. It is therefore not surprising that there was little difference among the Norwegian political parties about the need to manage the consequences of enlargement for Norway, though there were some nuances over detail. The main point was that the EEA should continue for an enlarged EU.

Agreeing the terms for an enlarged EEA proved not to be so easy. Norway had free trade agreements with the new member states, but these covered certain agricultural and fisheries exports which had to take on the common external tariffs of the Common Agricultural Policy. Norway had four main concerns in its negotiations about the extended EEA: keeping in line with the EU enlargement, finance, fisheries and agriculture.

The first issue required the negotiations to finish in time so that all twenty-eight states (the twenty-five members of the enlarged EU and the three EEA EFTA states) could ratify any agreement to allow it to start on 1 May 2004, together with the EU enlargement.[3] So negotiations could not be allowed to continue for too long. The question of a 'technical updating' of the EEA agreement had already been considered from the Norwegian side. This involved changing those elements in the EEA agreement that were reflections of Treaty of Rome articles that had been changed by the Maastricht, Amsterdam and Nice treaties (Traavik 2002). However, this hope was placed to one side and the main aim of enlarging the EEA to cover the new members was pursued. Even so, the process, which lasted from January through to March 2004, was not made easier by the multilateral nature of the negotiations. Though the European Commission was negotiating on behalf of the then fifteen EU member states, with a mandate from the European Council, the talks were joined by all ten new members and the three EEA EFTA states, though Norway stressed close cooperation with the other two EFTA states and bilateral links with the EU states and the new adherents (*Stortingsproposisjon* 3 2003: section 4.2).

In the period 1994 to 1998 Norway had paid Nkr926 million to the EU's structural funds, with an unused Nkr75 million being given back. In the five-year period 1999–2003 Norway paid out Nkr942 million. There would anyhow be a need to consider the period after 31 December 2003, and the Storting was willing to vote Nkr996 million for the following period. However, the negotiations to extend the EEA intervened and the European Commission wanted the EEA EFTA states to pay in the new period something like twenty to thirty times what they had previously contributed. Contributions from these states were to be judged along the same lines as those of member states, an approach that the EEA EFTA states rejected. They pointed out that factors such as the CAP and the fisheries policy were not included in the EEA agreement, and that payment should only reflect policies related to the agreement. The Norwegian Minister involved in the negotiations stated that 'we do not consider the principles presented by the European Commission for calculating the future financial contributions of the EEA EFTA states to be either fair or balanced' (Traavik 2003b).The EU tied payment to the increased market access gained by broadening the EEA.

The EU brought the extension of the EEA into question and, in the end, Norway decided that a special Norwegian contribution was needed, extra to any agreed EEA sum, to keep the EEA afloat (*Stortingsproposisjon* 3 2003: section 5.2.4). This solution was accepted and Norway agreed to pay an *annual* contribution to the two funds – one EEA EFTA and one purely Norwegian – of Nkr1,882 million, some ten times the figure it was paying in the previous period.[4] Money from the EEA EFTA fund would contribute to social and economic solidarity in the EU, especially in the case of the new members, while all the Norwegian fund would go to the new members, and would be spent particularly in the areas of the environment, better border controls and improved administration of justice, all areas of particular concern to Norway (ibid.: 5.2.5). The government's evaluation was that the negotiations satisfied Norwegian interests 'even though the economic contribution was increased manifold compared with the current loan and grant arrangement' (ibid.: section 8, author's translation). A price had been paid to keep the EEA link. Nevertheless, the government was keen to claim that the contribution was worth while in political and economic terms and had nothing to do with other aspects of the deal. Traavik (2003b) declared that 'it is misleading to claim that our contributions should be considered merely "payment" for herring and mackerel, as some commentators have'. While this was no doubt true, the payments certainly helped to mollify doubters on the EU side of the negotiating table.[5]

Indeed, access for its fish exports was an area of real concern to Norway during the negotiations. Norway had had free trade agreements with the eight Central and East European states that were to join the EU and on their accession this would be changed for the less favourable Protocol 9 which regulated Norwegian fish and seafood exports to the EU. From

Norway's side, 'the EEA regime for trade in fish is not very satisfactory . . . there are high duties on certain marine products . . . [and] we are not protected against threats of anti-dumping and countervailing measures' (Traavik 2003b). Indeed, Traavik noted the shortage of fish within the EU and the need to keep free access for the sake of the EU processing industry as well as Norway's fishermen (ibid.). Nevertheless, EU fisheries policy has been hard enough to manage within the Union of the fifteen, and 2003 was not unusual in seeing a battle between the Commission and some members over fish stocks. It was unlikely that the members were going to alter an important part of the fisheries policy – its external dimension – at the behest of Norway, even when joined by some of the processing industry in new member states, in particular Poland. Norway wanted to be compensated for the loss of its free trade access to the Central and East European markets. It wanted no new barriers to trade in fish and seafood exports. Norway had a relatively strong bargaining position: the fishing and fish-processing industry at home, with its entrenched political power, was looking over the negotiators' shoulders, again creating a two-level game (see above, pp. 163–4). Furthermore, Norway had sympathetic backing for its position among the Central and East European states, not least Poland. Nevertheless, the Commission not only rejected this claim but also held out the prospect of raising the issue of Norwegian (and Icelandic) exceptions from freedom of investment and establishment in the fisheries sector. After several rounds of negotiations, an agreement was reached that represented a compromise the Norwegian government could recommend (*Stortingsproposisjon* 3 2003: section 2.3).

The new agreement gave Norway duty-free annual quotas for five years of 67,000 tonnes for frozen herring fillets and flaps ('butterflies'), 44,000 tonnes for frozen herring and 35,000 tonnes for frozen mackerel. Exports of the herring 'butterflies' over the quotas would bear a 3 per cent duty, meaning a reduction from 15 per cent from 1 May 2004 for this important export to the new EU member states. There was a promise of an examination of the quota level before 2009. The duty-free quota for frozen peeled shrimps was increased from 5,500 tonnes to 8,000 tonnes (EFTA Secretariat 2003c: *Stortingsproposisjon* 3 2003: para. 5.3.5.2). This agreement, which was in the form of a protocol to Norway's free trade agreement with the EC of 1973, thus still keeping it separate from the EEA, was portrayed by Kim Traavik (2003b) as containing 'quite generous duty-free quotas for herring and mackerel with an inbuilt allowance for growth' which would give 'the Norwegian fishing industry the compensation for the loss of free trade access to the acceding states that we set out to achieve'.

Agricultural exports proved to be relatively uncontroversial. Agricultural trade between the new adherents and Norway was small, the most important element being the duty-free Norwegian import of soft fruits and apple juice for processing. The export to Norway, mainly from Poland and Hungary, of frozen strawberries and raspberries, apple juice, rye-grass seed and cat food were all given duty-free quotas (EFTA Secretariat 2003c).

The one main domestic political issue was whether the free movement of labour between the new member states and Norway should be allowed from 1 May 2004 or whether it should be postponed. The existing EEA states were allowed to choose. The division of opinion was less within the government than between the NHO, the Confederation of Norwegian Business and Industry (2003), and the Norwegian Confederation of Trade Unions (2003). The Conservatives, reflecting the NHO position, favoured free movement of labour from the first day, while a number of Labour Party voices and the Centre Party (Kleppa 2003) wanted to postpone its early introduction. The Socialist Left Party decided that workers in the new member states should not be kept from relatively well-paid jobs, and this decision made it easier for the Labour Party leadership to accept the earlier starting date (Jagland 2003). However, a majority in the Storting – the Labour Party, the Progress Party, the Socialist Left Party and the Centre Party – attacked the government for potentially undermining Norwegian work conditions (*Aftenposten* 2004c). In the end the outside pressure of all the other EEA states (except the UK and Ireland) taking advantage of transitional measures and internal opposition took their toll. The government proposed that workers from the Central and East European new members could gain access to the labour market within Norway provided they had a work permit which would be issued 'for full-time employment at normal rates of pay and under normal working conditions' (Kommunal- og regionaldepartementet 2004: 1).

Assessing the developments

The changes that have affected the relationship between Norway and the EU in the lead-up to the 1 May 2004 enlargement are ones that Norway has had to take in its stride. In some ways, developments were kind to Norway. Sweden's rejection of EMU and the failure of the UK government to press for EMU membership have allowed Norway not to be an EEA outsider on this issue, but to have 'cover' from important (for Norway) EU members. Doubts about the running of the EMU have slowed progress in perhaps the most vital area of EU integration outside the single market. The failure by early 2004 to adopt a new treaty on the constitution has also placed a brake on the speed of the integration locomotive, though it has by no means stopped it. Even the open method of coordination points to a less *communautaire* approach to European integration. The negotiations for extending the EEA to include the new members, while not without a little drama, helped the EEA agreement to keep in step with EU enlargement.

Yet all these developments point to a greater gulf between the EEA EFTA states and the EU members. The new states will eventually have to sign up to the euro, and the governments of Denmark, Sweden and the UK have not ruled out membership. A greater emphasis on the open method could sidetrack the network of links with EU decision-making made by Norway through the EEA. Finally, enlargement has given a further tilt to the balance between the EU and EEA EFTA elements within the EEA, and it is a move away from non-EU states. Norway has shown itself skilled in adapting to all the changes, when needed, but the gains in terms of influence are becoming smaller for each adaptation demanded.

The choice for Norway

What are the options open to Norway in its relations with European integration in a post-Nice EU involved in the process of enlargement? The move from fifteen to twenty-five members brings the map of the Union closer to that of all Europe. It also means that the line of European interlocutors with the EU, of which Norway was one, has been substantially reduced, but the number of players within the system has increased. This has led to a consideration of Norway's relationship with the EU (Eide *et al.* 2003; Emerson *et al.* 2002). Three basic options seem to be open: stay with the EEA; try to change the link with the EU into something different from the EEA but which is not membership; or to apply for full membership. These options will be considered in turn.

Carry on regardless

There would be little need to consider a change from Norway's EEA link with the EU if a majority of politicians, interest groups and the public thought it to be working satisfactorily and expected it to continue to function well. Of course, all groups could be deluded, in which case alternatives should at least be examined. Nevertheless, while there is a strong current of opinion in Norway that considers that the EEA has worked well, there is perhaps a larger section of opinion that sees it coming to the end of its useful life. Opponents of the EEA want Norway to leave it, but some suggest that in the meantime Norway negotiates changes that will give greater freedom for the country to operate its own policies (for example, in regional policy, the environment, natural resources and public transport). While it seems unlikely that the EU would be interested in such a reform of the EEA agreement, the opponents make the point that if the EEA is to last for some time then an effort should be made to deal with the areas that have provoked Norwegian opinion most (Boye *et al.* 2003: 33).

However, there seems little appetite for change in Oslo. The European platform of the 'cooperation government', agreed in February 2002, opined that 'The EEA agreement is a good agreement for Norway for most sectors' (*Stortingsmelding* 27 2002: 107, author's translation). In a 2003 survey of members of the Storting, sixteen out of the twenty members responding from government parties considered that the EEA had worked 'as expected' for Norway, with only three considering that it worked 'worse than expected'.[6] The Labour Party has also been supportive of the EEA, though with less enthusiasm than the Christian Democrats: their spokesman said in May 2001, when Labour was in power, that 'we do not have any alternative to the agreement we have today' (*Stortingstidende* 2001: 3136, Haakon Blankenborg, author's translation). The White Paper of the 'cooperation government' presented a number of ways by which Norway could improve its effectiveness in the EEA, but these are unlikely to counterbalance the loss of relative weight in the EU firmament suffered after enlargement. Furthermore, as the EU undertakes more activity outside the single market the agreement will age more rapidly. This faces Norway with a dilemma, expressed by Kim Traavik:

> We have already agreed with the Commission that a limited, technical updating of the agreement should be conducted after the ten new members have acceded on 1 May [2004]. But in view of the many pressing challenges facing the enlarged EU in coming years, it seems unlikely there would be much interest in anything more than this sort of limited exercise on the part of the EU. A more comprehensive upgrading is not in the cards.
>
> (Traavik 2003c)

In Traavik's words (ibid.) the agreement is 'as good an agreement as we are likely to get under the present circumstances'.

A bilateral agreement

For those political parties and groups within Norway that are not satisfied with the EEA and firmly reject EU membership, there is a need for an alternative. Practically all recognize that some agreement has to be made with the EU, and some, such as the Christian Democrats, are satisfied with the EEA. Others want something that is less compromising of Norwegian sovereignty than the EEA, let alone EU membership, and more in line with their own vision of Norway. A booklet from the 'No to the EU' organization criticizes the EEA for undermining Norwegian sovereignty and advances alternatives. These are variations on a theme: Norway should get out of the EEA, base its trade relations with the EU on the 1973 free trade agreement plus any necessary revisions and underpinned by WTO rules, and on agreements similar to those negotiated by Switzerland. Norway would no longer be subject to the ESA or the EFTA Court and would be able to introduce its own regional, health and environmental policies, and to protect certain sectors (such as the postal service) from liberalization (Boye *et al.* 2003: 31–3).

Although Switzerland was a member of EFTA and engaged in the negotiations that led to the EEA agreement, its electorate rejected this option in a referendum on 6 December 1992. Negotiations started in 1993 between Switzerland and the EU over a bilateral solution to their relationship and an agreement was signed in 1998 and came into force in 2002. This covered seven sectors,[7] but there was no obligation on Switzerland to adopt the *acquis communautaire*, nor was there reference to institutions such as the ESA and the EFTA Court (Boye *et al.* 2003: 33). A second series of negotiations began in 2002 and covered issues such as Schengen and trade in services, but these had not reached a conclusion by the time the EEA agreement had been renegotiated (Swiss Parliament 2003).

Sverre Jervell's study of the Swiss option (2003) has also pointed to a number of differences between it and the EEA. His view is that the main difference is in the manner that the two agreements adapt to the EU's relevant regulations. The EEA agreement is an association that gives the EU the leading role, but its purpose is to translate EU laws into those of the EFTA member states which are consulted about the new laws. The Swiss agreement has no such duty to translate EU law into Swiss law, though there is an understanding that the EU and Switzerland will develop into a common legal area in the seven relevant areas of agreement. The Swiss are bound by EU law on an informal and voluntary basis – in effect they copy the relevant EU laws into their own statutes – whereas the EEA countries are bound by EU law-making through common institutions such as the ESA. The Swiss do not have a formal input to EU decision-making as do the EEA EFTA states, and the EEA is more dynamic than the Swiss agreement. The latter is, however, more intrusive in the areas of agriculture and air travel than is the EEA (Jervell 2003: 27–8).

Jervell (2003: 29–32) also points out a number of consequences of a Norwegian effort to obtain a Swiss solution. Norway would have to take over from the EEA the process of monitoring its own adoption of EU laws, allowing it to retain more of the trappings of formal sovereignty but in effect producing the same results. In exchange it would lose what influence it has on EU decision-making, and it would also have the European Commission looking over its shoulder to ensure it was keeping to the straight and narrow. Moreover, negotiations could be fraught. They would have to start from the basis of Norway leaving the EEA (which it can do with a year's notice) and using its thirty-year-old free trade agreement with the EC as a starting point. A whole range of issues would be on the table, from fisheries, veterinary controls and agriculture to the right of investment. The negotiations over the revised EEA treaty demonstrate that there is a 'harder negotiating climate' than when the EEA or the Swiss agreement was first agreed (Jervell 2003: 31, author's translation).

Furthermore, in giving notice to leave the EEA, Norway would have just a year to get another agreement in place, compared with almost ten years that were required for the Swiss agreement.

Another aspect of such an agreement is whether the EU would wish to negotiate such a deal. Jervell (2003: 29) considers that the EU is pragmatic and would try to find a practical solution with which all parties could live, and the Swiss agreement would be a precedent. However, Traavik's view is that 'a bilateral agreement of the type that the Swiss have is not a current option for our country' (2002, author's translation). This may refer to the desirability rather than the possibility, but it is in the gift of the EU to make the possible undesirable. It seems unlikely that the members of an enlarged EU would be willing to grant Norway more favourable conditions than those of the EEA agreement, unless Norway could offer an incentive. This would mean payment on a grander scale than required for the revision of the EEA in 2003 and/or payment in kind such as access to fishing grounds.

Perhaps the main reluctance about negotiating an alternative to the EEA is not in Brussels but Oslo. As recognized by those advancing other options, the EEA has support among those who opposed membership in 1994. Not only is it the preferred option of the Christian Democrats and the Liberals (and probably of the Progress Party), it is seen as the best alternative to EU membership by the Conservatives and the Labour Party leadership. Even the Social Democrats against the EU (SME) and the Labour Youth Organization and trade unions against the EU supported Norwegian adherence to the EEA (Boye *et al.* 2003: 38). Indeed, it has been left to Åslaug Haga, leader of the Centre Party, to sing the praises of the Swiss model (*Aftenposten* 2004d: 1)

Should the EEA structure collapse, there would be some sense from an EU viewpoint in having in place something like the Swiss agreement for those EFTA states that wanted it, but the European Commission would take on the task of overseeing parallel implementation of EU legislation in those countries, and access to decision-making would be dropped. The EEA may have led to some disappointments for Norway in areas such as oil and gas and trade in fish, and its institutions may challenge Norwegian autonomy, but the mechanisms had become a useful means of promoting Norwegian interests within the EU of the Fifteen. However, this is likely to be challenged by the 2004 enlargement.

Become a member

While Norway opening negotiations with a view to EU membership is not an option before the September 2005 election, there is every likelihood of just such a move after that date.

There was general agreement among the political parties that no Norwegian application should be advanced to the EU in the 2001–5 Storting.

This was the firm opinion of the Christian Democrats and the Liberals (Kristelig folkeparti 2003; Venstre 2003) and the Conservatives were obliged to accept a European Platform for the government that made no mention of EU membership. The Labour Party's manifesto for the period talked about an application 'earliest in 2005–6' (Det norske Arbeiderparti 2003). As Kim Traavik (2003b), a Conservative, described the situation: 'there is no majority favouring EU membership in the present [2001–5] Parliament'.

What chances are there of a Norwegian application in the 2005–9 Storting? The first section of this chapter has outlined how the EU has undergone change itself in the 2003–4 period, not least with enlargement. The EEA has been changed to take into account the new membership but the notion of two pillars in the EEA looks even more a fallacy than before. Enlargement at least provides an opportunity for a rethink of the question. Internally, there have been shifts in opinion concerning membership by the public, interest groups and politicians.

Public opinion

The change in public opinion can be seen from 2000 onwards. Until then opinion had been largely against membership, but thereafter views were more evenly divided until the summer of 2002, when the 'yes' to membership side started pulling away from the 'no' side. Throughout 2003 the 'yes' element had a sizeable lead, though it narrowed by the end of the year (Opinion 2003). Traavik (2003b) explained this swing to membership in terms of the enlargement process and 'the growing awareness of the shortcomings and the limitations of the EEA agreement'. It may also have reflected a greater sympathy for the EU at a time when Germany and France led the opposition to the war in Iraq and when the East and Central European countries were signing accession treaties with the EU, factors that faded by the end of 2003 when the Swedish electorate's rejection of EMU, trouble over the EMU's Stability Pact and the failure to agree on a constitutional treaty were more in the news. The sustainability of any public support for EU membership will depend primarily on the perception of the Union and the extent to which it may impinge on Norwegian interests and identity. With an opinion poll in early 2004 giving the 'yes' side a nine-point lead over the 'no' supporters (*Aftenposten* 2004e), it would seem that opinion is malleable and more likely voting for its interests. Those that see membership as a challenge to Norwegian identity seem to be a much smaller group than in 1994 and certainly than in 1972 and are mostly confined to the Centre and Christian Democrat parties. The unknown factor is the extent to which Progress Party voters are irreducible opponents, who see the EU as being 'foreign', or are opponents mainly because of their interest or are supporters of membership for economic reasons.

Interests

As well as changes in public opinion, there were also some significant shifts in views expressed by those leading interest groups. During the campaign leading to the 1994 vote the Norwegian Confederation of Trade Unions (LO) was split on the issue, with a special congress voting narrowly against membership (Archer and Sogner 1998: 71). By 2003 the leader of the LO, Gerd-Liv Valla, was re-evaluating her opposition to membership in the light of enlargement. While she was unwilling to support membership, she saw enlargement as removing one reason against Norway joining and called for a 'nuanced debate' (*Aftenposten* 2003b).

A survey of employers' associations and trade unions conducted at the end of 2003 showed all eleven of the former that replied in favour of a new EU application by Norway, whereas the ten trade union replies were split down the middle (see Appendix 1). Indeed, the 'No to the EU' campaign was still able to claim that support from the trade unions was increasing, with the largest amount of funding coming from the LO's biggest member, Fagforbundet, which has 300,000 members, mainly in the public sector. They were also receiving support from their traditional bankroll of the main agricultural organizations, Norges Bondelag (Norwegian Farmers' Union), Norges Bonde- og Småbrukarlag (Norwegian Farmers and Smallholders Union) and Norsk Landbrukssamvirke (Federation of Norwegian Agricultural Cooperation) (*Aftenposten* 2003c). One industry that had been key in the previous campaigns was fisheries. The threat to Norway's markets for fish exports as long as the country remained outside the EU meant that there was a much greater division of opinion between those fishing, who wanted to maintain Norwegian control of territorial waters, and those selling the final product. Indeed, one of the main fisheries organizations (FHL) joined with the main employers' association (NHO) to form 'Kysten for EU' (The Coast for the EU) in early 2004 (Udgaard 2004). Also since 1994, the EU had, through the EEA, involved itself in Norway's oil and gas industry and the industry had a much greater incentive to work from within the EU. The leader of the National Association of Processing Industries, which included industries making refined oil products, wrote in favour of full membership, noting that the EEA was 'no longer good enough for Norwegian industry' (*Aftenposten* 2003d, author's translation). The shift in the views of key elements of business and commerce may make a difference in the financing of a referendum campaign. However, the views of the trade unions will be important politically – their split in 1994 seemed to have confirmed Labour opponents in their determination to vote 'no'. Should the LO come out in favour of membership the Labour Party will feel more comfortable in running a pro-EU campaign.

Political parties

Most important, there have been developments in the view of the political parties and the members of the Storting. The Conservatives remain committed to Norway becoming a member of the EU 'as soon as possible' (Høyre 2003, author's translation). The Centre Party has, if anything, sharpened its criticisms of the EU (Senterpartiet 2003) and the Socialist Left Party has promised to 'work against Norwegian membership of the EU' (Sosialistisk Venstreparti 2003, author's translation).[8]

The four parties where there could be fluidity are the Christian Democrats, the Liberals, the Labour Party and the Progress Party. The Christian Democrats is seen as a 'no' party but it leaves open the possibility of a new application, though only after the electorate have agreed that course in a referendum, with a second referendum to be held on the outcome on any negotiations (Kristelig folkeparti 2003). Furthermore, Kjell Magne Bondevik, the Christian Democrat Prime Minister, stated that he would reconsider the whole question of membership in the light of changes (*Aftenposten* 2003e). He placed the question of Norwegian membership in the context not just of enlargement and the proposed constitutional treaty but also of 'whether we will see an EU with more differentiated integration, where groups of member states will move forward and seek enhanced cooperation in certain specific areas' (Bondevik 2003). This was interpreted by some as the Prime Minister raising the question of possible EU membership without participation in all the dimensions of integration, 'EU light', a concept that was received with little enthusiasm in Brussels (Hellstrøm 2003). The negative reaction from key party members (Spence 2003) led Mr Bondevik to confirm that he remained a 'no man' (*Aftenposten* 2003f). Nevertheless, he was also willing to 'look at it [membership] anew' (ibid., author's translation).

The Liberal Party is also a traditional 'no' party that has shown some willingness to think again. In its 2001–5 programme it promises not to bring the issue up and considers that any new application can be considered only after a referendum. Nevertheless, it notes that enlargement, closer cooperation over defence and strengthened and more comprehensive economic cooperation will make a new evaluation and discussion of Norwegian membership necessary (Venstre 2003).

The Progress Party has been the quiet man of the EU issue. The reason is simple – it is an issue that splits the party. The leadership has thus chosen to ignore it for as long as possible and not to treat it as a party issue. The party's leader, Carl I. Hagen, teased the parliament by disclosing that he had moved from being personally in favour of membership to being a 'maybe' (*Stortingstidende* 2001a: 3146). Of the nine Progress Party members that replied to a survey in late 2003, three declared themselves in favour of membership, three against and three had no opinion or 'did not know'. Considering this was a third of the parliamentary party, the leadership's tolerant approach has some justification. The party programme insists that a referendum should be held before a new application is submitted, and that such a vote should only be called once it was apparent that a shift in public opinion about the EU had taken place. Until then the 'people's no' of 1994 should be respected. The party would allow its representatives to campaign for either the pro- or the anti-side in a referendum but would be united in voting for whatever the people decided (Fremskrittspartiet 2003). Meanwhile it established an EU committee to consider a variety of questions related to the membership issue (Natland 2003).

As in 1972 and 1994, the reaction of the Labour Party will be a key element in any renewed application to the EU. However, it should be remembered that the party in the early years of the new millennium is not as large and dominant in Norwegian politics as it was in 1972 or even in 1994. Also it has the experience of recommending membership twice and seeing its advice rejected by the electorate on both occasions, in 1972 in a battle that split the party (see Chapter 3). Its leaders are thus likely to approach the question with some caution. Nevertheless, the party's foreign affairs spokesman, Thorbjørn Jagland, confirmed his role as a strong campaigner for membership when he launched his book *Ten Theses on the EU and Norway* in late 2003, containing arguments for Norwegian membership as soon as possible (*Aftenposten* 2003g).

While the anti-membership group within the Labour Party remains active, there were signs that it was losing support in the parliamentary party. At the start of 2004 four Labour members of the Storting, Torstein Rudihagen, Asmund Kristoffersen, Gunnar Halvorsen and Kjell Engebretsen, announced that they were moving from a 'no' position to that of accepting membership, enlargement being an important factor in their decisions (*Aftenposten* 2004a). Another former 'no man', Bjarne Håkan Hanssen, the leader of the party's European committee, declared himself to be rethinking the issue and to be on the fence (*Aftenposten* 2004b). While it seems that the Labour Party is becoming more of a 'yes' party than in 1994, it should be remembered that, with the strong growth of the Socialist Left Party, there is another home for left-wing membership opponents.

One hundred years: enough?

The general election of September 2005 will be key in determining Norway's course in relation to the EU for two reasons. First, it will determine the colour of Norway's government. Should the centre-right government continue in place, it seems unlikely that the Conservatives will continue to be bound by a promise not to raise the membership issue. However, the price to pay could well be a referendum before an application is sent to Brussels, as well as one after the negotiations. A Labour victory could lead to a coalition with the Socialist Left and Centre parties, an idea backed by Jens Stoltenberg (Economist Intelligence Unit 2003b: 7–8). Nevertheless, both potential coalition partners have warned that they would not join a government that applied for membership (*Aftenposten* 2003h). A referendum before an application could take the decision out of the hands of the politicians and place it firmly with the electorate.

The other importance of the election lies in the necessity of passing a treaty leading to Norwegian membership by a three-quarters majority of the Storting. Given that the membership of the Storting will be increased to 169 at that election, forty-three members could block such a law. If a referendum was in favour of Norway joining, the Conservatives, the Progress Party and the Labour Party (with possibly a handful of dissenters) would support the motion. Probably most of the Christian Democrats and any Liberals would also give way to 'the people's will'. However, the Centre Party would maintain its opposition, as would most of the Socialist Left Party. Both these parties will be campaigning hard in 2005 on the EU issue, especially in the shadow of celebrations of 100 years of Norwegian independence. The vote in parliament could be close.

What sort of treaty will members be voting on? Of course, Norway has already negotiated a membership treaty, in 1994, but the EU has moved on since then and Norway will have had almost a decade of experience of the EEA. The key issues will be agriculture and fisheries, especially the latter (Eide *et al.* 2003: 103). As mentioned, Norwegian interests there are more divided than they were in 1994, but there is also recognition that the EU's fisheries policy has been a failure. Especially if Iceland were to apply for membership at the same time, Norway could have a strong hand in negotiations, with the prospect of the EU moving to a fisheries policy closer to those of the two applicants. Norway would also be a net contributor to the EU budget, which would make it an attractive partner for the new EU members. Norway could complete negotiations in order to enter the EU with Bulgaria and Romania (and possibly Croatia) some time in 2009.

Should there be two referendums, one before negotiations start, one after they finish? By holding a referendum after negotiations have been concluded, as in 1972 and 1994, there is the chance of a 'no'. This may affect the EU's willingness to spend time and trouble on such negotiations and the prospect could deter at least the Labour Party from risking a third bloody nose. While having one referendum before negotiations would solve that problem, it might be considered handing the government a blank cheque. Some groups, especially the farmers and fishermen, may reasonably want to see the details of the deal they were being asked to accept. A referendum both before and after negotiations would address this argument. However, it would be more likely to lead to a dual 'yes'. Sceptics (not opponents) may more readily vote for negotiations to start, on the grounds that they could reject the outcome. After the negotiations, having voted 'yes' once, they could decide that a second positive vote was not too difficult. More important, the first referendum would allow the pro-membership groups to start their campaign at the same time as the 'no' side. In both 1972 and 1994 the 'yes' side was unable to campaign fully until the results of the negotiations were known, by which time opponents were in charge of the battle. A referendum on opening negotiations would not see the pro-membership groups so restrained.

In the end any move would again depend on the will of the people. All that has been written here suggests that a third referendum will not be a re-run of that in 1972. It will not even be about a straight 'in' or 'out' but more about the form of relationship with the EU: membership, the EEA or some new form of agreement. The campaign will resemble more that of 1994 but with arguments even more balanced and less clear-cut. Should the vote again be 'no', it will mirror not just Norwegian desire for autonomy, possibly boosted by the centenary celebrations, but more a reflection on the state of the EU. Should the vote be 'yes', it will reflect more a consideration of the best way Norway can gain influence than any great enthusiasm for European integration. Should Norway join, other members of the EU would soon find (if they did not already know) that Norwegians will continue to maintain many of their preferences, traditions and traits, born of their history, institutions and identity.

Conclusions

By 2004 Norway had been in the EEA for a decade. It spent that time voluntarily outside the EU, yet has become closely tied to all aspects of the EU. What can be said about Norway's relations with the process and aims of European integration during this time?

The functional areas

The EEA

The form of Norway's link with the EU by the EEA is different after some ten years from it was when first envisioned. It is more skewed towards the EU side and basically provides a means of transposing EU single market legislation on to the statute books of the EEA EFTA countries. Nevertheless, it has gone beyond that, allowing Norway, especially, to be tied closely to the EU decision-making domain in the relevant areas. This has led to a substantial blurring of what previously could be regarded as external to the Norwegian political system. To what extent do Norwegian laws and regulations have their genesis in EU law? It is hard to tell, as much of the *acquis communautaire* adopted in 1992 was either outdated or was not relevant for Norway. It is certainly more than the 5–10 per cent given as an estimate of the amendments to Norwegian laws (OECD 2003a: 17), as this does not include secondary legislation. The external – EU – legislation has become an important and regular part of the Norwegian domestic polity.

Furthermore, an element of the Norwegian state and society has become more internationalized. The central administration has become Europeanized, though in a partial and limited way. Likewise, some elements of civil society have become more engaged in the EU decision-making through expert committees. The wider public has been least engaged in the process of integration, though this has also been the case in EU member states. The danger is that of a widening gulf between a more Europeanized civil service, political community and economic interest groups and a population at least indifferent to the subject. Decreasing the extent of Europeanization would limit influence. One option is to inform the public more widely of what is happening, as suggested by the 2002 White Paper (*Stortingsmelding* 27 2002: para. 0.2.7). This could more effectively be done – and in a critical way – by those elements of civil society engaged in decision-making in Brussels. There is a role here for the employers' association – and the NHO has sponsored a study of membership and its alternatives (Emerson *et al.* 2002) – and the trade unions, the leadership of which has stayed fairly mute about the EU.

Schengen

Cooperation within the Schengen framework has been more intergovernmental than has been the case with EEA issues. Nevertheless, there has been a move towards using the 'Community method' in these areas and Norway remains locked out of the decision-taking, though present at the decision-making stage. The whole process has been made easier by the pre-existing Nordic arrangements and the presence of three Nordic states within the EU. The Nordic states collectively have now chosen the EU framework as a major arena for their response to the increased international demands on justice and policing policies. Norway is part of this system, with a voice but without a vote. Nevertheless, the Schengen II arrangement is a sweet deal for Norway though it arose from specific circumstances and may be eroded by the EU's Council increasingly defining issues as 'non-Schengen', by the pressure of new demands from new members and by a lack of understanding of Norway's special position by those members.

CFSP and ESDP

Norwegian foreign policy has been both focused on its immediate neighbourhood, especially Russia, and global in its range. Norway has been a member of the Security Council, has participated in UN peacekeeping, has a strong record on aid to poorer states and has engaged itself diplomatically in a number of peace-building efforts. It has thus raised its profile, perhaps in an effort not to be marginalized in post-Cold War Europe, but also to implement some of its own foreign policy norms. It has gone along with a number of EU initiatives, but is by no means in the shadow of the CFSP.

Norway's defence and security have been managed not just nationally but, since 1949, through the Atlantic Alliance. Increased nervousness about the US underpinning for NATO at the time of the 1994 referendum and after led the Labour government to seek greater involvement with the WEU. Since then, the WEU has been enveloped into the ESDP and Norway has trodden a path-dependent route. The link with the operative side of ESDP seemed less preferable than that of the WEU, but the main issue has not been the mechanics of association with the ESDP (despite Turkish efforts) so much as the wider relationship between ESDP and NATO. If the ESDP fails as an enterprise with any substance, then Norway's relationship with it will matter little. Should it start to act separately from NATO, then the link becomes important, not least as many more Central and East European EU member states join NATO. By early 2004 the EU seemed not too concerned about involving Norway as a non-member in its enterprise and Norwegian policy-makers seemed to have decided that the ESDP has little substance, especially compared with NATO.

The general relationship

It should not be forgotten that in 1994 Norway signed a membership treaty with the EU. Most of its political establishment, a sizeable part of its civil society and almost half those who voted in the referendum considered that this would be an appropriate relationship with the EU. With the triumph of the 'no' vote, Norway fell back on the EEA agreement which was already in place. It has been involved in Schengen issues from the same time as the Nordic EU states and has been engaged in European security and defence issues through NATO and through its association with the WEU before the ESDP was elaborated. Since 1994 Norway's relationship with the process of European integration, as led by the EU, has been as close as possible without full membership.

The wider context of this close relationship was provided in Chapters 2 and 3. The link was made between how Norway had reacted to the prospect of EC, then EU, membership and the history of its relationship to Europe more widely. This connection was particularly strong in 1972, and provided a source for references understood by a wide section of the population. Positive references to autonomy meant something: they played on the foundation of Norway in 1814 and 1905, on memories of the Second World War and on previous battles over the ownership of resources. Negative references to Europe pointed to religious, political and cultural differences, a dislike of 'union'. Those interest groups against membership were able to reach out to a wider public with a warning against the EC's siren song. By 1994 the question was less one of identity than of how best to manage the trade-off between influence and autonomy. For many the EEA, already in the bag, was good enough and for those who thought that it bit too deep into the kernel of autonomy, EU membership was certainly not an option.

The question was asked whether Norwegian policy towards European integration was determined more by interests, politics or identity and ideas (pp. 6–7). The answer by Ingebritsen (2003) that it is both interest and identity is supported here, but needs to be taken further. First, the Norwegian response has to be placed in the wider international environment. The EU in 2004 is different from that in 1994, and that was different from the EC of 1972. Second, the relationship between interests, politics and identity needs is complicated. Gstöhl (2002: 13) has linked together interests and politics, showing that engagement in European integration is more likely when favoured by the economic interests and political elites. The claim in Chapter 3 is that, after the 1960s, the grip that the Labour Party had on Norway's identity, often mediated through interest groups, was loosened. The European issue allowed the counter-culture, supported by particular interest groups and a minority of the political parties, to draw on historic sources and popularize the notion of Norwegian autonomy, as opposed to influence within the EC. By 1994 the campaign was less a struggle for the soul of the nation than about interests. However, after ten years within the EEA system, a number of these interests have started to calculate the costs of reduced influence in Brussels and have re-evaluated full membership. Furthermore, the distance between Norwegian and 'European' identities has narrowed, partly because of the effects of Europeanization and partly through the more general effects of globalization (Udgaard 2004).

The specific nature of the relationship with the EU has been summarized above and can be seen in more detail in Chapters 4 to 7. The relationships built up with the EEA, Schengen and, to a much lesser extent, security and defence cooperation has brought the EU into Norway's internal space as far as the political and interest elites are concerned. It is now much more a part of their life. This is increasingly the case for the wider population – it has affected what they can buy and when, their terms of employment, their security and how freely they can travel abroad.

What is surprising is the relative lack of attention paid to the relationship by the representatives of the people in the Storting. They have discussed the issue, though in a set-piece fashion, when key decisions such as acceptance of Schengen had to be made, and there have been two White Papers on the wider issues. Otherwise EEA legislation and Schengen matters are normally nodded through. The 2002 White Paper (*Stortingsmelding* 27 2002) offered some ideas about greater involvement by Norway in the whole relationship with the EU but the follow-up has been patchy. A broader consideration of the overall effect of EU legislation in particular policy areas compared with that of alternative policies (including pre-existing Norwegian ones) might help in creating a more proactive response to EEA membership, and could even help in improving EU policies. This is not to say that Norway is always ahead of the Union. Indeed, Traavik has claimed that:

> Norwegian legislative standards have been substantially raised in key areas as a result of our EEA membership. Standards for the protection of health, safety, consumer interests and the environment have indisputably been enhanced. This actually came as a surprise for many in Norway who had thought that Norwegian legislation in areas such as environmental protection was superior to that of the EU.
>
> (Traavik 2003a)

If such has been the case, then the substance of the evidence behind this claim could bear parliamentary scrutiny. It would help treat policies out of Brussels firmly as domestic politics instead of being 'neither democracy nor diplomacy' (Claes 2001: 23).

Looking at the model

A small state such as Norway may find much of the environment for its policy-making in the areas covered by this book set externally by larger powers and by events in the international system. Nevertheless, a set of opportunities, however limited, is provided for the decision-makers. By agreeing to the EEA, Schengen and cooperation in CFSP, Norway has channelled these opportunities through a series of institutions which have produced certain institutional limitations. The agenda is very much set in these areas by what is decided within the EU. However, these institutions also provide Norway with an element of influence in the decision-making, almost unique for a small non-member state.[9]

Two key questions arising from the model outlined in Chapter 1 (Figure 1.1) are 'To what extent has Norwegian adaptation to the EU affected the balance of influence and autonomy?' and 'How has the process of adaptation affected the elements within Norway that themselves feed back into policy-making?'

The report from the functional sector above paints a picture of disappearing Norwegian autonomy. It is hard to judge whether this is a result of 'globalization' or more specifically a reaction to Europeanization. There are certain areas of trade and economic autonomy that Norway might have lost had it not had the EEA but had abided by WTO rules and decided to make its markets more attractive to international investment and transnational firms. Both would have been choices to buy economic benefits (at least for certain groups) at the price of reduced autonomy.

This was part of the calculation with the EEA, the extra elements being that the deal was with Norway's closest and largest market and involved a Norwegian input into – influence on – some of the decisions made by the EU. The same calculations have been made with the relationship in the fields of justice and security. The influence bought may be small but it seems well in proportion to the relative size of Norway and the EU. Indeed, the suggestion is that it is relatively large in some spheres such as aquaculture and peacekeeping.

The feedback process may have an effect on the choice about eventual Norwegian EU membership. Norway has already adapted itself in a massive way to the EU by adopting the *acquis communautaire* and by using the EEA to keep up with EU internal market legislation. This has helped change the balance of interests within Norway concerning the relationship with the EU. With particular exceptions, much of Norwegian trade and commerce continues to be tied to the EU market and therefore concerned about the conditions for trading in this market. Processed metals no longer face the challenges they had before the EEA, salmon exports have precarious access, and the oil and gas industries know that the EU can indeed affect their conditions of trade in Europe. Though the EEA provides some access, membership of the EU would entrench Norway's position in the decision-making and would provide a more important point of access – to decision-taking. The experience of the EU through the EEA has helped to 'reproduce and reconstruct' (Jepperson *et al.* 1996: 63, see p. 10) the cultural and institutional structures within Norway so that they are more familiar with and closer to the habits and institutions of the EU.

Europeanizing and adapting

The twofold nature of Europeanization was noted in Chapter 1 (pp. 15–16). Clearly the first aspect, that of European integration, has continued independent of any Norwegian input. The second, as far as Norway is concerned, the way that process impacts on the country's 'political structures and processes' (Börzel 2002: 193), has gathered pace since the referendum of November 1994. Norway has indeed attempted to get a 'close fit' between its policies and most of those of the EU in order to lower the adaptation costs for businesses, consumers and others in public life affected by any mismatch between existing national laws and those that will dominate from Brussels. The most efficient way to do this is to ensure as close a fit as possible between EU and Norwegian legislation at the point at which EU law is made. The tactics of pace-setting, foot-dragging, least resistance or fence-sitting could be used either in the making of policy or, later, in its implementation, reflecting types of adaptation (see pp. 16–18).

In most cases, Norway has been acquiescent, accepting EU legislation without qualms, taking the line of least resistance to gain some influence. However, there is evidence that by gaining respect for expertise in the decision-making committees (see Chapter 4), it has been able to undertake a modest amount of low-level pace-setting, especially in areas such as the environment and aquaculture. In the implementation of most legislation Norway has been thorough, even an enthusiastic pace-setter. This front-loaded any costs for consumers, business, local government or other organizations, with the aim of allowing them to reap an early benefit of being 'in step' with regulations governing the EU's single market. In non-EEA areas, especially the ESDP, Norway has benefited from already having adapted to the new international security situation on a national basis and as a member of NATO. Norway has shown a degree of acquiescence in the wider ESDP arrangements (unlike Turkey) but has been intransigent on the key issue of involvement in the planning of any operation to which Norwegian troops are contributed.

On other occasions Norway has shown a degree of intransigence both in policy-making and implementation. This was particularly the case in areas where Norway had an advantage compared with the EU (such as gas) or which were not EEA mainstream subjects and were of importance economically and politically for Norway, such as fisheries. The surprise is that Norway did not exert more clout in the case of the Gas Directive, which may have been the result of an expectation that the European Commission would back down because of opposition within the EU, which proved unfounded in the end. In the case of fisheries, the state of stocks and wider market conditions have also had an important impact on agreements. In other areas within the EEA remit, such as the ownership of natural resources, the sale of alcopops and types of regional aid, Norway's attempts at foot-dragging, especially at the implementation stage, have been encouraged by identity and cultural factors, as well as those of economic interest. In negotiations for a Schengen II agreement, where Norway was not bound by an EEA format, had strong allies with common interests within the EU and had domestic pressure at home, a deal more to Norway's liking was negotiated.

Acquiescence may lower the adaptation costs of the EEA for Norway and promotive tactics could certainly advance Norwegian ideas within the EU system. Nevertheless, the Europeanization provided by the links with the EEA makes autonomy more expensive and helps change the balance of interests in favour of continued integration. It also blurs the distinction between 'European' and Norwegian, making opposition to full membership from an identity-based perspective less likely.

What can be learnt?

Norway is a European country and a rich, West European democracy. It is also a Nordic state. It can thus be seen as one of a type, whether of some thirty, sixteen or five states. Do its experience of and reaction to European integration chime in with those of other countries?

Rather than conduct a comparative study, it is worth noting here the elements that make Norway the same as and different from others in the pack. The sameness can be summed up in the phrases already used: Western, democratic, rich, European. Also, placed beside other states, it shares an element of smallness, though the definitional problem with this concept is even greater than those associated with 'democracy'.[10] A brief examination of the Norwegian economy shows it to be as service-based and export-dependent as those of many West European states, and growth, inflation and unemployment to be fairly similar, though with all three veering to the lower end of the scale. The economy has been as touched by globalization as that of its neighbours.

The differences can be seen in current conditions, but more so in the history of the country. It is richer than other West European states, with only Luxembourg and Switzerland challenging this happy position. It has a smaller immigrant share of the population than most West European nations, though this has been rapidly changing. It is an oil producer and exporter in a way that outstrips other North Sea states, and is more global in its petroleum, shipping and fisheries sectors. With its possession of Svalbard, it is the most northern of European states outside Russia (Greenland, part of the Danish realm, being in America), and with its long coastline is perhaps one of the most Atlantic.

Like the rest of Europe, Norway has never been able to stand outside events on the continent of Europe. From the Reformation to the Napoleonic Wars to Hitler's expansion and the Cold War, they all washed up on Norway's shores. However, a mixture of its geographical position, its social construction and its political development has allowed the Norwegians, until 1940, to choose some of the major policies that affected their lives in a way that was less familiar in many other European states. They (or their representatives) made major constitutional choices in 1814 and 1905. They made lesser but still important choices in 1884, 1913 and 1949. Arguments about language and alcohol resounded throughout the nineteenth and twentieth centuries, and control of the country's natural resources remained an engaging issue. In 1940 the Germans were not greeted as liberators either from domestic tyranny (as in parts of the Soviet Union) or from foreign occupiers (as by some in the Baltic states). The Norwegians seemed to have a well-established feeling of self rooted in their history and social make-up and which had political consequences. It played an important part in the 1972 referendum on EC membership. That event was then added to the stock of national self-understanding.

However, since then, that understanding has changed and has been challenged. The capacity for autonomous decisions has slipped. The outside world increasingly impinged on Norway as improved communications 'shortened' distances and economic and some social barriers were reduced in the rise of globalization. Autonomy had already been diminished in the area of defence where membership of NATO had locked Norway into policies made elsewhere. International institutions provided the means to both spread and implement globalization and instruments of defence against some of its aspects. The EC, then the EU, was perceived by some politicians (for example, those in the Socialist Left and Centre parties) as part of the globalization process that deprived Norway of its autonomy in policy-making, while others, such as leading members of the Labour Party, saw it as a means by which small states such as Norway could affect the process. Increasingly the elements of Norwegian society and economy that encouraged autonomy have become more echoes of the past, whereas involvement itself in the EEA has increased both the habit of and benefits from influencing the EU. The one element that has run counter to this trend is the growth of Norway's petroleum economy, which itself is part of a global economy. However, even here the EU involvement in the gas market has trimmed Norwegian autonomy and provided an incentive to further engagement with the EU process.

The economic strength provided by the petroleum industry, the agricultural and fisheries interests, added to memories of those elements of Norwegian life that make the country distinct from the rest of Europe, could be enough to produce a third, and probably final, vote against EU membership. Much will also depend on the image of the EU within Norway. A multi-speed association of most European states will be seen as less of a threat to Norwegian values than a supranational European state-in-the-making. Should Norway join the EU, its voters will observe the Union's activities with a sceptical eye and will be insistent on exercising their influence.

Appendix 1
Questionnaire

In late 2003, all the members of the Storting were sent by e-mail a short questionnaire in Norwegian and were asked to reply to the following questions. They were given the option of expressing views and of any views being open to citation or not. A similar survey was conducted of editors of newspapers and leaders of various interest groups and organizations, chosen from a registry of these in Norway.

Survey results: the Storting

I EEA agreement: expectations–experience (by party affiliation)

Party	*In your opinion has the EEA agreement, for Norway, worked*			
	As expected?	*Worse than expected?*	*Better than expected?*	*Total*
Labour	5	2	1	8
Conservative	11	1	1	13
Progress	5	3	1	9
Socialist Left	6	6	–	12
Christian Democrat	5	2	–	7
Centre	–	2	–	2
Liberals	–	–	–	–
Total	32	16		51

II Attitude towards membership in the EU (by party affiliation)

Party	*Do you think Norway should apply to become a member of the European Union?*			*Total*
	Yes	*No*	*No opinion/ don't know*	
Labour	6	2	–	8
Conservative	13	–	–	13
Progress	3	3	3	9
Socialist Left	–	12	–	12
Christian Democrat	–	7	–	7
Centre	–	2	–	2
Liberals	–	–	–	–
Total	22	26	3	51

III Evaluation of likelihood of EU application in near future (by party affiliation)

Party	*Do you think Norway will apply for membership of the EU in the period 2005–9?*			*Total*
	Yes	*No*	*No opinion/ don't know*	
Labour	6	1	1	8
Conservative	12	–	1	13
Progress	5	2	2	9
Socialist Left	–	12	–	12
Christian Democrat	1	6	–	7
Centre	–	1	1	2
Liberals	–	–	–	–
Total	24	22	5	51

IV Personal conviction and predictions about the future

		Is Norway going to apply for membership of the EU in the period 2005–9?			
		Yes	*No*	*No opinion/don't know*	*Total*
Should Norway apply for membership of the EU in the period 2005–9?	Yes	20	–	2	22
	No	2	22	2	26
	No opinion/ don't know	2	–	1	3
	Total	24	22	5	51

V Evaluation of EEA agreement and attitude towards membership in the EU

Attitude towards membership	*Experience of the EEA agreement*			*Total*
	As expected	*Worse than expected*	*Better than expected*	
Yes	16	5	1	22
No	14	10	2	26
No opinion/don't know	2	1	–	3
Total	32	16	3	51

Response rate

	No. of MPs	*No. of replies*	*Response rate (%)*
According to party affiliation			
Labour	43	8	18.6
Conservative	38	13	34.2
Progress	26	9	34.6
Socialist Left	23	12	52.2
Christian Democrat	22	7	31.8
Centre	10	2	20.0
Liberal	2	0	0.0
Coastal	1	0	0.0
Total	165	51	30.9
According to constituency			
Finnmark	4	0	0.0
Troms	6	1	1.7
Nordland	12	3	25.0
Nord-Trøndelag	6	2	33.3
Sør-Trøndelag	10	3	30.0
Møre og Romsdal	10	3	30.0
Sogn og Fjordane	5	1	20.0
Hordaland	17	5	29.4
Rogaland	11	4	36.4
Vest-Agder	5	2	40.0
Aust-Agder	4	0	0.0
Telemark	6	2	33.3
Buskerud	7	4	57.1
Hedmark	8	0	0.0
Oppland	7	0	0.0
Akershus	15	6	40.0
Oslo	16	8	50.0
Vestfold	8	2	25.0
Østfold	8	5	62.5
Total	165	51	30.9

Survey results: civil society

I EEA agreement: expectations–experience

Group	*In your opinion, has the EEA agreement, for Norway, worked:*			*Total*
	As expected?	*Worse than expected?*	*Better than expected?*	
Press/media	8	3	2	13
Employers' associations	9	1	1	11
Trade unions	7	3	–	10
Political youth organizations	2	2	1	5
Agriculture and fisheries organizations	–	1	–	1
Total	26	10	4	40

II Attitude towards membership in the EU

Group	*Do you think Norway should apply to become a member of the EU?*			*Total*
	Yes	*No*	*No opinion/ don't know*	
Press/media	8	5	–	13
Employers' associations	11	–	–	11
Trade unions	5	5	–	10
Political youth organizations	2	3	–	5
Agriculture and fisheries organizations	–	1	–	1
Total	26	14	–	40

III Evaluation of likelihood of EU application in near future

Group	*Do you think Norway will apply for membership of the EU in the period 2005–9?*			*Total*
	Yes	*No*	*No opinion/ don't know*	
Press/media	8	4	1	13
Employers' associations	11	–	–	11
Trade unions	6	3	1	10
Political youth organizations	2	1	2	5
Agriculture and fisheries organizations	–	–	1	1
Total	27	8	5	40

Response rate

	No. potential respondents	*No. replies*	*Response rate (%)*
Press	41	13	31.7
Employers' associations	24	11	45.8
Trade unions	45	10	22.2
Political youth organizations	6	5	83.3
Agriculture and fisheries organizations	3	1	33.3
Total	119	40	33.6

Appendix 2

List of interviewees

Arne Bjørnstad, MFA Oslo
Anne Marie Borgvad, MFA Brussels
Anders Eide, MFA Brussels
Bjørn Tore Godal, former Minister of Defence and former Minister of Foreign Affairs
Knut Hauge, MFA London
Steinar Hernes, adviser to Marit Nybakk
Nils Holme, former head of the Norwegian Research Development Establishment
Bård Bredrup Knudsen. Ministry of Defence
Olav Bjørn Knutsen, Norwegian Research Development Establishment
Janne Haaland Matlary, NUPI
Marit Nybakk, Labour member of Storting and chair of Defence Committee
Chris Prebensen, DNAK
Annlaug Rønneberg, MFA Brussels
Per Sjaastad, MFA London, Brussels
Øyvind Stokke, MFA London
Bjarne Syrdal, Secretary, Defence Committee
Else Børmer Underdal, MFA Oslo
Guttorm Vik, MFA Oslo
Elisabeth Walaas, MFA Brussels
Kåre Willoch, former Prime Minister

Key

DNAK	Norwegian Atlantic Committee
MFA Oslo	Ministry of Foreign Affairs, Oslo
MFA Brussels	Norwegian representation to the European Union
MFA London	Royal Norwegian Embassy, London
NUPI	Norwegian Institute for International Affairs

Notes

1 Introduction

1 In their case the authors are concerned with security policy.

3 Norway battles with European integration

1 Rokkan (1970: 72–144) identified these as: geographical (centre versus periphery); linguistic (Nynorsk versus Riksmål); morality (especially over the availability of alcohol); religion (evangelicals versus the State Church bureaucracy); urban–rural (producers versus consumers); the rural class struggle (owners versus employees); and the industrial class struggle (capital versus labour). Many of these overlapped.

2 Ironically, one of the casualties of the vote was the Liberal Party that split into two and was reduced to a rump party.

4 Norway and the EEA

1 By 2002 Norway had an average gross national product (GNP) of US$31,800 per head, ranking third globally in terms of GNP per head behind Luxembourg and the US (Archer 2003). The unemployment rate was more than half that of states such as Germany and Finland (Statistics Norway, 2000, table 648). The revised budget for 2003 foresaw a fiscal surplus of Nkr128 billion, equivalent to some 9.7 per cent of GDP. The state's surplus income has been placed in a Petroleum Fund to assist in meeting the welfare demands of Norway's ageing population from 2010 onwards (Archer 2003).

2 The largest sectors are local government (19.7 per cent of total employment), trade (14.1 per cent), and personal services (10.2 per cent) (Archer 2003).

3 State Secretary is the equivalent of a junior minister in Norway.

4 The Progress Party had suffered an internal split and its two committee members had parted from the main party led by Carl I. Hagen.

5 This 'right of reservation' can refer to the right of the EFTA EEA states to refuse to transpose legislation, even though this may lead to a response by other contracting parties (the EU) such as the suspension of the part of the agreement directly affected by the relevant legislation (Article 102.5). However, there is also a right to take safeguard measures under Articles 112 and 113 where if 'serious economic, societal or environmental difficulties of a sectorial or regional nature liable to persist are arising, a Contracting Party may unilaterally take appropriate measures…' It seems that these two elements were sometimes confused in debates but here it refers to the 'right of reservation'.

6 See, for example, OECD 2003a, b; Statskonsult 1998, 2001a, b, 2002, 2003a, b, c; Statsministerens kontor 2001, 2002, 2003; *Stortingsmelding* 12 2000; UD 2003a, b, c, d; Andersen 2000; Eide *et al.* 2003: 63–72; Narud and Strøm 2000; Nordby and Veggeland 1999; Olsen 2000; Sejersted 1996; Trondal 1998, 1999; Trondal and Veggeland 1999; Veggeland 1999a, b).
7 The five areas of particular weight in Nordic cooperation over EU issues are gender equality, openness and transparency in EU activity, welfare policy, the fight against criminality and drugs, and research policy (Statskonsult 2002: 94).
8 UD (2003a) lists 214 committees in which Norway participated in 2003.
9 The coordination of Norway's input into the EEA process is outlined by the Prime Minister's Office in Statsministerens kontor (2001).
10 Of the twenty-two Norwegian special committees on EEA issues, only one is led by the MFA. The Ministry of Trade and Industry leads six, Health, Transport and Communications, Culture and Church Affairs, and Labour and Government Administration heads two each and eight other Ministries one each (UD 2003b).

5 The EEA in action

1 Article 16 EEA reads: '1. The Contracting Parties shall ensure that any State monopoly of a commercial character be adjusted so that no discrimination regarding the conditions under which goods are procured and marketed will exist between nationals of EC Member States and EFTA States. 2. The provisions of this Article shall apply to any body through which the competent authorities of the Contracting Parties, in law or in fact, either directly or indirectly supervise, determine or appreciably influence imports or exports between Contracting Parties. These provisions shall likewise apply to monopolies delegated by the State to others.'
2 The country was divided into five tax zones with varied employer contribution rates: Zone 1, central municipalities in southern Norway, 14.1 per cent; Zone 2, rural districts in southern Norway, 10.6 per cent; Zone 3, coastal area mid-Norway, 6.4 per cent; Zone 4, northern Norway (except zone 5), 5.1 per cent; Zone 5, Spitzbergen/Finnmark/northern part of Troms, 0 per cent.

6 Norway and the CFSP

1 An example is the *Kongsberg* case of 1987 (Tamnes 1991: 293–4).
2 The three approaches to bargaining suggested by Hirschmann (1990) are 'exit, voice and loyalty', the first being a threat to leave negotiations or an institution, the second being critical within an institution, and the last representing an attempt to make gains by exemplary behaviour. Within NATO, France exercised the 'exit' option, at least from the military command structure, Greece and Denmark tended to be the most vocal, and Norway one of the most loyal members.
3 The share of GDP devoted to defence has been cut from 2.8 per cent in 1985 to 1.9 per cent in 2002 (International Institute for Strategic Studies 2003: 335).
4 The WEU Petersburg Declaration of June 1992 allowed planning in the area of crisis management, peacekeeping, humanitarian and rescue actions and other similar tasks. These became known as the Petersburg tasks. In 1995 Norway declared a number of its forces to the WEU as available for these tasks.
5 This section is informed by interviews conducted in Oslo, London and Brussels.

7 Norway and Justice and Home Affairs

1 This was pursuant to Article 6 of the Treaty of Amsterdam's protocol integrating the Schengen *acquis* into the framework of the EU that stated that 'the kingdom of Norway shall be associated with the implementation of the Schengen acquis and its further development...' and allowed for procedures to be agreed to this end and an agreement to be concluded to cover the rights and obligations as between the UK and Ireland and Norway and Iceland 'in the domains of the Schengen acquis which apply to these states' (Duff 1997: 282–3).
2 In the 1993–7 Storting, Labour had sixty-seven seats, the Conservatives twenty-eight and the Progress Party ten. Labour and the Conservatives together thus had a majority of seats. The Christian Democrats had thirteen seats, the Centre Party thirty-two, the Socialist Left thirteen, and the Liberals and the Red Electoral Alliance one each. A minority Labour government was in power.
3 The governing parties only held forty-two seats, while the three pro-Schengen parties had 113 votes. Labour and the Conservatives together had a majority in the Storting, had they cared to use it.
4 The detailed reports by four of the group ran to forty-four pages. Of these only one definitely plumped for the use of paragraph 93 in the constitution, which would have required a qualified majority in the Storting, while three others accepted that paragraph 26, which only needed an ordinary majority vote, was sufficient, though with some reservations (*Stortingsproposisjon* 50 1999: vedlegg 7).
5 This was certainly the view of some of the judicial experts (see, especially, Boe at *Stortingsproposisjon* 50 1999: vedlegg 7).
6 After the September 1997 election Labour had sixty-five seats, the Conservatives twenty-three, the Progress Party twenty-five, the Christian Democrats twenty-five, the Centre Party eleven and the Liberals six. The Socialist Left dropped down to nine seats and the Coastal Party had one member. The centrist government had the support of only forty-two members. While in theory Labour and the Conservatives could press through Schengen-type legislation by a majority of the 165 seats, the presence of a handful of Labour rebels made this precarious. Meanwhile the Progress Party was becoming more neutral on European issues and could well have voted against a deal not backed by the judicial advisers. Foreign Minister Vollebæk admitted that had the institutional situation been different the advice of the experts could have been different on the use of a majority vote (*Stortingstidende* 1999a: 31).
7 Eurojust is a meeting of representatives of EU member states aimed at improving cooperation on the investigation and prosecution of serious crimes (European Communities 2002: 1).
8 See, for example, questions by the Counter-terrorism Committee of the UN Security Council (UD 2001).
9 Thus Sweden had cause for complaint when Denmark tightened its immigration and asylum laws in 2002–3. Denmark retains the right to act independently of the EU on such matters.
10 Even so, Norway sometimes refused to harmonize laws on matters such as marriage and abortion (Archer 1994a: 193).

8 Change, choice and conclusions

1 The Lisbon Strategy, advanced at the European Council meeting in Lisbon in March 2000 and developed in later European Council meetings covers macro-economic policy, the internal market, research, social security, employment and the environment and uses the open method of cooperation to achieve its aims.

Four key areas of the strategy are: increasing employment by training, improved mobility, bringing more women into the work force and helping flexibility in the labour market; structural and economic reforms to ensure functioning energy, transport and financial markets; increased investment in knowledge, in particular research and development; and placing the environmental dimension to the fore (*Stortingsmelding* 27 2002: section 5.4).

2 The EEA agreement actually refers to the relevant articles of the Treaty of Rome, as it was being negotiated at the same time as the Maastricht treaty (*Stortingsmelding* 27 2002: section 5.2).

3 They failed to do this. However, an exchange of letters between the EU and the EEA EFTA states on 1 April 2004 allowed a provisional application of the EEA enlargement agreement and its four related bilateral agreements as from 1 May 2004 until the ratification was completed (Mission of Norway to the EU 2004: 1).

4 The Norwegian contribution to the EEA-related activities was to be about Nkr4.7 billion for the five-year period (Nkr941 million per annum) from 1 May 2004 to 30 April 2009. The contribution to the solely Norwegian fund will be another Nkr4.7 billion for the period or Nkr941 million per annum.

5 Norway pays more (€205.8 million) to the EU structural funds in annual contributions than either Sweden or Denmark and is the main contributor to the structural funds in *per capita* terms (€137.2 per head) (European Observer 2004).

6 See Appendix 1. There are sixty-two members of the Storting from the three 'cooperation government' parties.

7 Free movement of persons, land transport, air transport, trade in processed agricultural products, technical barriers to trade, public procurement and research.

8 In the survey reported in Appendix 1, all twelve Socialist Left Party (SV) members of the Storting who replied were against applying for EU membership. The party provided the highest response rate (52.2 per cent), though it is perhaps unlikely that any member who was for membership would have replied, despite the offer of anonymity. None of the SV members thought that Norway would apply for EU membership in the 2005–9 period. However, a sizeable minority of SV voters continue to support membership.

9 Iceland and Liechtenstein have the same opportunities in the EEA, but not the same resources as Norway to take advantage of it.

10 For further discussions about small states, including questions of definition, see the special issue of *Current Policies and Economics of Europe* 11 (1), 2002, edited by C. Archer and N. Nugent.

Bibliography

Aardal, B. and Jenssen, A.T. (1995) 'Opinionsutviklingen 1972–1994' in A.T. Jenssen and H. Valen (eds) *Brussel midt imot. Folkeavstemningen om EU*, Oslo: Ad Notam Gyldendal, 31–44.

Aftenposten (2003a) 'Kluss og kaos med rusbrusavgifter' 14 June 2003, at http://www.aftenposten.no (accessed 5 January 2004).

Aftenposten (2003b) 'Valla har mistet et nei-argument mot EU', *Aftenposten*, 26 December 2003, at http://www.aftenposten.no (accessed 5 January 2004).

Aftenposten (2003c) 'Pengene strømmer in til Nei-bevegelsen', *Aftenposten*, 5 October 2003, at http://www.aftenposten.no (accessed 13 October 2003).

Aftenposten (2003d) 'EØS er ikke lenger godt nok for norsk industri', *Aftenposten*, 21 October 2003, at http://www.aftenposten.no (accessed 21 October 2003).

Aftenposten (2003e) 'Bondevik åpen for nytenkning rundt EU', *Aftenposten*, 20 July 2003, at http://www.aftenposten.no (accessed 24 July 2003).

Aftenposten (2003f) 'Bondevik: Jeg er forsatt nei-mann', *Aftenposten*, 10 October 2003, at http://www.aftenposten.no (accessed 13 October 2003).

Aftenposten (2003g) 'Jagland: Politikken dør uten EU-medlemskap', *Aftenposten*, 19 November 2003, at http://www.aftenposten.no (accessed 25 November 2003).

Aftenposten (2003h) 'Ap.s valg: Regjering eller EU-medlemskap', *Aftenposten*, 20 November 2003, at http://www.aftenposten.no (accessed 25 November 2003).

Aftenposten (2004a) 'Ap.politikere går fra nei til ja i EU-saken', *Aftenposten*, 4 January 2004, at http://www.aftenposten.no (accessed 5 January 2004).

Aftenposten (2004b) 'Regner med EU-avstemning i 2006', *Aftenposten*, 7 January 2004, at http://www.aftenposten.no (accessed 7 January 2004).

Aftenposten (2004c) 'Krever tøffere arbeidskontroll', *Aftenposten*, 6 April 2004, at http://www.aftenposten.no (accessed 6 April 2004).

Aftenposten (2004d) 'Hagas sveitsiske drøm', *Aftenposten*, 7 April 2004, at http://www.aftenposten.no (accessed 7 April 2004).

Aftenposten (2004e) 'Økende flertall for norsk EU-medlemskap', *Aftenposten*, 21 February 2004, at http://www.aftenposten.no (accessed 23 February 2004).

Akselsen, O. (2000) 'Gas Talk', *Statoil Magazine* 2: 11, Stavanger: Statoil.

Allen, H. (1979) *Norway and Europe in the 1970s*, Oslo: Universitetsforlaget.

Andersen, S.S. (2000) *Norway. Insider and Outsider*, Oslo: Arena, Working Papers 00/4.

Archer, C. (1994a) *Organizing Europe. The Institutions of Integration*, London: Edward Arnold.

Archer, C. (1994b) 'New Threat Perceptions. Danish and Norwegian Official Views', *European Security* 3 (4): 593–616.

Archer, C. (2003) 'Norway: Economy' in J. Love and J. O'Brien (eds) *Western Europe 2004*, London: Taylor & Francis, 504–7.

Archer, C. and Nugent, N. (2002) 'Introduction. Small States and the European Union', *Current Politics and Economics of Europe* 11 (1): 1–10.

Archer, C. and Sogner, I. (1998) *Norway, European Integration and Atlantic Security*, London: Sage.

Axtmann, R. (1993) 'The Formation of the Modern State. The Debate in the Social Sciences' in M. Fulbrook (ed.) *National Histories and European History*, London: UCL Press, 21–45.

Bache, I. (1998) *The Politics of European Union Regional Policy*, Sheffield: Sheffield University Press.

Bergh, T. (1987) *Arbeiderbevegelsens historie.* Bind. 5, Oslo: Tiden Norsk Forlag.

Bjerve, P.J. (1965) *Norges økonomi etter krigen*, Oslo: Statistisk Sentralbyrå.

Bjørklund, T. (1982) *Mot strømmen. Kampen mot EF 1961–1972.* Oslo: Universitetsforlaget.

Bjørklund, T. (1994) 'En reprise fra 1972?' *Dagbladet*, 30 November.

Bondevik, K.M. (2003) 'Speech at "Die Quadriga"/Werkstatt Deutschland, Berlin, 3 October 2003', Oslo: Statsministerenskontor.

Börzel, T.A. (2002) 'Pace-setting, Foot-dragging, and Fence-sitting. Member State Responses to Europeanization', *Journal of Common Market Studies* 40 (2): 193–214.

Boye, O., Kismul, A.H., Kristiansen, A.B., Seierstad, D., Strøm, B., Toft, A.K., Valle, Å. and Enebeck, P. (2003) *Alternativ til EØS*, Oslo: Nei til EU.

Brinchmann, E. (2000) 'Gas Talk', *Statoil Magazine* 2: 16, Stavanger: Statoil.

Bröms, P. (1995) *Environmental Security Regimes. A Critical Approach*, Stockholm: Swedish Institute of International Affairs, Research Report 23.

Brundtland, G.H. (1994a) *Norge-EU. Om forhandlingsresultatet, Preshefte, 16 mar 1994*, Oslo: Utenriksdepartementet.

Brundtland, G.H. (1994b) *Statsminister Gro Harlem Brundtland. Måløy, 15. august 1994*, Oslo: Statsministerens Kontor, mimeo.

Bull, H. (1999) 'Norge og Schengen. Forandre for å bevare?' in D.H. Claes and B.S. Tranøy (eds) *Utenfor, annerledes og suveren?* Oslo: Fagbokforlaget, 59–79.

Buzan, B. (1991) *People, States, and Fear. An Agenda for International Security Studies in the Post-Cold War Era*, London: Harvester Wheatsheaf.

Church, C. (2002) 'Redefining Swiss Relations with Europe' in M. Butler, M. Pender and J. Charnley (eds) *The Making of Modern Switzerland 1798–1848*, Basingstoke: Macmillan, 137–60.

Claes, D.H. (2001) *EØS. Demokrati eller diplomati?* Oslo: Arena, Working Paper No. 10.

Claes, D.H. (2003) *Energi*, Oslo: NUPI.

Claes, D.H. and Eikeland, P.O. (1999) 'Stormakt i utakt. Norsk energi og EU's indre marked' in D.H. Claes and B.S. Tranøy (eds) *Utenfor, annerledes og suveren?* Oslo: Fagbokforlaget, 151–73.

Collins (1979) *Collins Dictionary of the English Language*, London and Glasgow: Collins.

Confederation of Norwegian Business and Industry (2003) *Næringslivets Hovedor-*

ganisjon at http://www.nho.no/hovedweb/hovedweb.nsf (accessed 1 December 2003).

Dagbladet (1972) 22 September 1972.

Dagens Næringsliv (2002) 23 August, 20.

Dagens Næringsliv (2003) 27 May, 16.

Dagens Næringsliv (2004) 'EU skal granske norsk laks', 6/7 March, 9.

Danielsen, R. (1995a) 'The Political Sphere 1884–1918' in R. Danielsen, S. Dyrvik, T. Grønlie, K. Helle and E. Hovland, *Norway. A History from the Vikings to our own Times*, Oslo, Copenhagen and Stockholm: Scandinavian University Press, 297–313.

Danielsen, R. (1995b) ' The *embetsmenn* State. Golden Age, Decline and Fall' in R. Danielsen, S. Dyrvik, T. Grønlie, K. Helle and E. Hovland, *Norway. A History from the Vikings to our own Times*, Oslo, Copenhagen and Stockholm: Scandinavian University Press, 255–70.

Danielsen, R. and Hovland, E. (1995) '1814–1945' in R. Danielsen, S. Dyrvik, T. Grønlie, K. Helle and E. Hovland, *Norway. A History from the Vikings to our own Times*, Oslo, Copenhagen and Stockholm: Scandinavian University Press, 217–353.

Det norske Arbeiderparti (2003) *Det norske Arbeiderparti. Program for 2001–2005. Vedtatt på landsmøtet 12. november 2002*, at http://www.dna.no/assets/11964/140/Prinsipp%20og%20handlingsprogram%202001-2005%20(PDF).pdf (accessed 4 January 2004).

Devold, K.K. (2003) 'Defence Policy Aims and Priorities in 2003' at http://odin.dep.no/fd/engelsk/aktuelt/taler/statsraad_010011-09.../index-dok000-b-f-a.htm (accessed 15 January 2003).

Devold, K.K. (2004a) 'Norway's Participation in Multilateral Operations Abroad during 2004' at http://odin.dep.no/fd/engelsk/aktuelt/taler/statsraad_/010011-090091/index-dok000-b-n-a.htm (accessed 28 January 2004).

Devold, K.K. (2004b) '"From Course Change to Military Transformation", New Year address by Defence Minister Kristin Krohn Devold, Oslo Military Society, Monday 5 January 2004' at http://odin.dep.no/fd/engelsk/aktuelt/taler/statsraad_a/010011-090093/index-dok000-b-f-a.htm (accessed 28 January 2004).

DNAK [Den Norske Atlanterhavskomite] (2002) *Vollebæks PM til alle EU og NATO-land*, www.atlanterhavskomiteen.no/publikasjoner/andre/dokumenter/memo.htm (accessed 23 September 2002).

Duff, Andrew (ed.) (1997) *The Treaty of Amsterdam. Text and Commentary*, London: Federal Trust.

Dyrvik, S. (1995) 'Part II, 1536–1814' in R. Danielsen, S. Dyrvik, T. Grønlie, K. Helle and E. Hovland, *Norway. A History from the Vikings to our own Times*, Oslo, Copenhagen and Stockholm: Scandinavian University Press, 123–214.

Economist Intelligence Unit (1994) *Country Report: Norway, third quarter*, London: Economist Intelligence Unit.

Economist Intelligence Unit (1995a) *Country Report: Norway, second quarter*, London: Economist Intelligence Unit.

Economist Intelligence Unit (1995b) *Country Profile: Norway*, London: Economist Intelligence Unit.

Economist Intelligence Unit (1996) *Country Report: Norway, second quarter*, London: Economist Intelligence Unit.

Economist Intelligence Unit (1997a) *Country Report: Norway, second quarter*, London: Economist Intelligence Unit.

Economist Intelligence Unit (1997b) *Country Report: Norway, third quarter*, London: Economist Intelligence Unit.

Economist Intelligence Unit (2003a) *Country Forecast: Norway, September 2003*, London: Economist Intelligence Unit.

Economist Intelligence Unit (2003b) *Country Report: Norway, January 2003*, London: Economist Intelligence Unit.

Economist Intelligence Unit (2003c) *Country Profile: Norway 2003*, London: Economist Intelligence Unit.

EFTA Court (1998) 'Press releases' at http://www.eftacourt.lu/pr_98_6_98r.asp (accessed 29 November 2003).

EFTA Court (1999) 'Decided cases' at http://www.eftacourt.lu/dc_e_6_98.asp (accessed 29 November 2003).

EFTA Court (2002) 'Decided cases' at http://www.eftacourt.lu/dc_e_6_98.asp (accessed 29 November 2003).

EFTA Court (2003a) 'Introduction' at http://www.eftacourt.lu.introduction.asp (accessed 29 November 2003).

EFTA Court (2003b) 'Decided cases' at http://www.eftacourt.lu.decidedcases.asp (accessed 1 December 2003).

EFTA Secretariat (2002) *Forty-first Annual Report of the European Free Trade Association*, Brussels: EFTA.

EFTA Secretariat (2003a) *Forty-second Annual Report of the European Free Trade Association*, Brussels: EFTA.

EFTA Secretariat (2003b) *Agreement on the European Economic Area* at http://secretariat.efta.int/web/europeaneconomicarea/eeaagreement/eeaagreement/#_toc21163302 (accessed 27 November 2003).

EFTA Secretariat (2003c) 'Conclusion of EEA enlargement negotiations' at http://secretariat.efta.int/web/News/EEAenlargement (accessed 1 September 2003).

EFTA Surveillance Authority (1999) 'Press releases' at http://www.eftasurv.int/information/pressreleases/1999pr/dbaFile1840.html (accessed 29 November 2003).

EFTA Surveillance Authority (2000) 'Press releases' at http://www.eftasurv.int/information/pressreleases/2000pr/PR00-23.htm (accessed 29 November 2003).

EFTA Surveillance Authority (2001a) 'The EFTA Surveillance Authority: Root' at http://www.eftasurv.int (accessed 20 August 2002).

EFTA Surveillance Authority (2001b) 'Press releases' at http://www.eftasurv.int/information/pressreleases/2001pr/pr01-19.htm (accessed 29 November 2003).

EFTA Surveillance Authority (2002) 'Press releases' at http://www.eftasurv.int/information/pressreleases/2002pr/pr02-02.htm (accessed 29 November 2003).

EFTA Surveillance Authority (2003a) 'The EFTA Surveillance Authority: Root' at http://www.eftasurv.int (accessed 29 November 2003).

EFTA Surveillance Authority (2003b) 'AIDA and GENDA: Background Information' at http://www.eftasurv.int (accessed 1 December 2003).

EFTA Surveillance Authority (2003c) 'Press releases' at http://www.eftasurv.int/information/pressreleases/2003pr/dbaFile4115.html (accessed 29 November 2003).

EFTA Surveillance Authority (2003d) 'Press releases' at http://www.eftasurv.int/information/pressreleases/2003pr/dbaFile4231.html (accessed 29 November 2003).

EFTA Surveillance Authority (2003e) 'Press releases' at http://www.eftasurv.int/information/pressreleases/2003pr/dbaFile4508.html (accessed 29 November 2003).

EFTA Surveillance Authority (2004) 'Internal Market Scoreboard. EFTA States' at http://www.eftasurv.int/information/pressreleases/2004pr/dbaFile4716.html (accessed 6 April 2004).

Eide, E.B., Claes, D.H., Ulrichsen, H. and Toje, A. (2003) *Norge og EU. Medlemskap, EØS eller 'sveitsisk løsning'*, Oslo: NUPI.

Elias, N. (1978) *What is Sociology?* London: Hutchinson.

Emerson, M, Vahl, M. and Woolcock, S. (2002) *Navigating by the Stars. The European Economic Area and the European Union*, Brussels: CEPS.

Engberg, J. and Lane, J. (1980) 'Internationalisering och autonomi', *Statsvetenskaplig Tidsskrift* 4: 211–14.

Eriksen, K. E., (1977) 'Norge i det vestlige samarbeidet' in Trond Bergh and Helge Pharø (eds) *Vekst og Velstand. Norskpolitisk historie 1945–1965*, Oslo: Universitetsforlaget, 167–281.

Eriksen, K.E. and Pharø, H. (1997) *Kald krig og internasjonalisering 1949–1965. Norsk Utenrikspolitikks historie*. Bind. 5, Oslo: Universitetsforlaget.

European Commission (2003) 'The Reform of the Common Fisheries Policy' at http://europa.eu.int/comm/fisheries/reform/roadmap/index_en.htm (accessed 24 November 2003).

European Communities (2002) *Official Journal of the European Communities L63456 6 March 2002. 2002/187/JHA*, Luxembourg: European Communities.

European Observer (2004) 'Norway Main Contributors to new EU Member States' at http://euobs.com/index.phtml?sid=9&aid=14050 (accessed 9 January 2004).

European Union (2002) 'EU action in response to the 11th September 2001: one year after' at http://europa.eu.int/comm/external_relations/10901/me/02/187.htm (accessed 28 January 2004).

Featherstone, K. (2002) 'Europeanization in Theory and Practice' in E. Davidson, A. Eriksson and J. Hallenberg (eds) *Europeanization of Security and Defence Policy*, Stockholm: Swedish National Defence College, 13–20.

Finnish presidency of the EU (2000) *Summary of the Programme for the Finnish EU Presidency* at http://presidency.finland.fi/agenda.html (accessed 24 November 2003).

Fjærevoll, D.J. (1998) 'Challenges for Norwegian Defence into Year 2000. Address by Mr Dag Jostein Fjærevoll, Norwegian Minister of Defence, Oslo Military Society, 5 January 1998', mimeo.

Fjærevoll, D.J. (1999) 'Defence Minister Fjærevoll opening statement at the Leangkollen conference, 1 February 1999', mimeo.

Flora, P., Kuhnle, S. and Urwin, D. (eds) (1999) *State Formation, Nation Building and Mass Politics in Europe. The Theory of Stein Rokkan*, Oxford: Oxford University Press.

Førland, T.E. (1988) '1948 som "vendepunkt". Er NATO-medlemskapet bare kulisse?' *Internasjonal Politikk* 6: 69–85.

Folkebevegelsen mot norsk medlemskap i Fellesmarkedet (1972) *Folkebevegelsens melding om Norges forhold til de Europeiske Felleskap (EF)*, Motmelding til Regjeringens Stortingsmelding nr. 50, 1971–1972, Oslo: Folkebevegelsen mot norsk medlemskap i Fellesmarkedet.

Forsvarsdepartementet (2001) *The Long Term Defence Plan for 2002–2005*, Oslo: Forsvarsdepartementet.

Forsvarsdepartementet (2002) *Restructuring Year 2003*, Oslo: Forsvarsdepartementet.

Forsvarsdepartementet (2003) *The Norwegian Defence Budget 2004*, Oslo: Forsvarsdepartementet.

Forsvarsdepartementet (2004) *The Further Modernisation of the Norwegian Armed Forces 2005–2008*, Oslo: Forsvarsdepartementet at http://odin.dep.no/fd/engelsk/aktuelt/pressem/010001-070030/index-dok000-b-f-a.html (accessed 8 April 2004).

Forsvarskommisjonen av 1990 (1992) (Defence Commission of 1990), Oslo: Norges Offentlige Utredninger, 12.

Foss, P.-K. (2003) 'ESA godkjenner overgangsperiode' at http://www.hoyre.no/Saker/1068647470.25/artikkel_print.pt.

Foss, T., Matthiasson, T. and Ulrichson, H. (eds) (2003) *Iceland, Norway and the EC Common Fisheries Policy*, Oslo: NUPI.

Fremskrittspartiet (2003) *Prinsipp- og handlingsprogram 2001–2005. Norge og verden Norge og Europa*, at http://www.frp.no/article/?id=181#norgeeuropa (accessed 8 January 2004).

Frydenlund, K. (1982) *Lille land – hva nå?* Oslo: Universitetsforlaget.

Fure, O.-B. (1996) *Norsk utenrigspolitikks historie* III. *Mellomkrigstid 1920–1940*, Oslo: Cappelen.

Galloway, D. (2001) *The Treaty of Nice and Beyond. Realities and Illusions of Power in the EU*, Sheffield: Sheffield Academic Press, Contemporary European Studies 10.

Gellner, E. (1997) *Nationalism*, London: Phoenix.

Gerhardsen, T.S., Harsvik, W., Thoresen, F.E. and Strøm, S. (1994) *Sosialdemokratisk alternativ*, Oslo; Sosialdemokrater mot EU.

Godal, B.T. (1995) 'Foreign Minister Bjorn Tøre Godal's address to the Oslo Military Society, 2 October 1995', *UD informasjon*, Oslo: Utenriksdepartementet.

Godal, B.T. (1997) 'Innledning på Nordisk Råds konferense i Helsingfors 25.–26.8.97 om sikkerhet i Norden og de nordiske nærområdene', mimeo.

Græger, N. (2002) 'Norway and the EU's Defence Dimension: A "Troops for Influence" Strategy' in N. Græger, H. Larsen and H. Ojanen (eds) *The ESDP and the Nordic Countries. Four Variations on a Theme*, Helsinki: UPI, 33–89.

Grew, R. (1984) 'The Nineteenth Century European State' in C. Bright and S. Harding (eds) *Statemaking and Social Movements*, Ann Arbor, MI: University of Michigan Press, 83–102.

Grønlie, T. (1995) 'The Years since 1945' in R. Danielsen, S. Dyrvik, T. Grønlie, K. Helle and E. Hovland, *Norway. A History from the Vikings to our own Times*, Oslo, Copenhagen and Stockholm: Scandinavian University Press, 357–453.

Gstöhl, S. (2002) *Reluctant Europeans. Norway, Sweden and Switzerland in the Process of Integration*, Boulder, CO, and London: Lynne Rienner.

Haaland Matlary, J. (1993) 'And Never the Twain shall Meet. Reflections on Norway, Europe and Integration' in T. Tiilikainen and I. Damgaard Petersen (eds) *The Nordic Countries and the EC*, Copenhagen: Copenhagen Political Studies, 43–63.

Habermas, J. (1996) 'The European Nation State' in G. Balakrishnan (ed.) *Mapping the Nation State*, London: Verso, 281–94.

Hauksson, U. (2000) *Our Common Fishery Resource*, European Masters of Public Administration, Leuven: Faculty of Social Science.

Heidar, K. (2001) *Norway. Elites on Trial*, Boulder, CO: Westview Press.

Helle, K. (1995) 'Part I. Down to 1536' in R. Danielsen, S. Dyrvik, T. Grønlie, K.

Helle and E. Hovland, *Norway. A History from the Vikings to our own Times*, Oslo, Copenhagen and Stockholm: Scandinavian University Press, 3–119.

Hellstrøm, U.P. (2003) 'Kald skulder til "EU light" i Brussel', *Aftenposten* at http://www.aftenposten, 11 October 2003 (accessed 12 October 2003).

Henriksen, T. (2003) 'The Icelandic–Norwegian Maritime Conflicts' in C. Archer and P. Joenniemi (eds) *The Nordic Peace*, Aldershot: Ashgate, 112–34.

Hey, J. (2003) 'Refining our Understanding of Small State Foreign Policy' in J. Hey (ed.) *Small States in World Politics. Explaining Foreign Policy Behavior*, Boulder, CO and London: Lynne Rienner, 185–95.

Hirschmann, A.O. (1990) *Exit, Voice and Loyalty. Responses to Decline in Firms, Organizations and States*, Cambridge, MA: Harvard University Press.

Hirst, P. and Thompson, G. (2000) *Globalization in Question*, 2nd edn, Cambridge: Polity Press.

Historisk statistikk (2000) 'Resident Population', table 3-3-1t at http://www.ssb.no/historisk/tabeller/3-3-1t.txt (accessed 24 November 2003).

Hobsbawm, E. (1995) 'Introduction. Inventing Traditions' in E. Hobsbawn and T. Ranger (eds) *The Invention of Tradition*, Cambridge: Cambridge University Press.

Hodne, F. (1983) *The Norwegian Economy 1920–1980*, London: Croom Helm.

Hoel, A.H. (1999) 'Ikke en fisk å gi. Norge, EU og fiskeriene' in D.H. Claes and B.S. Tranøy (eds) *Utenfor, annerledes og suveren?* Oslo: Fagbokforlaget, 209–26.

Holm-Hansen, J. (2000) 'Internationalisation on the Local Level in Norway' in J. Gidlund and M. Jerneck (eds) *Local and Regional Governance in Europe*, Cheltenham: Edward Elgar, 77–94.

Holst, J.J. (1966) 'Norsk sikkerhetspolitikk i strategisk perspektiv', *Internasjonal Politikk* 5: 463–90.

Holst, J.J. (1967) *Norsk sikkerhetspolitikk i strategisk perspektiv* II, Oslo: NUPI.

Holst, J.J. (1991), 'The New Europe. A View from the North', Lecture to the Fundacion Jose Y Gasset, Madrid, 29 October 1991, Oslo, mimeo.

Honkanen, K. (2002) *The Influence of Small States on NATO Decision Making*, Stockholm: Totalförsvarets Forskningsinstitut.

Hovland, E. (1995) 'Modern Norway takes Shape 1875–1920' in R. Danielsen, S. Dyrvik, T. Grønlie, K. Helle and E. Hovland, *Norway. A History from the Vikings to our own Times*, Oslo, Copenhagen and Stockholm: Scandinavian University Press, 271–96.

Høyre (2003) *Høyres stortingsvalgprogram 2001–2005* at http://www.hoyre.no/Saker/program/1042326678.89/artikkel_print.pt (accessed 8 January 2004).

Ikenberry, J. (1991) 'The State and Strategies of International Adjustment' in R. Little and M. Smith (eds) *Perspectives on World Politics*, 2nd edn, London: Routledge, 157–68.

Ingebritsen, C. (1998) *The Nordic States and European Unity*, Ithaca, NY and London: Cornell University Press.

Ingebritsen, C. (2002) 'Norm Entrepreneurs. Scandinavia's Role in World Politics', *Cooperation and Conflict* 37 (1): 11–23.

Ingebritsen, C. (2003) 'New Perspectives on European Integration', *Cooperation and Conflict* 38 (2): 159–61.

Ingebritsen, C. and Larson, S. (1997) 'Interest and Identity. Finland, Norway and the European Union', *Cooperation and Conflict* 32 (2): 207–22.

Inglehart, R. (1990) *Culture Shift in Industrial Societies*, Princeton, NJ: Princeton University Press.

Inns.S. nr 248 1991–92 (1992) *Innstilling fra utenriks- og konstitusjonskomiteen om samtykke til ratifikasjon av avtale av Det europeiske økonomiske samarbeidsområdet (EØS), undertegnet i Oporto 2 mai 1992. Avgitt 29 sept. 1992*, Oslo: Stortinget.

Inns.S. nr 15 1992–93 (1993) *Innstilling fra utenriks- og konstitusjonskomiteen for godkjenning av en avtale i form av en brevveksling mellom Norge og om Det europeiske økonomiske felleskap om utvikling av det bilaterale fiskerisamarbeidet (St. prp. nr 102 for 1991–92)*, Oslo: Stortinget.

Inns.S. nr 229 1996–97 (1997) *Innstilling fra utenrikskomiteen om samtykke til ratifikasjon av samarbeidsavtale av 19. desember 1996 mellom partene i Schengen-avtalen og Schengen-konvensjonen, og Island og Norge om avskaffelse av personkontroll på de felles grenser*, Oslo: Stortinget.

Innst.S. nr 239 (2001) *Instilling frå utanrikskomiteen om Norge og Europa ved inngangen til et nytt århundre, St.meld.nr. 12 (2000–20001)*, Oslo: Stortinget.

Innst.S. nr 24 (2002) *Instilling frå utanrikskomiteen om EOS-samarbeidet 1994–2001*, Oslo: Stortinget.

Innst.S. nr 267 (2002) *Innstilling frå energi- og miljøkomiteen om samtykke til godkjenning av avgjerd i EØS-komiteen nr 123/2001 om innlemming av europaparlaments- og rådsdirektiv 98/30/EF om felles regler for det indre marked for naturgass (gassmarknadsdirektivet) i vedlegg IV til EØS-avtala (Energi), St. prp. nr 42 (2001–2002)*, Oslo: Stortinget.

International Institute of Strategic Studies (2003) *The Military Balance 2003–2004*, London: Oxford University Press.

Jagland, T. (2003) 'EU-prat med Jagland', *Aftenposten* nett utgaven Oppdatert 25 November 2003, at http://tux1.aftenposten.no/nettprat/jaglandeu2511/ (accessed 25 November 2003).

Jepperson, R.L., Wendt, A. and Katzenstein, P.J. (1996) 'Norms, Identity, and Culture in National Security' in P.J. Katzenstein (ed.) *The Culture of National Security. Norms and Identity in World Politics*, New York: Columbia University Press, 33–75.

Jervell, S. (2003) *Sveitsisk løsning*, Oslo: NUPI.

Joenniemi, P. (2002) 'Finland in the new Europe. A Hederian or Hegelian Project?' in L. Hansen and O. Wæver (eds) *European Integration and National Identity*, London and New York: Routledge, 182–213.

Johnsen, K.Ø. (2002) 'The new draft regulation in Norway' at http://odin.dep.no/krd/engelsk/taler/taler_politisk_lede.../index-dok000-b-f-a.html (accessed 2 October 2002).

Julsrud, O and Malmø, M. (2002) *Politisk Årbok 2002*, Oslo: Andante Forlag.

Kellner, D. (1998) 'Globalization and the Postmodern Turn' in R. Axtmann (ed.) *Globalization and Europe. Theoretical and Empirical Investigations*, London and Washington, DC: Pinter, 23–42.

Kelstrup, M. (1992) 'Introduction' in M. Kelstrup (ed.) *European Integration and Denmark's Participation*, Copenhagen: Copenhagen Political Studies Press, 1–12.

Kleppa, M.M. (2003) 'Sp krev overgangsordningar for arbeidsinnvandring' at http://www.senterpartiet.no (accessed 1 December 2003).

Knill, C. (2001) *The Europeanisation of National Administrations. Patterns of Institutional Change and Persistence*, Cambridge: Cambridge University Press.

Knill, C. and Lehmkuhl, D. (1999) 'How Europe matters. Different Mechanisms of

Europeanization', *European Integration Online Papers* 3 (7) at http://eiop.or.at/eiop/texte/1999-007a.htm (accessed 23 September 2002).

Kommunal- og regionaldepartementet (2004) 'The EEA Enlargement and Transitional Rules', *Press Release 19/2004* at http://odin.dep.no/krd/engelsk/aktuelt/pressem/016081-070196/index-dok000-b-f-a.html (accessed 24 March 2004).

Kosmo, J. (1995) *Norges forsvar. Hvor står vi – hvor går vi, Oslo Militære Samfund, 9 Januar 1995*, Oslo, mimeo.

Kostakopoulou, D. (1998) 'Is there an Alternative to "Schengenland"?' *Political Studies* 46: 886–902.

KPMG (2002) *Regulering av oppdrettsnæringen internasjonalt – en sammenligning av rammebetingelser i ulike lakseproduserende land*, Oslo: KPMG.

Kristelig folkeparti (2003) *Hva mener KrF om . . . EU* at http://www.krf.no/krfweb/politikk/hva_mener_krf_om/hva_mener_krf_om.asp (accessed 4 January 2004).

Lægreid, P. (1999) *Sentralforvaltnings Europatilpasning*, Oslo: LOS-senter.

Leira, H. (2002) *International idealisme og Norge* (Hovedoppgave i Statsvitenskap), Oslo: Institutt for Statsvitenskap, University of Oslo.

Lie, H. (1975) *. . . slik jeg ser det*, Oslo: Tiden Norsk Forlag.

Lindstøl, A. (1978) '"De 13". "Protesten mot atomvåpen" – et utenomparlamentarisk initiativ under atomdebatten I Norge, våren 1961' (thesis in history), Oslo: University of Oslo.

Løwer, E. (2000) 'Our Defence in an International Perspective', address to Oslo Military Society, 10 January 2000, Oslo, mimeo.

Lyng, J. (1976) *Mellom øst og vest*, Oslo: Cappelen.

Manners, I. (2002) 'Normative Power Europe. A Contradiction in Terms?' *Journal of Common Market Studies* 40 (2): 235–58.

Marks, G., Hooghe, L. and Blank, K. (1996) 'European Integration from the 1980s. State-centric *v.* Multi-level Governance', *Journal of Common Market Studies* 34 (3): 341–78.

McMichael, P. (1996) 'Globalization. Myths and Realities', *Rural Sociology* 61: 25–55.

Meyer, J.K. (1989) *NATOs kritikere. Den sikkerhetspolitiske opposisjon 1949–1961*, Oslo: Institutt for Forsvarsstudier.

Miles, L. (2001) 'Sweden in the European Union. Changing Expectations?' *Journal of European Integration* 23 (4): 303–33.

Ministry of Defence (1993) *Security Factors Determining the Activities of Norway's Armed Forces (translation of the Introductory Chapter on Security Policy in the Ministry of Defence's Budget Proposal to the Parliament for 1994)*, Oslo: Royal Norwegian Ministry of Defence.

Ministry of Defence (1996) *Defence Budget 1997*. Oslo: Royal Norwegian Ministry of Defence.

Ministry of Local Government and Regional Development (2002) *Newsletter on Norwegian Refugee and Immigration Policy* at http://odin.dep.no/krd/engelsk/016081-280007/index-dok000-b-f-a.html (accessed 2 October 2002).

Mission of Norway to the EU (2004) 'Simultaneous enlargement of the EU and the EEA ensured' at http://www.brussel-eu.mfa.no/News/default.htm.

Missiroli, A. (2003) *From Copenhagen to Brussels. European Defence: Core Documents* IV, Paris: Institute of Security Studies.

Moses, W.M. and Knutsen, T. (2001) 'Inside out. Globalization and the Reorganization of Foreign Affairs Ministries', *Cooperation and Conflict* 36 (4): 355–80.

Moses, W.M. and Tranøy, B.S. (1995) 'Norge i den nye verdensøkonomien' in T.L. Knutsen, G.M. Sørbø and S. Gjerdåker (eds) *Norges utenrigspolitikk*, Oslo: Cappelen.

Monar, J. (1998) 'Justice and Home Affairs in the Treaty of Amsterdam. Reform at the Price of Fragmentation', *European Law Review*, 23 (4): 320–35.

Mouritzen, H. (1996) 'Introduction' in H. Mouritzen, O. Wæver and H. Wiberg, *European Integration and National Adaptations. A Theoretical Inquiry*, Commack: Nova Science Publishers, 3–5.

Myrjord, A. (2003) 'Foreign policy diversification in Europe. The case of three-level co-operation in the Barents Euro-Arctic Region' (doctoral thesis), Manchester: Department of Politics and Philosophy, Manchester Metropolitan University.

Narud, H.M. and Strøm, K. (2000) 'Adaptation without EU Membership. Norway and the European Economic Area' in T. Bergman and E. Damgaard (eds) *Delegation and Accountability in European Integration*, London: Frank Cass, 125–50.

Nationen (2002) 6 May 2002.

Natland (2003) 'Birkedal skal gi Hagen EU-råd', *Aftenbladet*, 28 January 2003, at http://aftenbladet.no/nyheter/innenriks/article.jhtml?articleID=150878 (accessed 8 January 2004).

Nei til EU (1994) *Norge og EU. Virkninger av medlemskap i Den europeisk union*, Oslo: Nei til EU.

Neumann, I.B. (2001) *Norge – en kritikk Begrepsmakt I Europa-debatten*, Oslo: Pax-forlag.

Neumann, I.B. (2002a) ' This little Piggy stayed at Home. Why Norway is not a Member of the EU' in L. Hansen and O. Wæver (eds) *European Integration and National Identity*, London and New York: Routledge, 88–129.

Neumann, I. (2002b) 'Norges handlingsrom og behovet for en overgripende sikkerhetspolitisk strategi', *Det sikkerhetspolitiske bibliotek*, 3–2002, Oslo: DNAK.

Nordby, T. and Veggeland, F. (1999) 'Lovgivingsmyndighetens suspensjon. Stortingets rolle under EØS-avtalen', *Tidsskrift for samfunnsforskning* 40 (1): 90–8.

Nordlys, 22 July 1994.

Norwegian Confederation of Trade Unions (2003) *LO Brussel Rapport. Den nye EØS avtalen endelig godkjent. LO ber om overgangsordninger mot sosial dumping* at http://www.lo.no (accessed 1 December 2003).

Nugent, N. (1999) *The Government and Politics of the European Union*, Basingstoke: Macmillan.

OECD (2003a) *Regulatory Reform in Norway. Government Capacity to assure High Quality Regulation*, Paris: OECD.

OECD (2003b) *Regulatory Reform in Norway. Modern Regulation and Supervisory Agencies*, Paris: OECD.

Olsen, J.P. (2000) *Organized Democracy. Political Institutions in a Welfare State. The Case of Norway*, Oslo: Scandinavian University Press.

Olsen, J.P. (2002) *The Many Faces of Europeanization*, Working Papers 1, Oslo: Arena.

Opinion (2003) *Opinion AS Parti-barometer* at http://odin.Opinion AS.htm (accessed 8 January 2004).

Pedersen, O.K. and Pedersen, D. (2000) 'The Europeanisation of Local Interest in

Denmark. The Strategic Choice: to "Go through" *v.* to "Bypass" National Institutions?' in J. Gidlund and M. Jerneck (eds) *Local and Regional Governance in Europe*, Cheltenham: Edward Elgar, 51–75.
Pesonen, P., Jenssen, A.T. and Gilljam, M. (1998) 'To Join or Not to Join' in A.T. Jenssen, P. Pesonen and M. Gilljam (eds) *To Join or Not to Join. Three Nordic Referendums on Membership in the European Union*, Oslo: Scandinavian University Press, 13–36.
Petersen, J. (2003) ' "Norge og fremtidens Europa", Introduction to Conference on "EUs fremtid og Norge", Oslo, 30 October 2003', Oslo: Ministry of Foreign Affairs, mimeo.
Petersen, N. (1979) 'International Power and Foreign Policy Behaviour. The Formulation of Danish Security Policy in the 1870–1914 Period' in K. Goldmann and G. Sjöstedt (eds) *Power, Capabilities, Interdependence*, London: Sage, 235–71.
Petersen, N. (1998) 'National Strategies in the Integration Dilemma. An Adaptation Approach', *Journal of Common Market Studies* 36 (1): 33–54.
Pharø, H. (1991) *Norge, Norden og europeisk integrasjon som etterkrigshistorisk forskningsfelt*, Oslo: LOS-senter.
Putnam, R. (1988) 'Diplomacy and Domestic Politics. The Logic of Two-level Games', *International Organization* 42 (4): 427–60.
Radaelli, C.M. (2000) 'Whither Europeanization? Concept Stretching and Substantive Change', *European Integration Online Papers* 4 (8) at http://www.eiop.or.at/eiop/texte/2000-008a.htm (accessed 2 October 2003).
Ramberg, T. (1972) 'Sovereignty and Cooperation' in N. Ørvik (ed.) *Fears and Expectations. Norwegian Attitudes towards European Integration*, Oslo: Universitetsforlaget.
Ramsøy, N. (1974) 'Preface' in N. Ramsøy (ed.) *Norwegian Society*, Oslo: Universitetsforlaget.
Regjeringens informasjonsutvalg for Europasaker (1994) *Informasjon om EØS-avtalen*. Oslo: Regjeringens informasjonsutvalg for Europasaker.
Ribot, J.C. (1993) 'Market–State relations and Environmental Policy' in R. Lipschutz, and K. Conca (eds) *The State and Social Power in Global Environmental Politics*, New York: Columbia University Press.
Ringdal, K. (1995) 'Velgenes argumenter' in A.T. Jenssen and H. Valen (eds) *Brussel midt imot. Folkeavstemningen om EU*, Oslo: Ad Notam Gyldendal, 45–64.
Riste, O. (1965) *The Neutral Ally*, Oslo and London: Universitetsforlaget and Allen & Unwin.
Riste, O. (1984) 'Fra integritetstraktat til atompolitikk. Det stormaktsgaranterte Norge 1905–1983' in R. Tamnes (ed.) *Forsvarsstudier – Defence Studies* III. *Årbok for FHFS/FH 1983–84*, Oslo: TANO.
Riste, O. (2001) *Norway's Foreign Relations. A History*, Oslo: Universitetsforlaget.
Rokkan, S. (1967) 'Geography, Religion and Social Class. Crosscutting Cleavage in Norwegian Politics' in M. Lipset and S. Rokkan (eds) *Party Systems and Voter Alignments*, New York: Free Press, 370–89.
Rokkan, S. (1970) *Citizens, Elections, Parties*, Oslo: Universitetsforlaget.
Rosenau, J. (1970) *The Adaptation of National Societies. A Theory of Political System Behavior and Transformation*, New York: McCaleb-Seiler.
Rosenau, J. (1981) *The Study of Political Adaptation*, London: Pinter.

Ross, G. (1998) 'European Integration and Globalization' in R. Axtmann (ed.) *Globalization and Europe. Theoretical and Empirical Investigations*, London and Washington, DC: Pinter, 164–83.

Royal Norwegian Government Information Office (1943) *Norway. A Handbook*, rev. edn, London: Dent.

Russett, B. and Starr, H. (1996) *World Politics. The Menu for Choice*, 5th edn, New York: Freeman.

Salmon, P. (1993) *Foreign Policy and National Identity. The Norwegian Integrity Treaty 1907–1924*, Forsvarsstudier No. 1 1993, Oslo: Institutt for forsvarssstudier.

Sæter, M. (1985) 'Norge utenfor EF. Broer til Europa' in J.J. Holst and D. Heradstveit (eds) *Norsk utenrikspolitikk*, Oslo: TANO.

Sejersted, F. (1996) 'The Norwegian Parliament and European Integration. Reflections from Medium Speed Europe' in E. Smith (ed.) *National Parliaments as Cornerstones of European Integration*, London: Kluwer, 125–50.

Senterpartiet (2003) 'Derfor sier Senterpartiet nei til EU' at http://www.senterpartiet.no (accessed 8 January 2004).

Smith, S. and Baylis, J. (2001) 'Introduction' in J. Baylis and S. Smith (eds) *The Globalization of World Politics. An Introduction to International Relations*, Oxford: Oxford University Press.

Sogner, I. (1993) 'The European Idea. The Scandinavian Answer. Norwegian Attitudes towards a closer Scandinavian Economic Cooperation 1947–1959', *Scandinavian Journal of History* 18 (4): 307–27.

Solberg, E. (2002) 'The Political Challenges of Migration', welcome address by Erna Solberg, Minister of Local Government and Regional Development, to the seventh Metropolis Conference, 9 September 2002, Oslo: Kommunal og Regionaldepartementet, mimeo.

Sosialistisk Venstreparti (2003) *9.5 Partiprogram EU og EØS* at http://www.sv.no/mener/program/kap09/kap095/ (accessed 8 January 2003).

Spanou, C. (1998) 'European Integration in Administrative Terms: A Framework for Analysis and the Greek Case', *Journal of European Public Policy* 5 (3): 467–84.

Spence, T. (2003) 'Lilletun uenig i Bondeviks EU-åpning' at http://www.aftenposten.no, 5 October 2003 (accessed 13 October 2003).

Starr, H. (1997) *Anarchy, Order, and Integration*, Ann Arbor, MI: University of Michigan Press.

Statistics Norway (1995) *Statistikk årbok 1995*, Oslo: Statistics Norway.

Statistics Norway (2000) *Statistikk årbok 2000*, Oslo: Statistics Norway.

Statistics Norway (2003) 'Due to immigration population increased' at www.ssb.no/english/subjects/02/01/10/innvbe_en/(accessed 24 November 2003).

Statistisk sentralbyrå [SSB] (2000) 'Emigration' at http://www.ssb.no/emner/historisk_statistikk/aarbok/ht-020220-051.html (accessed 24 November 2003).

Statoil Magazine (2000) 'Links Market Force', *Statoil Magazine* 2: 5–7, Stavanger: Statoil.

Statskonsult (1998) *Handbok i EØS-arbeid. Utforming og gjennonføring av regelverket i EU og EØS*, Oslo: Statskonsult.

Statskonsult (2001a) *Norsk innflytelse gjennom EU-komiteer. En undersøkelser av komitéarbeidet innenfor utvalgte sektorer: sett fra dered egen og fra Europakommisjonens side*, Statskonsult Rapport 2001: 15, at http://www.statskonsult.no/publik/publikasjoner/2001-15/index.htm (accessed 14 November 2003).

Statskonsult (2001b) *Norsk deltagelser i og forvaltning av EU-programmer*, Statskonsult Rapport 2001: 13, at http://www.statskonsult.no/publik/publikasjoner/2001-13/r2001-13.pdf (accessed 14 November 2003).

Statskonsult (2002) *I komiteer og korridorer. Handbok i EØS-arbeid*, Oslo: Statskonsult.

Statskonsult (2003a) *EØS og tilsyn*, Statskonsult Rapport 2003: 3, at http://www.statskonsult.no/publik/rapporter/2003/2003-03sam.htm (accessed 14 November 2003).

Statskonsult (2003b) *EØS-arbeidet i norsk forvaltning*, Statskonsult Rapport 2003: 5, at http://www.statskonsult.no/publik/rapporter/2003/2003-05sam.htm (accessed 14 November 2003).

Statskonsult (2003c) *I kongens navn*, Oslo: Statskonsult.

Statsministerens kontor (2001) *Om departementenes arbeid med EØS-saker*. Oslo: Statsministerens kontor.

Statsministerens kontor (2002) *Om R-konferenser*. Publikasjonnummer B-0504B, at http:/www.dep.no/archive/smkvedlegg/01/01/nnma031.pdf (accessed 14 November 2003).

Statsministerens kontor (2003) *Om statsråd. Forberedseser av saker til statsråd*. Publikasjonnummer B-0501B, at http:/www.dep.no/archive/smkvedlegg/01/01/omsta035.pdf (accessed 14 November 2003).

Stenius, H. (2003) 'The Language Issue in Finland' in C. Archer and P. Joenniemi (eds) *The Nordic Peace*, London: Ashgate, 157–70.

Stirk, P.M.R. and Weigall, D. (eds) (1999) *The Origins and Development of European Integration. A Reader and Commentary*, London: Pinter.

Stoltenberg, T. (1994) 'Foreword', in Olav Schram Stokke and Ola Tunander, *The Barents Region. Co-operation in Arctic Europe*, London: Sage, ix.

Stortingsmelding nr 15, 1961–2 (1961) *Om det Europeiske Økonomiske Fellesskap og de europeiske markedsproblemer*, Oslo: Det kongelige utenriksdepartementet.

Stortingsmelding nr 86, 1966–7 (1967) *Om Norges Forhold til de Europeiske Fellesskap*, Oslo: Det kongelige utenriksdepartementet.

Stortingsmelding nr 92, 1969–70 (1970) *Om Norges Forhold til de Nordiske og Europeiske Markedsdannelser*, Oslo: Det kongelige utenriksdepartementet.

Stortingsmelding nr 50, 1971–2 (1972) *Om Norges Tilslutning til de Europeiske Fellesskap*, Oslo: Det kongelige utenriksdepartementet.

Stortingsmelding nr 9, 1973–4 (1973) *Hovedretningslinjer for Forsvarets virksomhet i tiden 1974–78*, Oslo: Forsvarsdepartementet.

Stortingsmelding nr 40, 1993–4 (1994) *Om medlemskap i Den europeiske union*, Oslo: Det kongelige utenriksdepartementet.

Stortingsmelding nr 38 1998–9 (1999) *Forsvarskomiteen Tilpasning av Forsvaret til deltagelse i internasjonale operasjoner*, Oslo: Forsvarsdepartementet.

Stortingsmelding nr 12, 2000–1 (2000) *Om Norge of Europa ved inngangen til et nytt århundre*, Oslo: Det kongelige utenriksdepartementet.

Stortingsmelding nr 27, 2001–2 (2002) *Om EØS-samarbeidet 1994–2001*, Oslo: Det kongelige utenriksdepartementet.

Stortingsproposisjon 100, 1991–2 (1992) *Utenriks- og konstitusjonskomiteen Samtykke til ratifikasjon av Avtale om Det europeiske økonomiske samarbeidsområdet (EØS-avtalen) undertegnet i Oporto 2. mai 1992* at http://www.stortinget.no (accessed 24 January 2004).

Stortingsproposisjon 42, 1996–7 (1996) *Samarbeidsavtale mellom Kongeriket Belgia, Forbundsrepublikken Tyskland, Republikken Frankrike, Storhertugdømmet Luxembourg, Kongeriket Nederland, Republikken Italia, Kongeriket Spania, Republikken Portugal, Republikken Hellas, Republikken Østerrike, Kongeriket Danmark, Republikken Finland, Kongeriket Sverige, som er parter i Schengen-avtalen og Schengen-konvensjonen, og Republikken Island og Kongeriket Norge om avskaffelse av personkontroll på de felles grenser*, at http://www.stortinget.no.St_prp_ nr_ 42 (1996–97).htm (accessed 24 January 2004).

Stortingsproposisjon 50, 1998–9 (1999) *Om samtykke til inngåelse av en avtale mellom Rådet for Den europeiske union og Republikken Island og Kongeriket Norge om de sistnevnte statenes tilknytning til gjennomføringen, anvendelsen og videreutviklingen av Schengen-regelverket. Tilråding fra Utenriksdepartementet av 26. mars 1999, godkjent i statsråd samme dag*, at http://odin.dep.no/ud/norsk/publ/stprp/032005-030049/index-dok000-b-n-a.html (accessed 24 January 2004).

Stortingsproposisjon 3, 2003–4 (2003) *Om samtykke til ratifikasjon av avtale om Den tsjekkiske republikks, Republikken Estlands, Republikken Kypros', Republikken Latvias, Republikken Litauens, Republikken Ungarns, Republikken Maltas, Republikken Polens, Republikken Slovenias og Den slovakiske republikks deltakelse i Det europeiske økonomiske samarbeidsområde (EØS) med tilliggende avtale. Tilråding fra Utenriksdepartementet av 10. oktober 2003, godkjent i statsråd samme dag*, at http://odin.dep.no/ud/norsk/publ/stprp/032001-030118/index-dok000-b-n-a.html (accessed 5 January 2004).

Stortingstidende 1966–7 (1967) vol. 7c, 13 July 1967, Oslo: Stortinget.

Stortingstidende 1987–8 (1988) vol. 7c, 7 June 1988, Oslo: Stortinget.

Stortingstidende 1989–90 (1989) Debate, 1 December 1989, Oslo: Stortinget.

Stortingstidende (1992) *Stortingsforhandlinger, 1992–93 nr 4, Debatter m.v. i Stortinget 15.–16. Oktober 1992, Sesjonen 1992–93*, 169–341, Oslo: Stortinget.

Stortingstidende (1997) *Stortinget Møte mandag den 9. juni kl. 11 1997. Votering*, at http://www.stortinget.no/stid/1996/sv970609.html (accessed 24 January 2004).

Stortingstidende (1999a) *Stortinget Møte mandag den 26. april kl. 12 1999. Instilling fra utenrikskomiteen om samtykke til inngåelse av en avtale mellom Rådet for Den europeiske union og Republikken Island og Kongeriket Norge om de sistnevnte statenes tilknytning til gjennomføringen, anvendelsen og videreutviklingen av Schengen-regelverket*, at http://www.stortinget.no/stid/1998/s990426-03.html (accessed 2 October 2002).

Stortingstidende (1999b) *Stortinget Møte mandag den 26. april kl. 12 1999. Votering*, at http://www.stortinget.no/stid/19986/sv990426.html (accessed 2 October 2003).

Stortingstidende (2001a) *Stortingsforhandlinger, Debatter m.v. i Stortinget, nr 31 22. mai 2001*, at http://www.stortinget.no/stid/2000/s010522-01.html (accessed 2 October 2003).

Stortingstidende (2001b) *Stortingsforhandlinger, Debatter m.v. i Stortinget, nr 31 01. mars 2001*, at http://www.stortinget.no/stid/2000/s010301-09.html, 1 March 2001 (accessed 2 October 2003).

Stortingstidende (2002a) *Stortingsforhandlinger, Debatter m.v. i Stortinget*, 14 November 2002, at http://www.stortinget.no/stid/2002/S021114-01.html (accessed 2 October 2003).

Stortingstidende (2002b) *Stortinget Møte mandag den 18. juni kl. 13.05 2002.Votering*, at http://www.stortinget.no/stid/2002/S021114-01.html (accessed 2 October 2003).

Swiss Parliament (2003) 'CH-UE Négociations bilatérales II. Communiqués de presse 2003: Généralités (22/10/2003)' at http://www.europa.admin.ch/nbv/medien/2003/f/gen.htm#22.10.03a (accessed 7 January 2004).

Tamnes, R. (1987) 'Integration and Screening. The Two Faces of Norwegian Alliance Policy 1945–1986' in R. Tamnes (ed.) *Forsvarsstudier – Defence Studies VI. Årbok for FHFS/FH 1987*, Oslo: TANO.

Tamnes, R. (1991) *The United States and the Cold War in the High North*, Oslo: Ad Notam.

Tande (2002) 'Alle gode ting er tre?' *Norsk fiskerinæring* 11/12: 9.

Thorhallsson, B. (2000) *The Role of Small States in the European Union*, Aldershot: Ashgate.

Tilly, C. (1990) *Coercion, Capital, and European States, AD 990–1990*, Oxford: Blackwell.

Torgersen, U. (1974) 'Political Institutions' in N.R. Ramsøy (ed.) *Norwegian Society*, Oslo: Universitetsforlaget, 196–220.

Traavik, K. (2001) 'Den nye regjeringens europapolitikk' at http://www.odin.dep.no/ud/norsk/aktuelt/taler/taler_politisk_ledelse/032001-090146/inde . . . (accessed 7 October 2003).

Traavik, K. (2002) 'EØS-avtalen under press. Hva gjør Norge?' speech to NHO's Brussels conference, 1 March 2002, at http://odin.dep.no/ud/norsk/aktuelt/taler/taler_politisk_ledelse/032171-090016/index-dok000-b-n-a.html (accessed 3 January 2004).

Traavik, K. (2003a) 'Social Partners in the new Europe. EEA, EU and EFTA', speech to conference of the EFTA Consultative Committee, Oslo, 27–28 February 2003, at http://odin.dep.no/ud/engelsk/aktuelt/taler/p10001532/032171-090110/index-dok000-b-n-a.html (accessed 3 January 2004).

Traavik, K. (2003b) 'EU and EEA Enlargement. The Norwegian View', address to a seminar on Norway and Poland, Oslo, 16 June 2003, at http://odin.dep.no/ud/engelsk/aktuelt/taler/p10001532/032171-990086/index-dok000-b-n-a.html (accessed 3 January 2004).

Traavik, K. (2003c) 'The Thessaloniki Summit. A Norwegian Perspective', *EU and EEA Enlargement. The Norwegian View*, at http://odin.dep.no/ud/engelsk/aktuelt/taler/p10001532/032171-090136/index-dok000-b-n-a.html (accessed 3 January 2004).

Trondal, J. (1998) *Mellom politisk styring og faglig uavhengighet*, Oslo: Arena, Working Papers 98/4.

Trondal, J. (1999) *Multiple Institutional Embeddedness in Europe*, Oslo: Arena, Working Papers 99/32.

Trondal, J. and Veggeland, F. (1999) *Norske myndigheter og EØS. Mellom utenrikspolitikk og innenrikspolitikk*, Oslo: Arena, Working Papers 99/10.

UD [Utenriksdepartementet] (2001) 'Report to the Counter-terrorism Committee' at http://odin.dep.no/ud/engelsk/publ/rapporter/032001-990580/index-b-f-a.html (accessed 1 October 2002).

UD [Utenriksdepartementet] (2002) 'The Norwegian Government's European Policy Platform' at http://odin.dep.no/ud/engelsk/publ/handlingsplaner/032 . . ./index-dok000-b-f-a.html (accessed 25 April 2002).

UD [Utenriksdepartementet] (2003a) 'EU-komiteer med norsk deltagelse' at http://odin.dep.no/ud/norsk/europa/eos/kontaktpunkter/komiteer/index-b-n-a.html, (accessed 14 November 2003).

UD [Utenriksdepartementet] (2003b) 'Spesialutvalg' at http://odin.dep.no/ud/norsk/europa/eos/kontaktpunkter/spesialut/index-b-n-a.html (accessed 14 November 2003).

UD [Utenriksdepartementet] (2003c) 'Kontaktpunkter for ulike sentral arbeidsområder knytter til EØS' at http://odin.dep.no/ud/norsk/europa/eos/kontaktpunkter/aktorer/index-b-n-a.html (accessed 14 November 2003).

UD [Utenriksdepartementet] (2003d) 'EØS-komiteens beslutninger, 26.09.2003' at http://odin.dep.no/ud/norsk/europa/eos/aktuelle/beslutninger/032141-130141/index-dok000-b-n-a.htm (accessed 14 November 2003).

Udgaard, N.M. (1973) *Great Power Politics and Norwegian Foreign Policy. A Study of Norway's Foreign Relations, November 1940–February 1948*, Oslo: Universitetsforlaget.

Udgaard, N.M. (2004) 'EU-terskelen høvles ned', *Aftenposten*, 20 February, at http://www.aftenposten.no.template/droplets/utskriftsvennlig.jhtml?articleID=736413 (accessed 8 April 2004).

Ulriksen, S. (2002) *Den norske forsvarstradisjonen. Militærmakt eller folkeforsvar*, Oslo: Pax.

UN Development Programme (2002) 'Norway still first, US sixth, in human development' at http://hdr.undp.org/reports/global/2002/en/pdf/HDR%20PR%20E5.pdf (accessed 24 November 2003).

Utenriksdepartementet (2002) 'Angår utenrikspolitikken deg?' at http://odin.dep.no/ud/niv/innledning/index-b-n-a.html (accessed 8 August 2002).

US Naval Institute (1986) *US Naval Institute Proceedings, January 1986*. Maritime Strategy supplement, Annapolis, MD: US Naval Institute.

Valen, H. (1973) '"No" to EEC', *Scandinavian Political Studies* 8: 214–26.

Valen, H. and Rokkan, S. (1970) 'The Election to the Norwegian Storting in September 1969', *Scandinavian Political Studies* 8: 214–26.

Väyrynen, R. (1993) 'Finland and the European Community. Changing Elite Bargains', *Cooperation and Conflict* 28 (1): 31–46.

Veggeland, F. (1999a) *Delegering, læring og politisk kontroll i EØS-arbeidet. Norges deltakelse I EU-komiteer på veterinær- og næringsmiddelområdet*, Oslo: Arena, Working Papers 99/28.

Veggeland, F. (1999b) 'Institusjonelle tilpasninger til europeisk integrasjonprosessen', *Norsk Statsvitenskapelig Tidsskrift* 15 (1): 3–39.

Veggeland, F. (1999c) 'Matpolitikk I Norge. Fra et beskyttet landbrug til frihandel og forbrukervern' in D.H. Claes and B.S. Tranøy (eds) *Utenfor, annerledes og suveren?* Oslo: Fagbokforlaget, 227–48.

Venstre (2003) *Personlig frihet og sosialt ansvar. Venstres stortingsvalgprogram 2001–2005*, Aktiv Europapolitikk, at http://www.venstre.no/programmet (accessed 8 January 2004).

Vink, M.P. (2001) 'The Limited Europeanization of Domestic Citizenship Policy. Evidence from the Netherlands', *Journal of Common Market Studies* 39 (5): 875–96.

Vollebæk, K. (1998) *The Transformation of European Security. New Challenges for Norway*, address to Oslo Military Society, 9 November 1998, Oslo: Ministry of Foreign Affairs, mimeo.

Warleigh, A. (2002) *Flexible Integration. Which Model for the European Union?* London: Continuum.

Wiberg, H. (1996) 'Adaptive Patterns and the Deep Roots. A European Overview' in H. Mouritzen, O. Wæver and H. Wiberg, *European Integration and National Adaptations. A Theoretical Inquiry*, Commack: Nova Science Publishers, 43–63.

Wilkinson, R. (2000) *Multilateralism and the World Trade Organisation. The Architecture and Extension of International Trade Regulation*, London and New York: Routledge.

Index

DENNIS RODGERS
Professor of Urban Social and Political Research in the School of Social and Political Sciences at the University of Glasgow. Previously a senior research fellow in the Brooks World Poverty Institute (BWPI) at the University of Manchester, UK, where he led their programme on Urban Poverty and Conflict.

JO BEALL
Director of Education and Society at UNU-WIDER, and member of the executive board of the British Council. Formerly Deputy Vice Chancellor at the University of Cape Town, South Africa, prior to which she was a professor of development studies at the London School of Economics, UK.

RAVI KANBUR
T.H. Lee Professor of World Affairs, International Professor of Applied Economics and Management, and Professor of Economics at Cornell University, USA. He has taught at the universities of Oxford, Cambridge, Essex, Warwick, Princeton and Columbia. He has served on the senior staff of the World Bank, including as Principal Adviser to the Chief Economist at the World Bank. He has also served as Director of the World Bank's World Development Report.

Studies in Development Economics and Policy

Series Editor: **Finn Tarp**
UNU WORLD INSTITUTE FOR DEVELOPMENT ECONOMICS RESEARCH

(UNU-WIDER) was established by the United Nations University as its first research and training centre and started work in Helsinki, Finland, in 1985. The purpose of the institute is to undertake applied research and policy analysis of structural changes affecting the developing and transitional economies; to provide a forum for the advocacy of policies leading to robust, equitable and environmentally sustainable growth; and to promote capacity strengthening and training in the field economic and social policy-making. Its work is carried out by staff researchers and visiting scholars in Helsinki, and through networks of collaborating scholars and institutions around the world.

UNU World Institute for Development Economics Research (UNU-WIDER)
Katajanokanlaituri 6 B, FIN-00160 Helsinki, Finland

Titles include:

Tony Addison and Alan Roe (*editors*)
FISCAL POLICY FOR DEVELOPMENT
Poverty, Reconstruction and Growth

Tony Addison, Henrik Hansen and Finn Tarp (*editors*)
DEBT RELIEF FOR POOR COUNTRIES

Tony Addison and George Mavrotas (*editors*)
DEVELOPMENT FINANCE IN THE GLOBAL ECONOMY
The Road Ahead

Tony Addison and Tilman Brück (*editors*)
MAKING PEACE WORK
The Challenges of Social and Economical Reconstruction

George G. Borjas and Jeff Crisp (*editors*)
POVERTY, INTERNATIONAL MIGRATION AND ASYLUM

Ricardo Ffrench-Davis and Stephany Griffith-Jones (*editors*)
FROM CAPITAL SURGES TO DROUGHT
Seeking Stability for Emerging Economies

David Fielding (*editor*)
MACROECONOMIC POLICY IN THE FRANC ZONE

Basudeb Guha-Khasnobis and George Mavrotas (*editors*)
FINANCIAL DEVELOPMENTS, INSTITUTIONS, GROWTH AND POVERTY REDUCTION

Basudeb Guha-Khasnobis, Shabd S. Acharya and Benjamin Davis (*editors*)
FOOD INSECURITY, VULNERABILITY AND HUMAN RIGHTS FAILURE

Basudeb Guha-Khasnobis and Ravi Kanbur (*editors*)
INFORMAL LABOUR MARKETS AND DEVELOPMENT

Basudeb Guha-Khasnobis (*editor*)
THE WTO, DEVELOPING COUNTRIES AND THE DOHA DEVELOPMENT AGENDA
Prospects and Challenges for Trade-Led Growth